ITEM GIRL

Richa Lakhera is a TV journalist by profession, an inorganic chemist by education, and an artist by passion. She lives in New Delhi and Mumbai with her husband and daughter. She is an Associate Editor at NDTV and her debut novel was *Garbage Beat*.

Twitter handle: @iamrichalakhera

Facebook: https://www.facebook.com/richa.lakhera.33

Website: www.Richalakhera.com

Email: richalakh@gmail.com

Praise for *Item Girl*

'*Item Girl* is a compelling whodunit. Highly recommended for fans of the crime fiction genre.' – **Madhur Bhandarkar**

'Dark...edgy...twisted...toxic! The author takes you to the darkest of places and into the savageness of the human heart!' – **Tisca Chopra**

'*Item Girl* is a savage tale of a world which is heavily guarded. Very rarely do you come across a book which balances emotions and atmospherics so unerringly.' – **Manoj Bajpayee**

'Evil! Addictive! The human mind can be a womb of deceit and pure evil. But *Item Girl* reminds us there is always a choice...' – **Viveik Oberoi**

'Unputdownable! Addictive! Visceral! A chilling murder mystery...a must must read.' – **Suniel Shetty**

'A dark drama replete with chilling revenge.' – **Richa Chaddha**

ITEM GIRL

Richa Lakhera

RUPA

First Published by
Rupa Publications India Pvt. Ltd 2014
7/16, Ansari Road, Daryaganj
New Delhi 110002

Sales centres:
Allahabad Bengaluru Chennai
Hyderabad Jaipur Kathmandu
Kolkata Mumbai

This is a work of fiction. Names, characters, places and incidents are either the product of the author's imagination or are used fictitiously, and any resemblance to any actual persons, living or dead, events or locales is entirely coincidental.

ISBN: 978-81-291-3480-6

First impression 2014
10 9 8 7 6 5 4 3 2 1

Typeset by Saanvi Graphics, Noida

Printed at Repro Knowledgecast Limited, Thane

To all the hard lovers and all the dark days

To all the hungry Gods and Goddesses

To those who thought I would not have the guts to tell it

and

To Djiah who holds my hand in dark nights

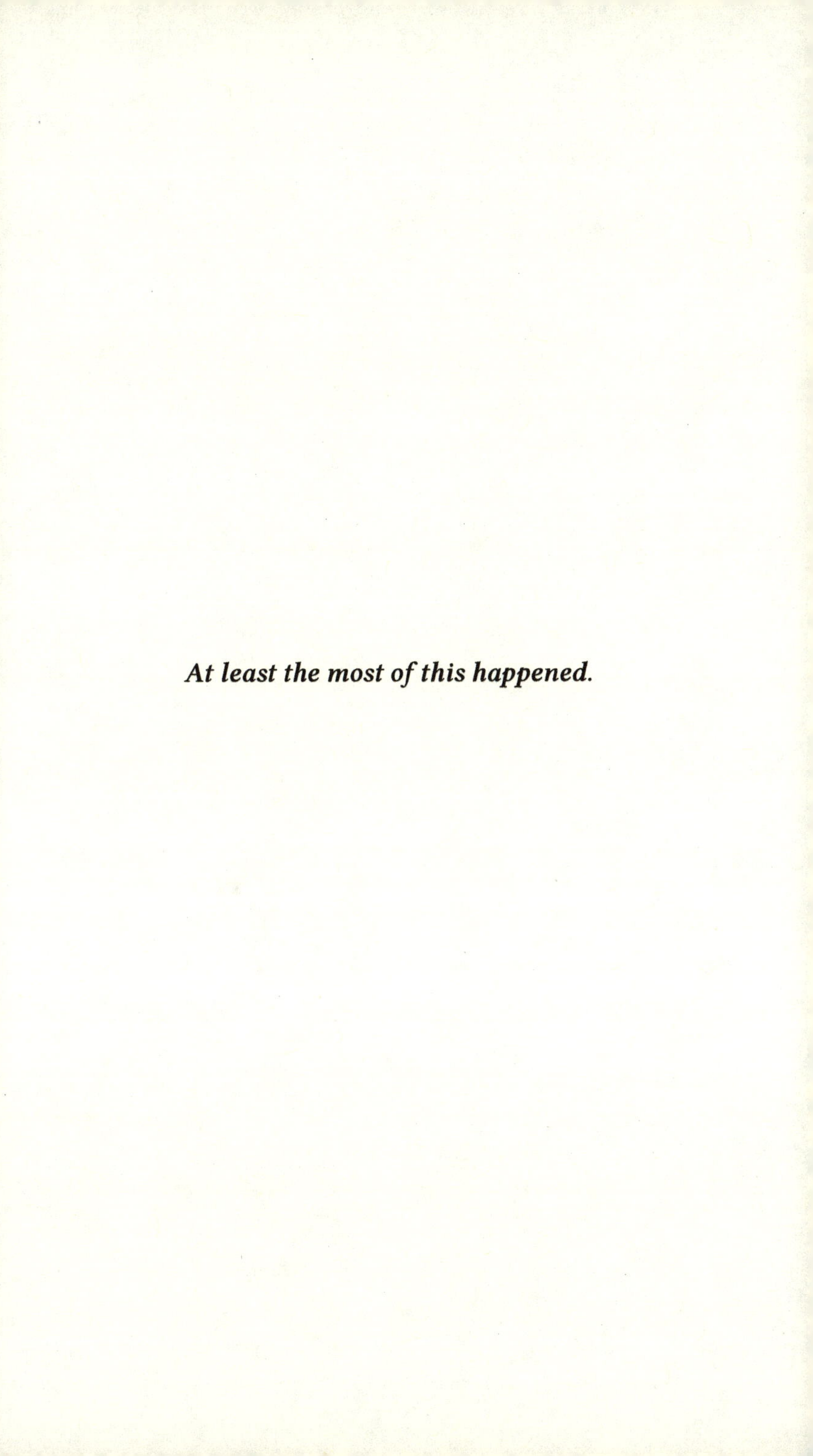

At least the most of this happened.

The Beginning

Tabu was the most beautiful girl he had seen in his life. He was fascinated and wonder struck. When he first gazed at her, he wanted to crunch her in his arms and fill her glittering golden light inside him. Tabu with her disturbing beauty and gypsy eyes spilling gold. Tabu the impetuous live wire who always seemed to sparkle and glow like a hoor. Tabu the merry girl with the explosive disordered laugh. She was the love child of top Bollywood actress Bina, the dream queen of seventies' Bollywood. Vishnu Kashyap, a young fledgling assistant director, on contract with Sitara Matinee, spent hours gawping at his dream girl at filmy parties feeling her sunny warmth thawing his heart, the heart which always seemed too cold and numb since he moved to Bombay. Bina never married, she was married to the screen. But she had had the time to indulge in a torrid affair with a married director and became pregnant. In the end the director refused to leave his wife and despite the huge scandal Bina decided against abortion and gave birth to Tabu. The strong-willed actress brought up her darling daughter single-handedly with great care and love. Years later when the repentant director came to Bina for forgiveness, she famously not only got him thrown out of her plush Juhu bungalow but refused to give Tabu her father's surname. Or any man's surname. She remained just Tabu. Of course Tabu did not care a damn about not having a father or any relatives to speak of. With her Boston education and her impeccable upper class English accent, the well read and evocative Tabu made quite an impression on Vishnu, himself an M.A. in Hindi from Lucknow University. On the outside, the gap between them seemed too wide to bridge, and in the beginning, Vishnu never thought of her as more than an unattainable fantasy. But the day Tabu smiled at him, Vishnu was totally riveted. Under her spell he found himself begging for invites to Bina's star-studded high-fangled soirees to get a glimpse of the unbearably beautiful creature. Desperately in love, Vishnu tried to fit in her hip filmy gang, even took to splurging his meagre post-war economy salary to spruce up his appearance. He shaved his small-town stubble and started patting his hair with carefully rationed Brylcream, the one extravagance he allowed himself since it seemed to work better than sugar and water. He took to wearing his solitary decent suit whenever he expected her to be around, but felt sure that in the starry sophisticated crowd which always seemed to hang around Tabu, he stood out as shiny and cheap. He knew he was no good at singing and dancing so he tried to talk fancy in a hurriedly acquired accent to impress his dream girl with fantastic tales of exotic destinations and ideas. There was no one more surprised than him when Tabu reciprocated his feelings and seemed to be genuinely interested in him. For, despite being surrounded by suitors from the crème of her starry society,it was with Vishnu that Tabu seemed to find an arcane chemistry, an inexplicable connection. Tabu fell in love with the tall and very silent young director with his clear probing eyes and strong sexy chin. And though she never bothered about the nitty gritties of status and class, Vishnu remained ill at ease with the ornate careless luxury which surrounded her. From her Olympic-sized Italian tiled pool to her monstrously opulent mansion and manicured gardens bursting with exotic blooms and orchids, even the electronically controlled gates and imported frilly drapes... a world untouched by recession utterly depressed him. The thought of his own transit camp, a tube-lit two room quarter, leased against the measly cheque he got as an assistant director, disheartened and dejected him. The 1962 war was just over and luxuries were scarce. His small fridge stuffed with rationed food and the oven which he purchased proudly with his first cheque from Sitara Matinee was just not good enough anymore. The shiny new sink and the four seater plastic dining table he had picked up at a bargain price left him disheartened. There was no way he, a lowly AD of little consequence, could match up to the affluent lifestyle of the top heroine's pampered daughter. But kismet ordained a sequence of events wherein the director of the film he was assisting in died of heart failure. It was left to the young and inexperienced Vishnu to complete the movie. The film was a surprise hit and Vishnu Kashyap's Aparichit Padosan *won all the major film awards that year. Sitara Matinee feted him with a celebratory bash, inviting the star cast including Bina, who came with her daughter. For Vishnu, Tabu was still the brightest thing in the room and his awards, his triumph,his victory seemed meaningless to him in front of her beauty. From that moment on, and forever, Vishnu knew he was madly and hopelessly lost in her love.*

It all seemed such a waste now.

There was bitter rage building in him. He was mad at her and at himself. What had he been thinking? At nights, staring at her drugged out on meth lying on their marital bed, he fiercely wished she would snub him so that he could hate her comfortably for the rest of his life. That would have been better than living with her love. At least it would have hurt much less.

The dream had turned into a nightmare.

1

'I am the result of you—you whore town—' he taunted rabidly pointing an accusing finger at Mumbai's misshapen skyline gorged and growing at 2.13 a.m. His face a monstrosity in the unforgiving night lights of Maximum City pockmarked after years of mainlining heroin. '—your flesh-eating cannibalistic womb of fuck and garbage and whoring harlots and size zero maadarchodds!' KD ranted at the kaleidoscopic lights blinking contemptuously at him across the Queen's necklace. Racing down Haji Ali to *Hotel Fun & Sand* his heart pumped frantic amounts of adrenalin full tilt making him dizzy. The new Quad drug he was on to control his HIV must be A-grade or had he overdosed on his amitriptyline, he thought tensely. Switching from the regular Atripla to the formidable four-drug combination left him twitchy and unsettled. Usually the multi-coloured anti-depressants helped, knocking him out like a well-timed hammer. But today even the extra dose of painkillers failed to calm him. KD was furious at the scorn and humiliation that had been heaped on him minutes ago.

'—*aichalavdemaachuda*! You can't handle a two-penny whore—*chutiya chaarchaar ghante phone nahin uthata*—'

Except that four hours ago he was dead to the world. Indifferent to the electronic whirring of his gem-studded 3G iPhone crammed under his pillow. It was the pain from the stinging blisters on his arsehole which seeped into his consciousness first. Zoning out from a black haze he awoke to a body leached by tiny sores oozing agony and a penis as hard as nails. And the incessant metallic drone that just wouldn't stop. Screwing open his eyes, he froze at the 18 missed calls. Then the ear-splitting profanities—

'—cuntshop—arrogant *badtammeez naashukree haramzadi*—that girl has the devil in her—' the high-pitched voice steeped inputrid anger and grated offendingly. Caught by surprise, KD opened his mouth to cuss back but the rabid tongue-lash shut him up for a good 43 seconds while the call lasted. The number finally connected to the face and the name. Salem al Khalifa bin Hassan. Biggie film financier and chief sponsor of Bollywood events in the entire Middle East circuit.

'*Film mein nangi nachti hai yahan problem hai*! Huzoor sahib offered her more than her rate card—but that Sunny has got more *nakhras* than a heroine!' KD sensed the menace in the voice barking insults at him.

'Listen let me talk to h—' his cloying tone disgusted him and bitter acid shot up his gullet nauseously cramping his tongue. The men from Dubai were pissed. Their lavish benefactor, the ageing and extravagant Bahraini Prince Salem al Khalifa bin Hassan, third cousin of the reigning royal family of Bahrain, was furious. He was 69 year old and loaded with dollars, dinars and dirhams, Salem Hassan was the reason why Kay the Dee Krafts manager Kalidas was driving like a maniac to the remote Navi Mumbai hotel in the dead hours of the night.

'Your bitch disrespected Salem bin Hassan! How dare that snatch forget her place, randichodd?' Wiping his clammy palms on his sullied designer suit KD was scared to even ask what she had done. It was the Sheikh's obsession with Sunny which brought him within sniffing distance of the man's big bulging mid-East pockets. And he was not ready to blow it now.

'Let me handle Sunny—' KD pleaded.

'SHUTUPP SISTERFUCKER! Tell your pathetic whore to become a nun. Her mother was a damn better slut than her. And don't bother us about the Dubai dates—sheikh huzoor has no time for you or your doped out sluts.'

'No no—one minute—I ha—' He was pleading to dead cold static. Two gloomy blackholes of defeat stared back at him from the rear view mirror. He could already feel the blisters in his arsehole bursting with tension.

Bitch bitch bitch.

He should have just locked up the whore and thrown away the keys. He should have just made an excuse and sent the other girls. He Except he never imagined it would play out so nightmarishly. KD wolfed down a fistful of capsules, his minute five-feet three-inch frame a tight knot of fury, and wondered gloomily whether lying to his doctor that he was off Prozac had been a dumb thing to do. He just wanted to be done worrying, done wheedling with two-bit producers and whores. Done with looking over his back constantly. He knew time was running out. He needed to bail out before Mumbai's shit exploded in his face. A gratified Salem would have speedily opened doors for him in the mid-East, but that was before. Before Sunny shat on his parade. Swearing hotly he bounded across *Fun and Sand*'s glass floor glaring at the bloated fish lazily shuffling under his feet.

'Where is the fucking lift?' he hollered. By now the sores on his penis felt hard as nails but he was past caution.

KD burst into Suite 909. The lights were dim. He moved menacingly towards the four girls who stood frozen like dumb mannequins.

'Time out. Chop chop. Why are you cunts still here? Tamasha over. *Chalo phutto.* Get your tits and asses out. Out out OUT,' he roared and three frightened girls scampered out of the room.

'You! Stay here!' Face contorted frightfully, he turned around to face Sunny bathed in the ghostly glow of the television.

'You lunatic bitch! Trying to diss people who got you where you are today?' he hissed, 'How dare you?! Have you forgotten, if the client says dance you hop-skip-jump and do plenty more besides. But what... what... what did you do? If you were even half the rand your mother was,' his jaws clenched in a tense knot.

'I will teach you how to be a good randi your uuuudkkkghHH–'

As he lunged forward towards Sunny, his eyes red with rage, something unexpected happened. The air was knocked out of his lungs; KD's expression of incredulous disbelief was almost comical. He did not register it for the first few fatal moments and then his world dissolved into a hellish agonising pain. Dumbfounded, he stood watching his hands and chest being slashed open demonically by a knife-wielding Sunny. Recovering his senses, he jumped on her but missed his mark and was knocked off balance and onto the floor. The razor-sharp knife met soft skin and carved deeply. With the weapon tightly gripped in her hand, Sunny jabbed viciously about his aorta making cruel punctures on the blood vessel carrying the red life force away from his panicking heart. A thin stream of crimson blood sprayed on her skimpy top turning it red.

'Uhhhg ggggdkkk youuu...' He started hurling invectives but stopped abruptly holding his stomach, struck dumb at the sight of his own blood spurting freely. She gashed him every time he tried to move. He grabbed a silk mattress wildly. The last thing KD heard before passing out was his own scream of pain. Sunny clasped the knife tightly and sat on the bed trying to regain sanity, looking at him, trying to let the situation sink in. After what seemed an eternity she got up, wiped the knife and kept it on the table. She thought she heard a soft knocking sound. Someone was talking to her, trying to tell her something from very very far.

◆

She creates her own chaos.

The ground was nowhere. The earth dissolved under her feet... the evil soil made a slurping sound and guzzled her in greedily... the gloomy black mud entered her eyes her nose her ears her arsehole. She was again four years old, breathing drinking eating fetid mud and mother stood there smiling. Next instant the air turned malevolent, sucked her out of the cavernous ground, and twisted her in a tight coil. KD's face leered from the dark and she lost all bearings. She was suspended in the air but not floating. One minute she was a four-year-old rocketing up, and in the next breath she was a ten-year-old plummeting down wildly flapping hands...she plunged into the demonic ground again. And mother was fading. Every muscle every bone in her became rubbery, the soil and the stones grinding her limbs against each other. A misshapen moon looked pinkish and bloated as she moved towards her car. Its eerie light scattered and made everything around her menacing. The street had been newly charcoaled and smelled terribly of hell. Bloated clouds punctured the sky ready to drop their load craftily, even as the wind howled around her ears and dark glittering shadows beckoned her. Where was her mother? She walked rapidly, heart in her mouth, jumping over the cracks in the street and ran into KD's bloodied face one minute, Salem's leering face the next. The night refused to release her from its grip. She was numb outside, but agonisingly alive underneath, her cries and screams muffled at the throat. A piercing screech brought her back to reality, shattering her parallel universe. With great effort she opened her eyes.The world still seemed hazy but at least she was in her own bed.

'*Aaa rahee hain. Arrey sor kyon machaye ho? Arrey kya bawaal hai...aaahhkuthriyaa—benchdd—ruko aa rahee hain—*'Kaanta, her maid, stumbled against the heavy sofa, and swore.

'*Aap kon? Rukiye...arrey madam jee rukiye! Didi andar hain.* Sunheri *didi... didi ...police ke hain! Police waalee aayee hain* Sunny didi—' The maid's hysterical yelp fell like lightening on her ears. Her heart thundering in her chest, she got up groggily and stared at the bedsheet in dismay. She had wet her bed. Kaanta's bulging raccoon eyes leaking kohl swam into focus. The haze was now accompanied by a throbbing pain in her head. In front of her appeared three robust-looking khaki-clad policewomen entering her bedroom. Sunny Kashyap was still trying to get up from her damp bed when beefy policewomen clanked big iron shackles on her reed-thin wrists.

2

Suhana was infuriated by the nasty campaign on the internet linking her with actor Sumraan Ibrahim. There was no truth in the absurd rumours and she knew who was behind the gossip, but there was little she could do about it. After all, Jerome Mangwani was a powerful producer-director who could make or break careers in the film industry. A promising young director herself, Suhana perceived she was in very real danger of falling behind production schedule if she let the vile talk distress her. At Noir Studios, like at any film studio, all publicity was welcome, but the studio bosses would not be as tolerant if she cost them expensive production time. She realised how intensely bitter director Jerome Mangwani was with her bagging *Mumbai City Mein Maut*, Noir Studios' much-hyped mega-budget multi-starrer and most ambitious film till date. A stream of bitchy tweets authored by Jerome had flooded social networking websites. Just a day earlier Jerome took a dig at her for having cucumber snacks at the producer guild's party:

@therealjeromesays: when she ordered a cucumber and a knife at the bar last night, I thought she was going to perform a vasectomy.

Jerome tweeted a photo of a tray with a cucumber, a knife and sliced lemons on it. This was retweeted so many times it trended majorly and was followed by a barrage of even more foul tweets from his followers. He then attacked her with:

@therealjeromesays: daddy ghost directing shhhhh don't tell

Suhana had proof the director was feeding a powerful clique of producer-wives crappy lies about how unsafe it was to have their men around her. At the producers' guild party she overheard Jerome bitching about her to to her business contacts and she almost lost her cool when the obnoxious man cheekily raised a toast to her! Exercising utmost restraint, she managed to smile through her ordeal. Inside she was seething, wanting to yell—*You paunchy balding lame-brained bitch, leash your lip! You are so insecure about your work... well you should be because you truly sssuckkkk!'*

Shit. She could not let this get to her. Suhana was resolute. She refused to get goaded into a fight with Jerome Mangwani. A frivolous fight was all it would take to divert the media's attention away from her hard work. *Mumbai City Mein Maut* or MCMM was her first big ticket film with the most exciting script that she had penned. Suhana could not blow her big chance. She was juggling through a production logistics nightmare since the movie spanning three decades and was to be shot at different locations.

For Suhana, converting the MCMM script to screen was an enormous challenge but she was finding the work exhilarating. Along with her trusty cinematographer, Iyer, she had tirelessly checked out locations and zeroed in on some exciting possibilities. It was a shitload of work but happily the crew was not giving her any attitude. She put it down to her hand-chosen tightly-knit staff being young, hungry and still not versed in the rickety ways of old Bollywood. Ever since MCMM began, she had spent every waking hour on the script, thrashing out scenes, adding lines, changing characters, beefing fleshing rehashing slashing. It was like giving birth, she thought excitedly. She was eating, living, breathing the film. It was now time to cast for important assisting roles. Suhana took a deep breath and stared at a young actor Aneel Naathh standing in front of her waiting impatiently for his audition. She tried not to look at his crotch shining at her like a beacon through his extra-tight jeans. Instead, she glanced at his bio-data. TV-serials, modelling, a walk-on part in a shootout movie. Aneel Naathh moved towards her with a studied action-hero walk. Stupidity in motion, she told herself, suppressing a smile. They were coming for the film audition in droves. Eager to please. Dying to impress. Hungry. Pompous. Very young. Old trying to look young. Very pretty. Really ugly too. All armed with their photos and portfolios and DVDs of their work and dances and dialogues. She preferred to meet her actors face to face, instead of through coordinators and handlers, and had instructed her team to keep tiresome secretaries, pushy managers and PRs out. Suhana had herself avoided the all-enveloping cocoon of a protective PR. She felt annoyed by their deal pitches:

Want a cheap Katrina lookalike? A thin Vidya? A young Shahrukh! The new Salman? Desi Sunny Leone bhi hai!

No thank you! Fact was she did not want known faces for these parts. She sought new faces, raw, uncertain, edgy. What she wanted were actors.

'Hi ... I am Aneel Naathh. You will love my act! Lurve it!' She looked up at a not-so-bad face.

'Oh so you are a clairvoyant!' Suhana smiled.

'No! I am Aneel Naathh. That's a double 'e'.'

'Right Aneel, read these lines please.' She sighed.

'Okay but I must say you are heroine material. Maybe when we both are free—' she ignored his suggestive remark. Ever since she had started casting for *MCMM*, she had been accosted by models and actors and junior artists in all sizes and shapes.

I'll do anything for you... annniiieeetheeeng! Strange men, women talked to her suggestively on the phone, but it did not stop there. She was hounded by obscene calls, some used phony names to get through to her. She wanted to change her number but it would have meant loss of time. She could not afford that. But how did the despos get hold of her number? Did they comb through Bollywood directories or did they prowl parties to extract contact details from her sloshed ADs? Suhana sighed and handed Aneel Naathh his audition lines in Hindi.

'Here goes... *main is sheher se nahin.. yeh sheher mujh se hai—*'

Suhana tried to keep a straight face trying not to get distracted by his nervous pouting and prancing.

'*Haan—maa—khooni hai tera beta—inn haathon se—*'

'Ehh... you have soft looks. Good profile. But we need edgy, slightly ugly,' she suggested after a while.

'I can do ugly,' Aneel grimaced uglily.

'Okay. We will get back to you...' Suhana said patiently.

Rejecting someone was never easy.

'But can I dance and show you my moves...' Aneel got up, raised his arms and did an impromptu pelvic thrust, a massive movement of his groin which alarmed her. '—like? I can do even more—'

'No. Arrey no. Aneel please stop! This is not a dance film,' she tried to not sound unkind.

'I can be serious—real killer mean—'Aneel's face twisted into a mean grimace. She felt bad for him.

'Look this part is not for you, but we will see...' she tried to smile.

'When can I call?' he took out his crystal-covered cell.

'We will get back to you, okay? Don't be pushy. I am sure there is something better for you out there. Only not here.'

'I can show you my abs—' he said, ripping off his shirt with a single swipe.

'Hey. Stop that. STOP. PLEASE.' Suhana was startled.

'Just look at these babies once—'Aneel pressed on flexing his muscles. '—I can make you happy... Very happy,' he leered unpleasantly.

'You need to go. Now. By the way Aneel, your fly is open,' she said without blinking an eye.

'Okay. Chill chill. I will be back,'Aneel said in Arnie style, his hand covering his crotch as he walked out jutting his butt in the air behind him..

Bollywood. Tinseltown. The place where most dreams came to die. She lit her Du Maurier Special Mild which she had come to prefer for its soft lemon aftertaste over the Mistys and the Capris and the Virginia Slims. She took a long satisfying drag and observed the men in her production team as a stacked teenage girl walked in for her audition. Suhana could guess precisely what they would do and they did not fail her. The men leisurely checked out the girl's breasts and butt, a few nudge-nudge-wink-wink comments followed, a lewd remark and some sniggers. Average conduct from regular and entirely civilised men we believe women to be just tits and cunts.

Absolutely normal behaviour. Suhana did not want to think what her 'perfectly decent' all-male crew normally thought about her. The male-dominated industry had not exactly been a cakewalk for her. Being the daughter of Vishnu Kashyap and Tabu had raised more eyebrows than she could count. She had dropped her surname and became just 'Suhana'. Hitch was she was still a girl. In the two and a half years she was in the industry, she had fobbed off more men wanting to take her to bed than in her entire life.

"What's a glam doll like you doing behind the camera!"

"There are easier ways to make cash—for a woman who looks like you!"

There had been plenty of crude propositions and lewd 'tough tit' and 'conceited cunt', remarks. Initially, some left her in tears. But over time, she developed a thick skin apretended not to notice what they were talking about. Things changed only when she held steadfast and achieved the and seemingly impossible. A small but important road movie, entirely with newbies, and with a theme considered too risqué and offbeat for the Hindi film industry. The film hit the jackpot and became the toast of festival circuits. Suhana got a few prestigious awards but more importantly, men-who-mattered were suddenly interested in the goods above her neck. They looked at her differently now.

Suhana wished Aneel Naathh good luck and stubbed her cigarette. Bosomy Bidishaahh with an obvious nose-job and a practised bubbly smile moved in. 'Bubbly Bindaas Bosomy' she had written in the attributes section on her resume. Waiting in line was leather-clad Karizmaah with I-will-kiss-your-arse-and-anything-else written all over her tight face. Then a lacy Mausemeh. Suhana looked up at her assistant running towards her with a TV remote. She was livid. The rules were clear. No disturbances. But then her phone ringer also took off and she heard the caller screaming at her to switch on the TV. There was something about Sunny on it. Something not good. Alarmed, she grabbed the remote. The screen flickered on, and all hell broke loose. White-faced she stared at a grainy shot of Sunny being taken away by the police. Suhana frantically dialed home desperately hoping she reached her father before the news did.

3

ACP Kabir Bhonsle had slept poorly and awoke with the sun on Saturday. He skimmed through his unopened mails, lined up important newspapers and magazines to read, cleared his unpaid bills, cleaned his two-bed sitter until it sparkled, fed the Black Mollys and the orange and gold Koi and had just started netting the debris out of his fish aquarium when he was called in urgently from his day off. A high-profile Bollywood murder at Hotel Fun & Sand sounded intriguing. Thirteen years of carnage, mutilations, killings, rape, robbery, assaults, pimps, pushers, junkies and muggers. And they seemed to be getting more vicious each day. Bile rose in his throat. Some event manager, they said, had been attacked by an item girl. As it turned out, the police officer had not seen anything like this in his thirteen years in the force and he had seen some very ugly things. The hardened police officer winced recalling the mutilated corpse sliced and strung up like a piece of meat. Kabir went over the medical examiner's findings:

1. The death scene was a brutal parody of auto-erotic-asphyxiation, a sort of a sex-game.

2. In a bid to increase the victim's agony, the perpetrator of the crime had tied the victim's long hair with a rope and had almost scalped half his head.
3. Talcum powder on the victim's face, lipstick graffiti carved on his body before or after he was forced to swallow underwear.

This was the intensity of the violence a woman, mad with rage and frenzy, was capable of committing. That, of course, was the police assertion and they already had the accused in custody. ACP Kabir Bhonsle spent the rest of the day at the hotel doing ground work and talking to witnesses.

WITNESS#1:'I heard a cry of pain from Room 909. The door was not locked, so I peeked inside. He was on the carpet... Mr KayDee... covered by our huge red silk duvet. Maybe that's why I did not see any blood at the time. She told me—Sunny Miss said they were rehearsing a film scene—of course I mean Sunheri Kashyap—everyone knows her as Sunny—I was quite nervous about our duvet, it is hotel property you see. It was a very expensive eiderdown comforter made of authentic Chinese silk—yes yes of course—Sunny Miss was sitting on the sofa looking strange and sad.' The witness's eyes protruded with uncertain self-importance.

'I was appalled when I saw our mahogany Sri Lankan Buddha bar kept next to the lounge leaning oddly towards the wall. I set it right immediately. Guests have to pay for all damages, we are very strict about it. The 61-inch Sony XBR TV we have provided in the emperor suites was tilted. I did see that the guest was on the floor.

Sunny Miss dismissed me saying it's a private matter or something. People do all sorts of things, it is their personal matter. These are delicate private issues, we can't afford to be intrusive. Some guests are offended if we are pushy. Besides, I did not see any cause for alarm—at that time—and she is a regular here. Nice lady. No *hallabazi*, polite and well-behaved with our staff. She Visited often with her filmy crowd and guests. Lots of famous people come to our hotel. Anyway, I apologised to madam, and excused myself. If I had any idea, if I had any—

'No, no—she—Sunny Miss did not threaten me or anything. Sir, we do not interfere with the guests' activities, er, legal activities. *Sir it* is policy at our hotel,' he added self-righteously.

'Oh! I heard he was her uncle? Someone said they heard that on television but I did not believe them, these days they say anything to sound important... *uncle bolne se uncle thodee ho jaata hai!* But, how can the hotel know these things? We are quite respectable.'

'I don't know when and how she trussed him up with rope and his—his—you know his genitals were all tied up and twisted with a nylon rope. And he was very dead. I threw up when I saw him like that—he was really her uncle?'

WITNESS#2: 'HIV. We got to know later. The cleaners refused to go in at first. And the housekeeping staff were so terrified. No, of course, we do NOT differentiate but in these matters we have to think of other hotel guests. We do not want any talk of AIDS associated with our hotel. Of course we know HIV does not mean AIDS! But we got the whole room quarantined and sanitized by professionals.'

'But there was so much blood. He had tried to drag himself on the floor... I could see from the marks. His shirt had been ripped away. His right hand had been almost severed. He was left spread out on the bed with a woman's silk underwear stuffed in his mouth, his socks around his neck and whore written on him with red lipstick. I have never seen so much blood. I fainted Sir.'

WITNESS#3: 'I almost collided with Sunheri ma'am in the lobby. She was leaving. No, not running. Just walking, looking rather lost, she had chocolate stains on her dress, at least I thought they were chocolate stains at that time. I warned her about the stains, but she...I remember she said "Alibaba", that's my name—Alibaba...she said, "Alibaba, some stains make you cleaner."

In the department, they always gave him the prettiest of the cases, and this one was the prettiest of them all. Kabir headed for the café wishing he could wipe out the vision of the disfigured cadaver from his mind. Along the way, he found a cameraman's pack of cigarettes lying limply on the table, and he stole one. His assistants Shinde and Holkar were already seated at a table with some papers and a shiny sleek tablet, a gadget recently made mandatory for the police department.

'Mutton and hash Saab?' The cafe boy asked indifferently. Mutton and hash. His favourite. Succulent red meat stewed in its juices and fried in fat and a liberal mix of tomatoes, ginger and green chillies. Delightful when washed down with chilled beer.

'No. Get me chilled beer.' He had lost his appetite. He gulped down the beer so quickly it made his diaphragm ache.

'Thoda nimbu daaloon,Saab?' the boy asked in concern. Kabir nodded dismally, his stomach tossing.

'*Maa ki aankh,* what a piece of work this item? Too beautiful for any one person.' His goggle-eyed assistant Shinde remarked on Sunny with his habitual disregard for syntax.

'Hmmm.'

'Nasty bleeder! Slashed like a pig. Her own uncle!' Shinde held up his sleek tablet showing a photo of KD, mean-looking and droopy-eyed, but projecting a hard-edged scrap for survival and a greasy duck's ass hairdo.

'I looked up his sheet, pretty extensive—been in for extortion many years ago, tried to squeeze money from small-time film-makers, drunk disorderly behaviour, strong arm stuff, threatened some producers too, even a lewd conduct charge by a model—not your ideal citizen here. The Girl probably did us a favour. But filleting him like a fish—there are less painful ways to go!' Holkar said. Shinde greedily slurped his drink,tucked in his chin and belched loudly. Noticing Holkar staring at him in disgust, he grinned and cheekily retorted.

'That's nothing. Wait till you hear me fart!'

'*Bhenchodd. Soooar.*'

'But Sir, item claims she recollects nothing—' Ignoring Holkar, Shinde said to Kabir,' 'Total Blank!'

'Jail time will change that. Let her spend a few days at Bheesha—*jail mein jahannum ka trailer dikhega pooree film gaa ke sunaayegi!*' Shinde wisecracked.

'Yes, Bheesha Jail turns the hardest into mush, and she is just an item girl,' Holkar interrupted.

'Not that ordinary, our sunny little item.Full name Sunheri Kashyap. Fancy-ass star Prince Sulaiman Capure is her current boyfriend, gets ten crores per film. Arrey dada wha—I like bolly-shollywood—' Shinde, a true blue Bollywood fan, was defensive.'She is doing lots of drama, but we will nail her,' he concluded matter-of-factly.

Kabir stared at the girl's picture wondering where he had seen her before. She looked intriguingly familiar. Shinde smiled knowingly.

Leaning forward, he said in a lowered tone,

'She is Madam X's daughter.Vishnu Kashyap's scandalous first wife Tabu. Red hot mummy wearing nothing but a fur rug fame, was the centre piece of several filmy orgies, some interrupted by police raids way back in seventies. Toilet pin-up—queen of wet dreams—it's written on the net! Sir have you never seen her mummy's photos?'

Of course he had, as a curious ten-year-old. He had stared guiltily at the neatly stacked photos of a naked woman secreted from a friend's locker. He had been dazzled and disturbed for weeks since. Going by her photos in the glossies furnished by Shinde, Sunny was a replica, a carbon-copy of her mother. And as notorious by the looks of it.

'Mummy-beti both are listed on extremehotbindi.com, a banned interracial exotic sex site offering peek-a-boo nudies to people tired of everyday porn—horny young men swig bootleg liquor from flasks decorated with her and her mamma's pouting face and naked fanny.' Shinde elaborated with relish offering prized nuggets of tabloid tattle. 'But the family is jinxed. Very unfortunate *kismet.* Total jinx. *Panautee* hai, Sir *panautee.* They say in Bollywood, they have evil eye.' Holkar said bug-eyed.'You remember her step-sister drowned in some accident seven-eight years ago...Dannie right?' ACP Kabir Bhonsle remembered too well. Dannie, the dream girl, silver screen's breezy college sweetheart. No one typified the clean-cut college girl better than charming Dannie. When she disappeared from her luxury boat in a drowning accident, Kabir got his first high-profile case. Except that the young actress's body was never found. In the complete absence of clues, the case was closed amidst a burst of outraged public reaction. Just another unsolved murder. His team was almost torn apart by the media who launched a scathing attack on him and his men accusing them of goofing up.

'Bloody Bollywood!' cursed the officer dryly.

Not this time. This once it was an open-and-shut case, his superior had pressed on him smilingly. The body, the accused, the weapon, the witnesses were literally strung up and splayed out, Kabir reflected, as he got ready for the press briefing. The media was clamouring for a formal statement. As if that would deter them from glossing over facts and reporting pretty much what they wanted to, he thought grimly. With his monosyllabic replies and curt quotes, ACP Kabir Bhonsle's statements never made a sensational copy.

That hadn't changed, since Dannie.

◆

Outside Hotel Fun and Sand, traffic had crawled to a halt due to the milling crowds. News of KD's murder had spread faster than an out-of-control forest fire. The pavements on either side of the hotel were filled with people. The media throng was thickest at the colonnaded entrance porch which already smelt of dirty socks and burning tobacco. Many had positioned themselves against the sloping walls, frantically scribbling on paper, anxiously replying to SMSes, shouting wildly, smoking feverishly. The rest were standing shoulder to shoulder overflowing into the streets in front of the hotel. A grainy picture of Sunny leaving the hotel sourced from a camera-phone earned a fortunate hotel-guest a neat bundle. The lucky man soon trebled and quadrupled his wealth by hawking the grab to every publication accompanied by unsubstantiated quotes on 'stag movies' and 'flowing booze', 'item girls dancing nude' and 'professional party girls', indulgence in 'marijuana reefers' and 'young filmy-type women of loose morals' spouted with ghoulish relish.

'—Shameful! These filmy girls frequent the hotel and producers, casting agents, businessmen and councillors come—I have seen many with Sunny with my very own eyes—totally ticking—and did you read her outrageous tweets last week—out of control—'

The hotel-guest spoke waving his hands like a filmstar at the exploding flashbulbs and the hurled questions. The media lost no time in raking up Sunny's 'strange' and 'odd' behaviour with her fans exactly a week before. News channels flashed with reports of how Sunny had 'stunned' and 'angered' her Twitter followers with foul-mouthed tweets that had them abandoning her in droves on a social networking site. The tweets were played over and over again.

@sunnyhoney started off with an upbeat tweet:

'Nuff luv 2 all the muffins 4 evaa thankful 4 ur support #shoutout2thefans.'

However, the niceties soon became ominous and menacing as her mood seemed to shift:

'N as 4 all u f***** haters... u can kiss my f***** ass #gettingpaid #bothered? Gdsgdhdhdhdh hahaha'.

@sunnyhoney continued to post alarming drunken messages:

'Love it when me n the crew get crunked! we so craaaaaazzzzzyyyyyy... If God dropped acid would he see people?'

'Always lose a few thousand followers when I hav a drunken rant with a bit of harsh language... #wellworthit #f***em'

After being inactive for two hours, @sunnyhoney hinted that she would be hitting the bar again right away:

'Ooooooouuuuuuuuuccccccchhhhhhh MY HEAD HURTS... oh well... self inflicted I guess... round 2 any1? DING DING'

A pattern of 'deviant' and 'frightening' behavior by the actress was easily established with week-old headlines, retrieved from archives. Now with a grisly murder to boot, the broadcasts were crammed with the 'ticking' itemgirl's horrific act. Imaginative re-enactments of the sensational crime at the hotel filled TV screens. Some TV stations already sentenced Sunny to animated padded cells with 3D VFX effects.

GLAMOUR AND GORE coming up in 00:23–

ITEM GIRL SLASHES UNCLE–

LEGENDARY DIRECTOR'S ESTRANGED

DAUGHTER FACES MURDER RAP–

A minor altercation broke out when the media rushed to get reactions from a garrulous DJ with questionable credentials.

'Excuse me... are you done with this guy...? Did you see the body? Was it entirely naked? Entirely?'

'Maybe I will answer if you stop screaming like a horse's arse.'

'Up yours.'

The DJ was promptly dumped when the police appeared. The journos raced towards ACP Kabir Bhonsle in a bid to elicit headline worthy quotes from him.

'Sir was she his niece? Real niece?'

'Sir, was she with three women? In bed?'

'Sir, the rope around his genitals and neck—what is this auto-erotic asphyxiation—?'

'Sir was there a sex toy too?'

'Yes, we found sex toys in the room. What sort? A dildo and a vibrator ma'am. I will get back to you in case you want to know the brand and the colour, whether it's ribbed or scented or tastes of strawberry?' ACP Kabir Bhonsle never hesitated in taking a dig at the media whenever he could.

4

'SUNNY KASHYAP ARRESTED–'

The screen abruptly jumped to 'Nirmal Baba's Third Eye' and then 'Barbie's World' on Pogo. Livid at pounding the wrong remote buttons, Silky Mehta swore nervously before hitting news. He did not want to miss himself on TV, but the anchor was taking her time.

'SEX GAME TURNS FATAL FOR BOLLYWOOD EVENT MANAGER? POLICE SUSPECT AUTO-EROTIC-ASPHYXIATION AS CAUSE OF DEATH–'

Mehta, dressed in bright orange striped pants and a chest-hugging tee with 'I ME MYSELF' written on it in bold letters, listened with mounting horror to the news of KD's death. The full implication of the murder and the way he had died was just hitting him. He sat down on his fading blue sofa, missed it and fell heavily with a whump on the floor. To be truthful, Silky did not give a horseshit about KD's death. Slashed to ribbons like a pig. Motherfucking thieving snake deserved it, he hissed loudly. *Oh man, he was on TV!*

'—Here is what Silky Mehta, KD's ex-partner has to say: "The whole thing makes me sick—yesterday he was alive, today he is dead—For the record I had not met KD for so lond... long. He was my partner but he had his own businesses... I know nothing about foul play. You say it was what murder? A sex game? Autosexual asphy—what? For your information I represent very high-profile cunCLIENTS—'"

Watching himself blunder in the press conference, Silky Mehta's baby face contorted into an ugly ball. His hennaed hair and light-watery eyes looked unflattering in the frasie-lit room where the media had accosted him. Worse, he was fumbling for words looking incredibly stupid. Bloody reporters with their big phoney smiles and fake accents and absurd questions! They pestered him about the sex angle as if he was some kind of authority. Auto sex auto erotit—tik—what the fuck was that? He still had not got the goddamned word right. He had been on his way to the pub when TV reporters had assailed him with their LIVE mikes and volleys of questions which included phrases like 'genitals slashed' and 'sex game'.

'CHOKED TO DEATH BY NIECE—' screamed the bold red-blue-orange text on the four television screens in his room. His pride and joy, the four LCDs, bought in happier times, today looked ridiculous in his windowless third-floor Kurla garret apartment. My four faithfulls, he used to brag in front of cheering floozies who came for overnight romps in exchange of walk-in parts. Today, stupidity, his stupidity, caught from different angles. Silky flinched. Each screen stood split between his unflattering mug shot and his dead partner's morphed corpse.

'—in a ghoulish parody of the sex films his starlets were known for, KD was found nude and dead with his neck and wrists tied with a rope—'

He gawped at the dramatic pictures of the death scene splashed on his favourite tabloid. The high resolution grabs showed an entirely naked man except his face seemed paler than the rest of his body, his hair and testicles tied with a rope and strung up and something was jutting out of his mouth. The weak attempt at digitally morphing the picture had entirely failed and he wondered whether someone would get into trouble for that. Silky shuddered to think that the mangled pathetic remains were that of cocky KD. He could not believe that they could let a picture like this be published.

'—That little tramp is not my daughter—she is the devil's seed! You want the truth?'

Startled, Silky turned to look at Kala's zoned out vacuous eyes; she stood shrieking standing next to a TV reporter with a mike. Kala Kashyap. Or ex-Mrs. Kashyap. Sunny's stepmother. Or ex-stepmother. And KD's sister. Furiously stroking her pet bitch Diva, who she had dyed blonde, with eyes as frighteningly empty black holes as its mistress.

'—Sunny was always a whore just like her mother. And now she is a murderer also. Just like her father—'

The anchor tried to butt in except there was no stopping Kala from ranting against the Kashyap clan.

'—Dannie...KD... both dead—first my daughter now my brother—both gone... He... that Vishnu Kashyap and his evil daughter. They are responsible. Her mother—and her seed is no different—the Kashyap women are manhooos—' Kala spat out shaking her fingers wildly at the camera till the stressed anchor abruptly cut her gibbering. Kala's bitch Diva started wailing forlornly in protest.

Silky had met Kala, Vishnu Kashyap's ex-wife, on his occasional visits to KD's house, when he had hoped to use her contacts in the film industry, but found her too offensive and unhelpful. Kala would ply him with alcohol to dig out the dirtiest details about every director, producer, actor and actress.

Fucking freaky cunt, Silky thought. Fucking freaking family. The TV channels got one thing bang on—the cocky bitch was a ticking bomb! Refusing gigs, acting pricey, asking for contracts, demanding to see the script. *See scripts!* Sunny had recently been nothing but trouble. A far cry from the pliable seventeen-year-old girl KD had presented to him five years ago. Glorious looking, with heavily lashed champagne eyes and magnificent breasts—every inch a dazzling nymph. She had the kind of body men jacked off to in toilet rooms. Silky recalled their first meeting.

{'Firstly baby... loose the heavies! No meat no money—' Silky advised the seventeen-year-old Sunny when she had entered his cabin in a long-sleeved dress, her nipples straining against the fabric like rosebuds.

'No last names please. First name is Sunheri? But I prefer Sunny—is that your nickname—more sexy—Silky will make you famous.' She seemed shy but he sensed a disturbing attraction about her which could drive the audience mad.

'Trust me—they all do it—item girls as well as hero heroines! Sab nange hue hain. *There is no shame in this... be* besharam *okay. It's hard work...'*

'If a producer likes you, it's all good. All taken care of like family. That's what you need here. A sugar daddy. Just the other day, Salma's mummy dropped her at the producer's house at night. Ab raat mein kya kaam hota hai honey *all know. But aunty told me, look Silky, my baby has to become the hottest item number. And she will. Wait and see, Salma will be the hottest item number.* Arrey *talking part bhi* milega—'

'What about my audition?' she asked and he had laughed.

'Audition phodition se kya hoga? Karna toh wohi hai. *Also because I have begun to feel for you baby, cash upfront should be your policy. If someone offers you a film, remember it's all len-den. Give and take. No contract no cunt. No dough no dick. I tell each of my boys and girls. Remember, Mumbai is a tough place to stay in. You do no favours. No favours. Silky is here to make sure you don't sell yourself cheap. Remember you have bills to pay, sweetie pie. Don't worry there is no dearth of sheikhs wanting an Indian* tandgdee *for dinner...' Sunny had not replied, just stared expressionlessly at him with her disturbing brown eyes.}*

'—Sunny is not a criminal. There is a lot she has done, but this she has not—'

Presently, Suhana Kashyap's furious face filled his TV screens. She was trailed by a thin and frail-looking old man, her father, Vishnu Kashyap, looking visibly hassled by the media. Silky had never met him. But the sister was a different story! He never once forgot the look of hatred Suhana would give him and KD, especially KD, whenever she saw Sunny in their company. The two sisters were as different from each other as chalk and cheese. The ice maiden and Roxie. Suhana's pale face turned determinedly towards the screen, her clear brown eyes staring directly at him.

'—There is someone out there—who knows the truth—'

She was pointing at him with her finger. Or so he thought.

'Shit! I could have been in Dubai,' Silky said aloud.

If some of this rubbed off on him he would be cast off like a used sanitary napkin. An untouchable pariah in B-town. No. He could not let that happen. He had to stay ahead of the game. Like always.

◆

By afternoon, twenty hours after the news of the murder exploded, there was more bad news for Sunny. Her blood had tested positive for banned narcotics. The test report had been leaked to the media... psychotropic and memory depressing drugs beyond permissible limits. Experts spouting their theories on the crime filled TV screens:

'—Sunny's blood tests positive for psychotropic drugs and illegal narcotics—actress stares at jail term!'

'—Psychotropic drugs affect the central nervous system—the person remains unaware of what they have done—'

◆

By evening, 48 hours after the news of the murder exploded, a lewdly shot amateurish film tailer featuring Sunny surfaced on all major Bollywood websites. South Indian film producer K Lingaswamy announced that he was reviving a stalled film of Sunny titled *Sunny: The Scent of Love.* In a hurriedly summoned presser release, K Lingaswamy called it an explosive bold film starring Sunny Kashyap and southern actor 'Rocket Raju'. A clumsily shot trailer with some explicit shots of Sunny dancing with Rocket Raju netted 2,00,000 hits on YouTube alone and was still counting. The item song started with crude lyrics in Tamil and Hindi. In the first shot, the camera lingered on Sunny entering a hotel room where she promptly began to undress swaying to remixed Tamil lyrics. Subtitled in English, Sunny was seen inviting a reluctant'Rocket Raju' to sleep with her.

Sunny (lip-syncing): *chari. eedaakuudam nnaa enna? enna ippoo?* (subtitles: What if something unexpected happens? What now?)

Rocket Raju played hard to get.

Sunny (lip-syncing):*manacheyee koduththuddeen enne kodukkamaaddeenaa Ulle veliya-ulle vileya-ulle veliya*

(subtitles: I've given you my heart. Won't I also give you myself?)

At this point, a line inserted in the trailer flashed, 'They were just two people looking for solace first...'

In the item number, Rocket Raju played a cop assigned to ingratiate himself with Sunny in the hope that she will lead him to her gangster boyfriend. Sunny's dress abruptly changed from the coy saree to masks, underwear and a double barrelled bra before she launched on a soft striptease which became a full-fledged jig, all to the raunchy tunes of pop singer Ho Ho Monny's hit song *Rocket ki Socket.*

Tu meri sunny daru main tera rocket wocket chal maare shot whotban ja meri socket socket socket socket socket socket socket—

Swaying to the mindless lyrics, Sunny danced closely with Rocket Raju. The two then joined each other in a dance of such sensuality that the observer could only gape, feeling envy and lust.

The video ended with a frantic message from K Lingaswamy:

Releasing-soon-Sunny-Her-Looks-Can-Really-Kill!

5

'Swing her around. Kick her in the gut.'

Item girl Mink Mocovich staggered back when the beefy stuntman Ronny slammed his fist into her shoulder.

'That's better. Gimme a roundhouse punch. Pound her to the ground.' Mink bent backwards as the fist moved towards her face, she felt his hot knuckles swish past her nose.

'Better! We go with the sequence, okay? Fight as if you are battering your worst enemy. Kicks, uppercuts, tripping, sweeping, pull her hair. You kick him in his balls. Ram it into each other. Give me blood. ROLL.'

He punched. She ducked. He kicked. She twisted. He paused, listening for movement. The whisper of a footstep to his left. He turned, lashed out blindly, felt his fist connect with muscled flesh and heard a soft crunch. He hit the table with a thundering crash. Splinters stabbed her bare arms. Mink swung around and walloped Ronny in the gut. He sputtered out curses and crumpled to the ground ripping Mink's wide shoulder pad clumsily as he fell. A moment's distraction proved costly and Ronny yanked Mink's legs viciously making her crash face forward.

'CUT. I never... never... NEVER EVER want to see these ugly pads.' Jerome Mangwani rushed to shred both the shoulder pads off the terrified girl's dress.

The scene was resumed in seconds and Jerome instructed Ronny to whisper a stream of obscenities in Mink's ear. As Ronny became increasingly vulgar and started groping the Ukrainian girl, Jerome Mangwani winked at the close-cams and settled down enjoying the look of discomfiture on the jittery item girl's face. His films were for connoisseurs. Film aficionados. Want to entertain your fucking family, go watch a fucking circus or kingdom-of-dreams-or-nightmare or whatever. He, Jerome Mangwani, made 'real' films. The Ukrainian model Mink Mocovich with her edgy girl-interrupted look was perfect for the role of an American girl trapped in a kamatiputra whore shop.

Jerome nodded at his cameramen to get ready with the close cams focused on Mink's face. He wanted them extremely close. It was to stay like that no matter what happened on the set because Jerome had planned something which would shock everyone. Mink Mocovich's clothes would be ripped off her till she stood naked in front of the hundred odd men his ADs had slyly collected on the sets. And save his trusted cameramen none of the cast or crew were aware of his intentions. The raw fear on an unsuspecting girl's face when she stood naked in front of a lusting cheering crowd. Jerome felt orgasmic, close to god. That would knock the balls off them. Off everyone. Even the arty folks at Noir and their new fancy director slut Suhana.

'Puleeze! Darrling! Nobody really thinks that Suhana has actually written *Mumbai City Mein Maut.* The way they are going bosh and tosh in the papers—*Suhana inherits the undeniable talent of Vishnu*! Trust me I have it from a verrry trustable source that Vishnu Kashyap has actually written it and passed on the credit to his daughter. Poor man is desperate for at least one of his daughters be famous for what's between her ears rather than what's between her legs! Suhana could not write a decent line even if it climaxed over her cunty face.' Jerome bitched non-stop to his assistant.

'I, Jerome Mangwani, have more talent in my farts than Suhana has in her whole body. That Noir studios will fall flat on their avant-garde faces! Imagine they have given her MCMM. Bloody half-baked bitch. *Film making koi family dhanda nahin hai—ki baap ke baad ab beti karegi!* Just wait till their movie bottoms out—' A nervy stylist holding up a shimmering microscopic costume for him to approve interrupted Jerome's acidic diatribe. The filmmaker threw the tabloid and bellowed.

'YELO...?? Madam Fancy-Nancy do we have to wait a whole day for a whore outfit? Why do you get paid? For sticking sequins on underwear for a whore film?' he glared at the film stylist Nancy. 'Tell the item she has only three minutes to change—'

Nancy scampered off dragging Mink behind her.

He was almost done with the item girl. Now if only the fucking heroine would care to show up for the next scene. Fuck. Why did she have to take this long for makeup. He was an award-winning director; he did not have to put up with some award-winning heroine bitch. The pricey cunt was creating such a ruckus over her makeup-man taking off with some other heroine. Two whole days wasted for that dick-sucking makeup artist to return!! He could have fired her except she was dating the big shot producer's son. He could have fired the makeup man except he was registered with the *Bawlas* who would squeeze him by the balls with a list of labour law violations. Jerome Mangwani, was left with no option but to stuff his thumb deep inside his arse and instead begin the shoot schedule with the item girl. He stared at the fidgety girl clutching a thin diaphanous gauzy cloth. The costume left nothing to imagination. Mink Mocovich blushed at the huge suggestive hole right in front of the crotch.

'She won't wear it.' Nervous Nancy glared accusingly at Mink.

'Jerome but I ca*y*n't wear this outfeet—itz too too sleazy—' Mink objected.

'WHAT?? Now you want designer underwear to cover your gilted Ukrainian arse? Maybe Lulla or Malhotra will design chaddi for you? *Chicken work ki bra aur kachchee chahiye with zardosi?*' Jerome belted the frazzled Ukrainian girl with filthy Hindi abuses. A hard-driving bully with a monstrous ego and a short fuse, Jerome Mangwani did not take kindly to any actress, let alone a chint of an item girl, talking back.

'But it's too skeempy. I ca*y*n naawt, man.' Mink Mocovich stubbornly pulled the towel closer to her body, refusing to wear the outfit.

'And what secret you have left to hide?' Jerome spat out.

'Jerrome.. I—ca*y*'nt ca*y*'nt wear it—' The rest of the crew looked at the whole scene with amusement. Jerome appeared to have been waiting for a moment like this. Gesturing to the close-cams with a signal of his hand Jerome tore away the towel from Mink's body. He ripped off her shoulder laces first and the front portion just came off. He cut, slashed, hacked till the flimsy costume was lacerated beyond recognition. The hapless young girl stood frozen, too scared to the director who was maniacally tearing off the remaining fabric from her body to ribbons, slashing and shredding in front of a crowd of leering, ogling men. Finally, the chief AD rushed in and stopped Jerome from committing a felony. The shaken girl was given a glass of water and some savlon for the bruises on her neck. Some of the spot boys had started filming the nearly naked item girl, for posterity or a quick buck. Finished and spent, the director threw the scissor on the floor and shouted.

'This is your debut. Remember to thank me for your big moment in a Jerome Mangwani film. You are famous now! Cunt be warned. I can get your work permit cancelled and your Ukrainian cunt will be banned from Mumbai. But I won't. Despite your indiscipline. I am giving you a talking line—say *main choot hoon.* Go on say it. Teach madame her lines someone. There is NO actress-wactress here–*sab choot hotee hain.*' Jerome shouted hysterically. No one noticed the girl till the remaining fragments of the dress slid down from her body on the floor and she let herself go. Someone snickered and hooted.

'Fancy-Nancy take Madam to the toilet.' Half fainting Mink Mocovich moved out of the room trying to stop the hot stain from spreading down her thighs. Her body moved towards the exit, her back burning with the leery eyes boring into her body.

'*Cayn't* make an omelette without breaking a few eggs yaa?*Cayn yaa now*?' Jerome's bloodshot eyes mimicked meanly. Now he had the scene pat down. His happiness was interrupted by the number flashing on his cellphone. Nisha Poddar, editor of the magazine *Bollywood Truths*, was calling him relentlessly. Shit. Now this had to be the madaachodd icing on the madaachodd cake. He was in the middle of his frigging film, and all the nosy hack wanted to talk to him about was the fight. His fight with KD. How did that witch get to know so soon? Must be one of the despo fucks on the set. His left eye twitching madly, Jerome looked around warily. Totally ignoring the umpteenth cup of dry black coffee in front of him. Today, he desperately needed something much stronger than caffeine. Last week's nasty public fight with KD had not been entirely his fault.

{'STOP. Stop this shoot. We object to—mooh-mein-de—words of this item song.' Bawlas' rowdies led by a sloshed KD had barged into his film set and disrupted his shoot.

'But we have changed the lyrics! Now it's—haath-mein-de-' Jerome was defensive. His new item song 'Mooh Mein Le' was quite popular on the internet, garnering 90,000 hits within forty-eight hours of being released on YouTube.But the Bawlas' Entertainment wing of Cine and TV steered by KD sharply objected to the lyrics of the song threatening to yank off the song from the movie print.

'—and all these Russian, Ukrainian, Checzkoslovakian chammiyaas in chaddis—do you have registration for all these imported items? I don't see local dancers? Don't you know 50 percent local is must?' There was no love lost between the filmmaker and KD who had forcibly stopped his shoot for the third time in a month. Jerome was furious because at this rate he would soon be losing more money than he was making.

'Don't bullshit me. Who says its 50 percent? I know the rates. Stipulated is 30 percent. I am going to complain to Munjal about you—and WHAT HEY—don't scare my crew—' Jerome was furious that KD was demanding an extra 50 percent fine on every foreign crew registration.

'Yeh koi goondaraaj hai or what? I am warning you bhenchod I will finish you in this industry. You will be over, you fuck, if your faggot army stops my shoot.'

'Hey Mumbaa Devi! Where do these people come from?! Stop the shoot stop the shoot stop the shoot—' Under KD's lead

the Bawlas' took up the chant and started hooting and clapping. The shoot forgotten, Jerome's foreign crew stood frozen in fear.

'You fuck I will get you for this. You are dead you fuck. I will bury you and your family...I WILL KILLYOU FAGGOT.' Jerome had threatened in front of his crew.}

He could not get the words to stop ringing in his head. If anything, he could only be accused of incredibly bad timing. The nineteen missed calls and messages from Nisha Poddar made him nervous. She must have heard about his stupid threat. Jerome felt hot under his great chunks of flashy jewellery. His neat hair always combed forward with dollops of gel to conceal his enormous balding pate was unsettled by his sweaty palms touching his head every now and then. The pimp had been sliced and left to dry and the press had smelled blood. Jerome Mangwani was worried that if he did not watch it, his sorry arse could very well be the main course.

6

The city court building situated in the heart of the city was a five-storeyed redbrick structure made of sandstone cornice mounted impressively with dominant viridian canopies. The building boasted of recently constructed interiors of gilded oak and a shiny new green-and-rose marble flooring. Inside, the court was so noisy, sometimes ACP Kabir had a hard time paying attention when they were finally silent. Witnesses never remembered anything in order, they messed up frequently, they lied and they thought a lot. Confirmations, substantiations, verifications, corroborations of the testimonies and presentation of evidence and proof took inordinately long with the finicky judge painstakingly reading, re-reading to himself each piece of information presented. The lawyers stopped and read notes, they repeated themselves annoyingly, stuttered, and kept on asking the same question in different ways.

Not all cases moved at breakneck speed, but this promised to be one. The circumstantial evidence in the homicide was loaded against Sunheri Kashyap. He knew if the defence actually believed her to be guilty they would not even try to put as much facts and evidence as the prosecution but may simply make a stab at softening the mood of the court towards their client. Although Sunny's counsel, PK Dang, was clearly relishing his moment in the limelight, the police officer groaned. After Sunny meekly admitted to attacking KD, his jubilant officers wanted to thank her for not wasting police and court time. Except Sunny not only rebuffed attempts to make her confess to defacing KD's body, she avowed complete ignorance to exactly how her uncle ended up with genitals trussed and a mouth full of underwear. But then she was an actress, he reminded himself, as he waited, uniformed and hot, on the marble bench outside the court-room for the hearing to finish. Either way, ACP Kabir Bhonsle knew he would need an army of crowd-pounders to keep the crush of media and hanger-ons outside the court under control. The news came out sooner than he expected. Bail denied.

News of Sunny Kashyap being sent back to Bheesha Jail spread like a wildfire. Policemen stood on high alert to check the ensuing chaos. Like a hound of ravenous dogs, the crowds edged her into a tight spot as she walked out shepherded by police, and shadowed by her sister and father. The shoving and pushing reached a crescendo with every one trying to get a better look. The shapely legs in blue jeans, gum boots, face scrubbed clean of makeup—her ferocious beauty was disturbing. The body of a *hoor*, the face of an angel. The child-woman whose sexy item numbers were the stuff of wet dreams. As if under a voodoo spell, they ogled at the screen seductress. The frenzied crowd pushed and heckled and jostled dangerously with the media for scarce space. The more adventurous photographers balanced on trees with wide-angled telephoto lenses.

'What's going to happen now?' Suhana choked in anguish.

'Whatever makes most money.' Sunny said impassively.

'God, the crowds 'Suhana could not keep her voice from trembling.

'C'mon they are fans in lurve with all that stupid fun all the shit I've done—expressing their admiration for my shitty life' Sunny said dazedly ignoring the policewoman's stern *chalo chalo.*

'Your magnum opus? Keeping the Kashyap banner flying high sis? Dad must be so proud of you.' Sunny said. Suhana glanced sideways at her unresponsive father, momentarily taken aback by how much he had aged. Vishnu's tortured solitary stare remained undecipherable.

'This is scary, there is not enough police here—god! Why aren't they controlling the crowd?' Suhana's anguished eyes locked on her sister's. Moist eyes with indifferent ones. A look passed between the two siblings. A look which spoke of them being yoked together in inviolable complicity of some old terrible secret.

'One half of life is fucking up. The other half is dealing with it. I think Nietzsche would approve of me—isn't it like... fight monsters and you become one, fight devils and you become one!

'Chaliye Madam. Talk-shalk over.' The crotchety lady police officer said bad-temperedly. Sunny appeared disquietingly calm. Mockingly unconcerned with the circus around her. Those present were disturbed by her contemptuous indifference to her fate. And fascinated too.

'Sunny...Sunny...your film with Rocket Raju is being released, would you please comment?'

'Yeah sure. I have some good lines in the film,' she said taunting the onlookers with her naked eyes, face shorn of grease-paint.

'Unless they have ended up on the cutting floor, then I will really feel ripped off!'she added with a cheeky smile. TV cameras went wild voraciously recording her each expression. Reporters thrust their mics greedily into her face, they wanted more. A reaction? A bite? A chat? A quote? Unexpectedly, she threw back her head and laughed a glittering golden laugh as if from some newfound freedom. Someone hooted at the actress and that broke the spell. Frantic jeers, hisses and boos and taunts rained down on Sunny.

'Oye cunt-shop,' they screamed, masking their perverted desire for her under a cloak of smug, self-righteous anger.

'Officer. Please. Tell them to mind their language,' Suhana tried to control the anger building up inside her.

'Hey cunt-shop.' Someone pushed and even as Suhana cried out in shock and anguish Sunny fell down. The photographers competed with each other, their news-cams rolling and flashing frantically to capture every scandalous celebrity moment, as additional cops pushed their way to the spot.

'Who is this? Where are you motherfucker?' screamed Vishnu shaking in anger. The crowd watched as the unfolding drama reached a climax.

The cops shouted: 'Everybody out, everybody out.'

Voices shouted: 'Let's take her with us!'

The cops shouted: 'Rasta dijiye—Please give way.'

Voices shouted: 'These filmy girls are into everything and everyone. They are all randis from age ten!'

'Don't you have women in your house? Wherever you are from—officer tell these—these sick people not to talk to her like that...HEY. *Ek minute, kya problem hai aapko?* Why did you touch her? They are trying to touch her officer!' screamed Suhana.

'Laga ke batayun? Will put a lot more than hands on you!'

'Ma'am, you control your sister first—or give your Sunheri Sunny to us. We will control her for you!'

'Shut up! Get away from my girls bastards—you—you—you try and touch me bastard,' Vishnu shrieked weakly, shaky from some inner brittleness. As his face crumpled with grief at what reality was scripting for him the photographers and TV crew shoved each other to snap him: *The anguished father.*

Voices shouted: 'Sunny is going to jail. How will you protect your killer daughter now?'

The cops shouted: 'Nobody will speak. Come on take it easy.'

Voices shouted: '*Buddhe mein dum nahin hum kissi se kam nahin*! That horrr should stay in jail.' The mob moved as a whole in a shameless voyeuristic frenzy desperate to strip the petite girl with golden eyes.

'Filthy pigs,' Vishnu muttered loudly, his veins straining against his neck like bulging harnesses.

Wild catcalls added to the mayhem as the police moved in to shield the mobbed family. The raging din had now made it impossible for anyone to hear anyone else.

'Whenever she is raging, she takes all life away, haven't they seen enough the shitty ruins of my world?' Sunny mumbled a ditty and Suhana shuddered in the claustrophobic heat of the court premises.

◆

'Family always gets screwed,' Shinde said watching the Kashyaps being escorted out. Kabir shook his head staring at the procession heading out of the court towards a waiting police vehicle.

'Like clockwork, the family is always the last to know.' Kabir stared at Suhana Kashyap, intrigued. A director of some sort, Shinde informed him. Had even gotten some important film award. Kabir was impressed. When he first saw her he thought she was an actress incognito or something. A knockout, long black hair and a lithe body although she played her looks down by wearing no makeup and functional clothes and tightly pulled back her hair in a severe ponytail. But she did not succeed in hiding her stunning eyes and sharp cheekbones. Not a tiresome bottle blonde starved to an inch of her life drowling in fake accents. He caught his own reflection in a car window and roughly settled his hair. ACP Kabir was not a conventional good looker, but the sum of the parts added up to a not-so-bad-looking man. He had a ruddy tanned complexion which was a result of sweating it out in the sun for years and a short army haircut. His sharp jaw and tight shoulder muscles gave him an air of authority and made many a female heart shudder with fascination when he walked by. As he made his way through the discarded Kinley bottles and stubbed out cigarettes lying on the road, he felt intrigued by Suhana. What was her story?

But first there were the three item girls to deal with. Nargis Khaled, Daisy Katta and the one Shinde really wanted to meet first: item girl Digital Dolly.

7

Nisha Poddar was suspended on a big blue yoga mat, her body stretched to a dangerous limit. Her mind was racing. She simply had to get more out of Benny Bhojwani but the botoxed broad was acting too pricey.

'One...two...three... Hold... girls do the tilt... One...two... three... pump the hips up girls. Holddd! We want them like taut buttons, don't we? So they can't get their hands off them. Hold to count five... C'mon Benny, Deanne, Mala, Nishaaa, move girls if you wanna cream the competition. Now relax.'

She loved to come to Pommy's gym, a hot favourite with the first ladies of Bollywood. Apart from getting superb massages and steam baths and exercises and head-to-toe-conditionings, the gym was simply the best place to gather the newest gossip in town. Her sources: the perennially bitchy women that frequented it. Important accurate news to begin with, like which actors were auditioning for which film, which project to be excited about, who was out, who was in. More importantly, the women were Nisha's hotline to Bollywood's big daddies' most intimate secrets. These wonderful powerful women confided in her. After all she was Nisha Poddar; the editor of *Bollywood Truths.*

'He is so short...and she insists on wearing jhatakk matak costumes to deliberately dwarf him...and then do you know she asked for a box for him to stand on...for their romantic scenes! But he got back at the bitch!' Benny Bhojwani was excited to be the centre of attention.

'How?' Nisha Poddar was all ears.

'He asked Biddoo...don't tell anyone but he was ready to slash his price if a slap scene was incorporated in the scene. Haah...you know how my Biddoo is...could not see his hero's agony...*maan gaya*...he is such a softie...and the bitch was floored with a left uppercut to her jaw! Haaaw hhhhhaaaw!' Biddoo Bhojwani, Benny's husband and co-founder of Noir films, was one of the biggest producers in Bollywood.

Nisha laughed, but not at the story. She already knew it. But then Nisha knew everything, for the simple reason that people confided in her. They disclosed, revealed, confessed their innermost secrets to her. She supposed she had the rare quality of listening. She supposed over the years she had become one of *them*. They told her everything about their married lives and their gynaec problems and plastic surgery and their super jocks on the side. She knew they loved her for the power she wielded. Reputations, love affairs, talent, looks, a come-back, a debut, all could be shred to bits with a few carefully arranged words by Nisha in her dreaded column. Of course, she had other sources too for her 'insightful' stories. Certain tarot card readers and gynaecologists and plastic surgeons and clap doctors and telephone switchboard assistants and florists and lab assistants at hospitals. But this, this 'Power Circle' was something else! She had smelled raw clout and immense wealth here. Nisha loved to cultivate these power women, just as they did her. It was often suggested that Nisha's powerful position in certain top studios required her to keep her mouth shut. It was not what she wrote about but, often, what she did *not* write about that mattered.

Nisha knew she had come a long way. It did not matter anymore that she was just four feet eight inches, with a face which could at best be called kindly, that too when hidden behind humongous glasses. In an industry where looks were everything for a girl, Nisha had surely triumphed with her quick sharp wit and talent for sniffing out stories.

She had got so many leads for her stop-the-press stories from the coots here that she had stopped counting. But Benny was being uncommonly cagey about her husband's new film at Noir, and that was reason enough to pique Nisha's interest.

'It's a big one. That's all I can say...EKHH THREE...EKHH FOUR...EKHH..'

'Good girl Benny. Five more to go—guess what? I have such dope naa.'

'EKKHHH...ONE...tell me.'

'I have dope on Prince's daily ritual!! Begins with hot water with Aloe Vera, three types of 'special' smoothies, including one made with spinach, banana, lemon and exactly twelve ice cubes! Breakfast ends with a bowl of oatmeal. Mr. Capure believes laughter is the best medicine and watches comedy circus for a perspective on life, as he admits to finding the news too serious!'

'Huh...ONE...how do you...know...TWO...THREE..?' Nisha couldn't care less. She had already done a piece on it. What she only cared about right now was Noir's new film which was being kept under a shroud of secrecy. What was MCMM about? What was the star cast? Who was doing what in the film? Who was doing the music, the item number? All she had was that the film was being directed by Suhana Kashyap.

'I have heard that Suhana Kashyap is a tough bitch?' Nisha prodded.

'Let's just say she has balls. Haa haa!' Benny exulted, happy to have the great tabloid queen Nisha Poddar on tenterhooks for a change.

'Jerome Mangwani swears Suhana did not write *Mumbai City Mein Maut*! He tweeted that Vishnu Kashyap ghost wrote it. I called him but the jealous dog is not taking my calls.'

'Who cares! She did it?! Daddy did it?! It's a winner–and it's OURS.'

'Yaaaa?'

'I can smell. It's going to be BIG! It will be one frigging hell of a blockbuster. Biddoo says so.'

'What's the script like?'

'No one has seen it Nisha. It's under complete wraps.'

'That's impossible! But there must be a pilot?' Nisha kept prodding.

'Dunno,' said Benny suddenly circumspect at having revealed what she should not have.

'Arrey Benny tell naa...what's it about?' Nisha had now given up all pretence of working out.

'Nothing I can talk about.' Benny was too guarded.

'A rom com?'

'Ehhhmmm.'

'A thriller or sex film??'

'It's a biggie. No slut stuff. Puleeze. Not a cheapie. Biddoo does not do cheapies. Big big budget.' She looked uncommonly secretive and evasive.

'It's a period film right?'

'I am not saying...you know this town...people are so bitchy...can't see a good thing happening...will sabotage it... spread rumours...I mean not you...you I trust naa...but the Mumbai air has ears darling—*yahan ki hawa hi kharaab hai.*' Benny said stubbornly.

'I heard Prince Sulaiman Capure had sent feelers?'

'Feelers?? Baaba he is desperate. Every night he plagues poor Biddoo for the lead role, is even ready to slash his market rate. But that'll never happen. Suhana is in charge of casting. She is dead against him. She would never take that old freak—' Benny Bhojwani abruptly clamped up.

'Yaa I agree. Plays all his roles with his nasal passages blocked. No wonder he can't smell his own shit. Bugger thinks he can snort up the whole world and still keep the pace—'

Nisha's mind was racing. So Noir films were casting for a period film and had rejected Prince and not the other way round as Prince's secretary Chaman was claiming all over town. She was not surprised. Prince Sulaiman Capure. Ace movie star. Super-hit romantic hero. First-class shit. She heard he constantly needed prompt cards to say his lines. Definitely not the Prince of old. She had seen too many of his kind. Golden stars corroding into swag-bellied insomniacs too fucked up again and again till no one could piece together their shattered lives. To keep up with the fast-paced world of high stakes they often took to drugs to fuel their fragile talent till they completely lost their moorings and sank into the sleazy world of drugs. Bottle nosed, bleary eyed and bloody wasted. But like every other star, Prince Sulaiman Capure had also started believing his own PR-machinery. That he was invincible. And he hated being told otherwise, as she found out after writing a withering article on the unsavoury aspects of super-stardom. Their faceoff had almost ended in a nasty fisticuffs. He called her a *midget—a weird little neutered midget who preyed off others to feed her sexless life.* He said a lot of other things which Nisha professed never to recall. But fact was she remembered every shitty thing he had said to her. Nisha Poddar never forgot an insult, never forgave a snub. She was dead sure she wanted to be at the finish line towards which Prince Sulaiman Capure was hurtling surely and swiftly. Especially with his coke and cunt fixation.

'Mm.. You know what... I will feature your store in my weekly and your photos will be in the socialite page for a month.'

'I don't know Nisha...' Benny sounded uncertain.

'C'mon! You mean to say *that* means nothing to you? Okay don't tell me the actual name of the movie. But at least tell me who the star is? Is it really Sumraan?'

'Yup,' a true gossip, Benny could not keep it in any more.

'Gosh! I have heard from Jerome there is something brewing between the two—Suhana and Sumraan?'

'Bitchery darling...sheer bitchery!' Benny was dismissive.

'Really? She must have inherited the writing keeda from her baap—and her sister...bechari, so horrible what happened with Sunny.'

'Please...that stupid murder spoiled my dinner party! Fucking everyone was only focused on that—no one noticed my new Italian chinaware! Let's be honest, this was waiting to happen—I have heard the girl is a major league user, crammed full of junk any time of the day—such a beauty, that Sunny though...what a frigging waste—*par* where is she now—you know very few girls can keep it all together! The easy money, the glamour, the fast life, the wild parties, the kinky sex—and some of these girls...their only ambition is to have sex with stars.'

'She was a regular item at Prince's party—his 'Sunny-honey'! *Uski* private squeeze and god knows what else—*tumne toh chaapa hai something naa*??'

'Benny sweetie, Nisha Poddar does not just "chaapo" something. I have the pictures darling. But tell me this MCMM...I mean *Mumbai City Mein Maut* is the final name? I have heard that there is a controversy and the title has already been registered by someone else?' Nisha asked.

'Nnnope yaa.' Benny sounded indifferent.

'Okay what do you want? Your photos for a month? I will get your NGO top coverage. Page one of supplement. Benny–right up there shining like a beacon.'

'If I tell you and you chaapo it, I'll be in big trouble with Biddoo.'

'Biddoo will in any case sell it to the press. But if you give it to me you will have your mug shot on every magazine. Your new boobies yaar, just think? Babe what's the point if the world does not see your load? Think about it...the party you are planning...the best party this side hosted by Mrs Benny Biddoo Bhojwani. Party queen Benny B. The Big B of parties... imagine!!'

'Sound good...!' Benny licked her lips. 'Come, walk me to the ice-spa...Oh—you know, Biddoo has such a fab idea...you will die when you hear it!

'Yaa?? Do tell!'

'But swear honey, you got this one from me. You know Biddoo wants a lot of publicity—he wants Sunny Kashyap to do an item number in the film—people will love to see her now... she has a murder rap on her—naa? What a genius my Biddoo...'

Yeah right. Best of luck on that. What a jackass.

'Very original idea! Except she is in jail.' Nisha said.

'Arrey she will be out—eventually—item numbers can be added even after the film is done. He is hoping she makes bail.'

With a sigh Nisha Poddar followed Benny into the special room, filled with crushed ice. Benny ran the shower and stood under the icy needles of water—

'Ahhhhh! Needed that. Does wonders for my mood. Okay Nishaa daaaarling, where exactly will you feature me and for exactly how many days?'

8

"CAPURE'S ARM CANDY STARES AT JAIL TIME—"

Bollywood star Prince Sulaiman Capure made no attempt to conceal his annoyance as he read the editorial. Columnist Nisha Poddar's piece hinting at his 'relation with the jailed item girl' incensed him.

'The garrulous old trout!! The old crow is at it again. Bitch begs for party invites and bites the hand which feeds her. Bitch! Dyke!' Prince Sulaiman vented his wrath on the tabloid ripping it to shreds.

It was not the first time she was persecuting him. From digging out the drug bust he was involved in, in his younger modeling days, to ensuring that his romantic escapades and bar room antics made tabloid headlines, Nisha Poddar continued to doggedly hound him over the years. Luckily for him, most of her catty pieces had instead of killing his career added to his draw, and increased his allure, by cementing his good boy with a bad-boys-go-to-hell-and-be-damned past. The additional hint of danger only made him more attractive to the public.

Prince Sulaiman Capure knew he was a lucky man, the public being indulgent towards his indiscretions. He loved his life as a superstar. He loved his multi-millionaire existence to match the size of his gold-fitted mansion with toilets the size of buses. He loved his swanky multi-level vanity van fitted with a capacious English cocktail cabinet and a miniature gold-rimmed splash pool. He loved that the phone never stopped ringing and brands never tired of chasing him for his nano-second appearances to sell their liquors and lotions. He loved his retinue of the beefiest bodyguards in the industry and he absolutely loved his five farmhouses named after his beloved dogs Aurangzeb, Razia Sultan, Lukhkha, George Bush and Ponty who, rumour had it,were fed imported champagne. But, most of all, he loved young girls screaming out his name, fresh faced ingénues hanging on his every word. *Aahhhh the unlimited groupies letting him do anything he wanted with them!*

But it all came at a price. It required of him to continue being a superstar. It required of him to never be *caught* crossing the line. With the help of his trusted secretary Chamanji, a past master in the art of covering Prince's peccadilloes, transgressions and follies, Prince supposed he had covered his bases pretty well. Till the devastatingly beautiful Sunny came along. It seemed a nice idea to flaunt the stunning young actress at a Holi rave party, or perhaps the coke mixed with quaaludes made him stupidly reckless. Worse still, getting photographed with Sunny was definitely bloody rash and unforgiveable! Because, for his adoring fans he had come a long way since his coke whores and feather-headed cocksman days and he, Prince Sulaiman Capure, could not afford a doped, crazy snatch denting his superstar image. He was angry at himself for allowing the photographers to click them together. Just one crappy jpeg was enough for the tabloids to spout yards of shit. Irritably he dialled Chamanji.

'I want to ram that Nisha's pen inside her gullet. And her reedy finger up her wrinkly arse. She has crossed all limits this time. Bitch writes—His teeth are newly capped, hair dyed and goes for chest waxes. Guess dearies, guess the superstar's name?! Worried about his blurring profile he is now experimenting with the nightingale poo facial—Are you listening...?? Just stop this Poddar whore Chamanji—I want her magazine to become less than toilet paper!' his voice was shrill as he yelled at his secretary of thirteen years.

'That vicious stupid pathological liar! She is mouthing complete fabrications—she can't say this—STOP HER—' Prince Sulaiman was shaking with anger till Chamanji's matter of fact clipped tone sobered him.

'Don't worry. We will hold a presser? Maybe throw a feel good party, fly the top journos there and send them on an all-paid luxury trip to Dubai or Bali. If that does not work... we will sue the cunt. I am already faxing your press note to you. Now shut up and GO give your award-winning shot!'

'My phone is jammed with calls for quotes, and my Blackberry has hung up thrice from the incoming SMSes. I have had a zillion missed calls from the press,' Prince complained.

'Best you tweet something like—*Saddened by this horrible tragedy. Did not know Miss Sunheri Kashyap personally, but we are all part of the same family and when this happens you feel the pain of someone from the industry*—How does that sound? Remember you are Prince Sulaiman Capure. Superjock. Superstar. Now give us an award-winning shot. GO! Floor them rockstar!!'

As if on cue, a couple of nervous assistant directors appeared at his plush van's door, sheepishly looking at their watches and peeking in.

'Just tell them Prince Sulaiman Capure will sue anyone who spreads malicious stories linking me to Sunny.' Prince warned as he descended from his cushy vanity van, and swaggered into the set of his new film *Indiawala Hero.* In a flash, the pretty makeup girl was all over him, blotting, puffing, filling, shading, touching, re-touching. The star gave her a pinch on her bony backside. She smiled slyly. He wanted to squeeze her tits.

'GUYS IN PLACE. Prince and Avani are here. Are we ready?' screamed Harry B, director of *Indiawala Hero.* The star did not bother to move and studiously ignored his heroine, the critically acclaimed young Avani Malan. Instead, he stared harder at the pretty makeup girl doing her up with his probing eyes. He rubbed his groin suggestively. The makeup girl blushed a carroty red and looked down in embarrassed nervousness.

'Okaieeeeee. Let's go then,' coaxed director Harry B once again. Every one stared at the star's next move. Prince Sulaiman Capure yawned widely and snapped at his assistant demanding a mirror. After studying his profile for a good ten minutes from every angle, he winked at the makeup girl and yelled for his ozonized water, finally making a show of noticing his heroine, Avani Malan.

'Avani, you have lost weight dearie! Still living on hummus and radishes! Major de-toxing haan?' Rumor had it that Avani Malan had been under strict orders to lose at least fifteen kilos for her new film in which she was playing a prostitute.

'You know Sulaiman...' she always used his middle name when she was about to say something caustic, 'the thought of bird poo on my face put me off. How is it though? Heard you are the expert...' she said waving Nisha's column on his face. The star coloured up.

'You know guys, I have heard the procedure involves mixing nightingale excrement with rice bran and water and applying as a face mask. Fantastic results haan, Sulaiman?' Avani smirked.

'Victoria Beckham is rumored to be a fan. Of course you wouldn't know her' Prince Sulaiman Capure did not see splashing out on the facials as being vain or weird, he knew there were much wackier fads out there.

'Au naturel sweetie—I hate the temptations of plastic surgery—is it painful? That bandage behind your ear darling—Harry Bhai we must avoid getting that on the cameras haan!' Clearly Prince was in no mood to relent now. It was common knowledge in Bollywood that Avani was not averse to a little nip and tuck to enhance her looks every now and then. Avani Malan turned a shade purple. All pretense of the shoot had stopped on the set and Harry was panicking.

'HA HA GUYS!—both of you have such a sense of humour—OKAY LET'S—!'

'Wow you are the funny guy, Sulaiman! Your eyes are shining too...are you happy to see me or is it the routine colon cleansing? And is the *drip* painful?' Avani retorted. Allegedly the superstar was put on a vitamin drip for a half-hour each week, during which he was given intravenous doses of vitamins B and C, and magnesium.

'Did it hurt when they sucked out the fat from your thighs and pumped it into your lips?' Prince shot back sarcastically.

'Guys guys—ha ha...very nice for an actor to be so humorous—get me the clap someone—'

So the bitch had read Nisha Poddar's article. She better drop the smart alecky act right now.

The scene began pretty fine. Prince was to mouth a pick-up line to Avani and walk out of the shot. Problem was, while Avani's bravura acting style won her spontaneous applause from the crew, he was blowing his simple lines.

The bitch was stealing his thunder. Was that Avani cunt trying to make him look bad? He would see to it the bitch ended up on the cutting floor. At least all her best lines would end up on the cutting floor. Let her play actress-actress for now.

After several takes, prompt cards were held up for the highly distracted actor, making him stamp his feet in childish petulance. Director Harry B screamed at his actors to focus.

Bad move buster. I don't even like the name of this film. So I guess I will change it. I will show you who the star on this set is. You don't mess with me. I am Mr Box Office. I am Mumbai ka King. Prince stomped out of the set without a backward glance leaving the heroine mid-sentence. Director Harry was bewildered.

'Fuck. What a whiney diva-bitch,' Harry moaned loudly, hands on his head, 'Who signed this nincompoop idiot I am working with—and good job Avani, but guys can we go easy on the applause? You know how angry Mr Superstar gets when he is upstaged? And who the fuck got this newspaper on the sets? And if a wiff of this shit gets out you motherfucking snoops, not you Avani, you are out of this industry. I don't want any press here. I don't want newspapapers. And I don't want anyone to talk about *that* case. Fuck now, who will go after that half-talent-full-pain-in-the-arse?'

'Sir, Prince's van is leaving the sets...' his AD whined piteously.

'Fucckk!' The director ran his fastest sprint and caught the gigantic vehicle shuddering to life. The actor made no move to stop his van forcing Harry to shuffle alongside half running, completely out of breath.

'Nothing we can't sort out Prince...huh...huh...Just tell me what you want and how you want it?' Harry panted anxiously. Inside the moving van, Prince Sulaiman Capure ignored the director and continued to switch TV channels.

'You are leaving then? So...so...Sulaiman...Prince...should we reshoot the sched tomorrow...huh...huh...I will send you the script...' Prince Sulaiman Capure signalled his driver to slow down, turned and stared at the director in the eye, sneering.

'Your *Indiawala Hero* needs new lines. *Naya maal do*, Harry brother. New script. New story. Why am I getting the same rehashed trash. Old wine in new bottle, it's *baasi* stale script. It stinks of last year. And I need a different name...I have said these dialogues before, I don't even need to fucking look at script lines. I want better scenes. More *dhaansoo*. The only thing fresh in this whole setup is that new hairstylist, so I guess I will do her first, haan?'

'Soooo what you want is...ehhhh...'

'I want a broad. Some fun.'

'Will send you three.'

'Sure. Three is better.'

'Certainly... anyone from the dancers? The makeup girl?'

'The one with the big titties. First row. Put her on ice till tonight. Send a couple more to my Bombay Hills pad—have biiiig men at my bash tonight! in future, do not—do not evver—send your spot boys crawling to my van to call me for my shot. I will come when I am ready. Okay?? Harry Bhai?? Now—go—go—go—I have to see this.'

The actor shooed away the hapless director, his eyes glued to the car's TV screen. She was exiting the city sessions court. His child-woman with her narrow waist and delightfully full hips, forever inviting caresses. A cheeky blend of innocence and wantonness, and her maddening smile promising secret delights. But all that was behind him now. Prince popped a pill. He was relieved that he had dumped Sunny before the shit hit the fan. The hyper TV anchor was trilling out macabre details of the crime with relish when the camera abruptly cut to an extreme close-up shot of Digital Dolly. The item girl, her pneumatic body and mammoth breasts poured into a crotch-skimming leopard skin dress and hooker heels,was ON LIVE.

''Kismet is a BITCH—and the BITCH can turn on you anytime—I was not there when she attacked him but everyone knows—its all sub—joo—diss you know—''

Prince laughed aloud staring at the boobsy item girl beaming from the TV screen jiggling her bountiful well displayed cleavage at the cameras. He found Digital Dolly's massive breasts wildly hysterical. Of course he was a breast man, but there had been so many breasts attached to so many floozies willing to let him do anything he wanted to with their bodies. Sunny had been different, with her provoking looks and puzzling naiveté, he thought as he combed through TV headlines. *Sex. Drugs. Betrayal. Murder. Bollywood Item girl.*Hell, could he do a film on it, he wondered stroking the rich interiors of his massive van heading towards his Bomby Hills penthouse. Bomby Hills—the highest priced spread in Mumbai a tiny pocket of mega-influence. Financially light years ahead of the rest of Mumbai but geographically only a mile or so south of the main studios. Traffic was heavy and people on the road gawked at his gargantuan tinted machine wondering at the identity of the occupant. The sleek vehicle, carrying its atmosphere of 19 degree Celsius and 25 per cent humidity, manoeuvred smoothly through a mass of sweaty office-goers mixed with surfers and sun worshippers coming from the beach and gawkers clutching maps to their favourite film star's homes. Prince Sulaiman rolled down his window with a whoosh and snapped at a roadside magazine vendor.

'Bollywood Truths *hai*?'

'Ohhhh.'

'*De de.*' Prince loved the look of disbelieving shock and incredulous awe on his fans' faces when they recognised him.

'Haannn,' his eyes glued to the star's face, the vendor robotically exchanged the magazine for the money. Prince enjoyed doing that. Sometimes they were so shocked they forgot to take money. Just stared at him. Some touched his car in wonder. Their demi-god of the silver screen. He loved being a superstar in Mumbai; the city knew how to treat stars, not like frigging Newark where they made him stand even at airports for hours to prove his credentials. Mumbai was different. His heart warmed up for the city as his vehicle glided silently through the dirt-filled broken streets, ranked the most expensive in the world. Fifty yards into Bomby Hills, everything went pastoral and hushed. And very very 'private'. The properties were immense, the houses concealed by high walls and, iron gates lined by their own mini forests guarded by attack dogs. A thin gathering of the most powerful distributors and cinema owners were coming to the bash tonight. It would be a big fantabulous party just like old times. Formidable men talking lots of money, snorting lots of harmless cocaine and, fucking lots of happy girls and boys. Not like the crap which happened last time when Sunny was there.

{Wherever he went whenever he wanted, there were girls and boys ready to do his bidding. Willing to crate themselves in boxes and just about do whatsoever to be near him. He knew he had had more girls than anyone he knew, a few boys too, out of sheer curiosity. His men would just round them up and get them to his room for him to look over. Increasingly, none of them took his fancy, and he would tell Chamanji to keep the best and the youngest ones on ice, Just in case he changed his mind. When he was in the mood for girls, they would route two to three of them through his room in a day, just the type he liked—stunningly beautiful, big breasted but not too big, but with the one key feature, very long and shapely legs. And he was totally put off by talking, thinking, intellectual broads. At his famous parties, he would sit on his legendary giant penis-shaped couch, sometimes with just a cowboy hat for cover, with dozens of girls parading in front of him till he smiled at the lucky winner after looking them over. The rest simply had to put up with being perks for his pals, his distributors and some favoured studio executives.

That was why he had asked for Sunny that night. Golden Sunny. Gloriously beautiful Sunheri Sunny. Legendary director Vishnu Kashyap's daughter. Occupation. Item Girl. Job. Cock sucker. He knew all she wanted was to smoke dope, take dope, lick, suck and fuck, dope and do anything it took to get to it. And was she wild that night. Making love to everyone in the room with her wild dance to celebrate the collections of his film. With her feathers and beads and plunging flimsy dress, with no bra and rose-bud breasts and eyes spilling brown sugar. Stomping and posing like an imperious whore. Enjoying men lusting after her pumping body. Stroking the mic, whipping her hair around. An original beauty who turned grown men into frenzied little boys without uttering a single word. A party with lots of coke and lots of cunts. He was especially grateful to his secretary Chaman Ji for the huge cut glass bowl brimming with cocaine and a pile of thoughtfully provided rolled up papers, and the XTZ, COK-N, Rave, Xplode, NeuroBlaster for the big boys and the Hi-Octane and Big Daddy for the scaredy cats. Not to mention the huge cake from which jumped out Digital Dolly wearing a wig and dressed as a cherry. Men hooted and women catcalled and the party roared to life. He had just started enjoying the edgy buzz of the party when Sunny's screams had jarred amidst the clinking of glasses and drone-like chatter of his buddies and bitches. She had spoiled it for everyone.

Slut slut slut.

Just who the fuck did she think she was? Playing dewy daisy all of a sudden! The mess she was in, it was her fault.}

It was definitely her own fault.

9

The sky was miserably bleak. The hot air a blazing inferno. Like hell was leaking onto earth. Boiling hot cars inched along, mostly waiting for the others to inch on first, their inflamed tail-lights leaking red like cruel gashes. Even hours after the scorching sun disappeared, Mumbai's summer nights offered little solace. The city contours dimmed into a gloomy dull grey hot smog, the air turned thick with haze. Power shortages had increased from 12 to an unbearable record of 20 hours.

Hot wind scorched Kabir's breath as he got out of his car with his men, dried brittle leaves snapping under his feet. A lone sad dog morosely watched the men cross a garden patch to enter KD's building. The apartment was locked, but luckily, the door's locking mechanism opened inwards. He had been trained to handle that. Kabir stood with his legs apart. He knew exactly where to aim his kick. He had done it many times. After a few mule kicks, the wood began to splinter. As expected, the deadlock bolt extended only an inch into the door frame. With a final blow which seemed to shake the building, the door leapt back against the locks and hinges, the lock burst and the wreck of the door fell inwards on the carpet. His men stood back for a moment and Shinde peered inside.

'It smells of shit. Hundred-year-old shit.' Shinde said, breaking open the remaining stub of the door. The putrid interiors smelled of vomit and decay. There was bird poop and feathers everywhere on the floor. Pigeons had shat all over the furniture, their white and grey downy feathers spread like dandruff on the TV, the carpet, the dining table. Bird shit and filth and garbage... Milk cartons sitting out of the refrigerator in 105 degree temperatures. The table was littered with leftover food, mouldy and decayed, and that explained the revolting smell.

'Yummy,' coughed Holkar, trying not to inhale.

'Looks like he grabbed what he wanted and left—in a hurry.'

'Wait. What's that sound? *Aaichigand*...running water?!' a constable stepped into the kitchen and found himself standing in half a foot of stinking murky water.

'*Maashichigaand*—where is this water coming—that's strange! The sink has not backed up...? Where is the frigging leakage? Checked toilet?'

'Water is dripping from the ceiling,' Shinde said tracing the mildew growth on the wall, his eyes resting on a spot right on top of the hallway which was murky black and spreading. Standing on a stool, Kabir craned his neck to inspect.

'That my friends, is the culprit. Water is dripping from the hallway ceiling down onto the soaking wet carpet. No wonder the house reeks of mould and mildew. Seems an added construction of some sort.'

'Hold me up' With the help of his men, Kabir stretched himself further and extended his hand to prod the crumbly, powdery roof. The ceiling was nearly featureless at first. It gave away unexpectedly and bits of the pink hallway ceiling disintegrated and collapsed to the ground. Kabir found himself staring at pinkish acoustical tiles peeking from under.

'Shiiiit!'

'At least now we know! That's not a pink carpet. That's pink attic insulation! I think the ceiling collapsed under the weight and sogginess of the water. The entire floor is wet and stinky. We will have to watch our steps in the room above.' Meanwhile, inside the bedrooms, it was much worse. Foul-smelling fetid water had reached the far end of the rooms and was wicking up the boards of the wooden bed. There was a kind of storage room out back, filled with dirty clothes completely coated in bird poop. The owner had enclosed the patio and made an addition room. A constable peered into the darkness.

'Hey...I think I can make out stairs here!' Gingerly watching his step, Kabir tiptoed through the little path to the doorway. The stench in the room was unbearable. Like something very sick was dying a slow painful death. The room was not as small as it looked.

'There has to be a light here some–' One of the men reached for the switch in the gloomy fetid darkness and their dismay turned to goggle eyed astonishment. A high-end home theatre system gleamed at them.

'Ayyyuiiihhk! Can live without anything but a TV...and what a TV!! It's a madachodd cinema-hall!' Shinde stared awestruck by the size of the screen.

'Lookiee here! You wont believe this. Fuck I don't believe this! '

Expensive bulgari swatch watches, golf shoes, alligator leather belts, several crystal encrusted iphones, 50-inch LCD TVs, limited edition white leather Jeremy Scott sneakers studded with gems...the men stared incredulously as a virtual treasure trove of luxury goods kept tumbling out of the squalid shabby apartment with its peeling paint and rickety windows.

'All floating in dirty stinky drain water and bird faeces!'

'This TV has provision for 1080i and 720p high definition picture—really expensive...just look at the workmanship. Destroyed by shit filled water.' Shinde's voice was hoarse with disappointment.

'*Yeh kya hai*? Cla ude pumps in gold leather for*Miss Daisy Katta*! This will increase height by five cms...and *Happy birthday Nargis Khaled* and hello we also have *Enjoy Sunny-honey...yeh kya hai*? Looks like our man had a habit of collecting gifts, not meant for him.' A small refrigerator revealed the most absurdly expensive drinks Kabir had seen in a long, very long, time—bottles of Crozes-Hermitage Red and *Pouilly Fume White Wine for Avani Malan.* At least seven 24-carat phantom solid gold watch under the mattress meant for seven different actors and actresses given by companies, studios, fans and admirers.

'*Puchhila chavla kutra!* Motherfucker was stealing gifts!!'

'Hey whaa—ts this??' His hands closed in on papers stuffed behind the copper welding carefully concealed under some wires.

'There are some numbers written here. Maybe locker numbers? Shit. Eyyyyeee! It's all soaked; the ink is running.'

'Its looks incomprehensible now. But you never know what comes up in the scans. Shinde will have to run a check—'

'It's going to be impossible to rescue the personal documents and several hundred DVD shere, or what's left of them.'

'Finally bull's eye! Sir come here!'

Kabir found himself staring at what appeared to be the medicine drawer. Inside it, in plain view, were cartels of drugs marked and labelled in neat stacks. Hallucinogens, antipsychotics, amitriptalines, anti-depressants and stimulants along with prescriptions for HIV treatment and painstakingly packed Quad pills, the new wonder drug for AIDS.

'Heaps of coke-N, rave & Xplode and Xtzees...very popular party drugs. Legal. You can buy these online. No big shit... except this stuff thrusts our man into a major league dope pusher—quite an illustrious career Mr KayDee—!'

'Hey, the plumber is still not here, the bloody toilet is running after every ten minutes,' Someone shouted from below as they inspected another drawer bundled with skunk and hemp and crates of phensidyl. Kabir knew about skunk, a favourite painkiller for AIDS or cancer patients. KD was obviously a man in pain.

'You know people who smoke skunk are twenty times more likely to develop psychosis. What's your theory?'

'My theory is that there's a lot of girls and boys that come here with a lot of dreams. And whenever you have a lot of pretty and hungry young girls and boys in one spot, it attracts every fucking idiot from all four corners of the world. Every douchebag, scumbag, scumsucker shows up and sets up shop and teaches them to snort and roll.'

'Like Salem. Number one degenerate fuck up whose idea of bliss is being passed out in a hotel room somewhere with four scantily clad women. I figured why they call that hotel Fun and Sand as 'Tits and Sand.'

'Pphissssss ...oye Shinde?—Hey what's this—it's a ciggie or what?' Shinde gave a rolled up cigarette to Holkar. A chain smoker, Holkar smiled widely in appreciation, his unflattering stained teeth beaming unevenly as he clutched the ciggy and lit it in a flash.

'Easy Holkar!This is not–'

'Shinde I know how to handle a damn ciggie–'

Before Shinde could stop him, Holkar took a deep drag, holding in the smoke for some time. The next instant, he began to cough frantically, his face red, he doubled up vomiting in the hallway.

'You fool, you don't know how to handle 45,000 an ounce 90 percent pure skunk–

'What's happened to him?' Kabir shouted.

'He smoked *that*!!'

'What the fuck is this? Are you a maadachod chootiya? Do you know what *this* is?? Benchodd take this chootiya out. Empty a bucket of water on his motherfucking head.'

'He–Sir–Shinde–Vwwaackk–' Holkar vomited again, staggering against the doorway.

'What did you do, Shinde?'

'I just asked him to tell me what it is? These ciggies–the bastard sampled it!'

'Fucker it's not a ciggie–it's a snort stoked with god knows what crap! It's to be taken in through the nose–not through the throat–take these samples for testing.'

Kabir was well aware about the pervasiveness of heroin and crack cocaine in the filmi circuit. 'Gotta perform', 'need drugs for the creative edge'were chanted like a Darwinian theory of evolution and used as pretext for any and every drug abuse, from smoking grass, coke-N, rave &Xplode and Xtzees to popping amms, acids and meths to gulping quacks to shooting speed. The phrase 'sex, drugs and stars' was interpreted as a devastatingly successful advertising slogan for an exciting life, but Kabir was far from amused when the super-rich and glamorous turned their druggy excesses into fashionable behaviour, because he knew it always ended in a crock of shit.

'Poor shit. Went out screaming. Check if this is the same stuff found in Sunny's blood—didn't the med guy say these drugs dangerously affected the central nervous system and made a person more violent and aggressive?' Kabir could not get KD's powdered and lipsticked corpse out of his mind. A very hostile woman could do that. Sunheri Kashyap must have has plenty to be angry about.

10

Her cell was icy grey with a stone cold soul. Her 8-feet by-8feet bunker held no promises. Her bed-plank-sink-bowl offered no hope. The stainless steel table was bolted tightly to the wall. Some more stainless steel in the form of a rectangular slab jutted into the cell sharply. Her bed. There were days when she preferred to sleep on the dry concrete floor. Straight-jacketed for hours at end, her eyes fixed at the small window mounted prohibitingly high on the southern wall. A forbidding steel door bolted from outside barricaded her inside her cell. Basically, there was nothing in the room that could be turned into a weapon. The chair she had requested had been refused.

Did they fear she would kill herself?

They were now taking every decision for her. A ventriloquist's dummy. When to eat. When to hope. When to shit.

She was inmate number 0486 in ward number 17 in Bheesha Jail and here for a terrible crime. The grey wall of her cell was punctured by a glittering red dot near the ceiling. She was being electronically monitored 24x7. The guard never opened her door until he looked in the window to see where she was. If she really wanted to injure herself it wouldn't take much to slam her head into a concrete wall since there were four of them pretty close by. But at least it was better than the non-ventilated cubicle in which she had to spend hours during her interrogation. Sunheri Kashyap stared at her metal and concrete cubicle bleakly. A half-inch thick piece of foam wrapped in coarse plastic was dumped on the steel slab after her lawyer had called in a favour with the prison superintendent. The coarse foam was supposed to act as a mattress for the iron bed, but instead, it cut cruelly into her soft skin, its customized pattern imprinted on her body. She was disoriented and drained, and every part of her body ached terribly. The relentless pain kicked off a defence mechanism and her body responded by becoming progressively numb. Feelings became indistinct, emotions unpredictable. In the day, her eyes grew weary of the unchanging concrete scene. At night, she thought she saw shadows, though never directly. The repetitive routine made thoughts hard to separate and capsulate.

'You can make it easy, Sunny Honey, or you can make it hard on yourself! And it will be harder for you given where you are coming from. So just lie lower than the roaches and maybe you will not be bothered.'

Some call Bheesha a control mechanism for the entire prison system—a penal cesspool where other institutions discard their waste. Sunny had heard horror stories about Bheesha from a girlfriend's junkie beau who did time here. That its dank evil interiors controlled you forever. That its putrid decaying atmosphere plunged through every conceivable pore of the body. That you could never be free of Bheesha. The truth is that Bheesha Jail was designed to subdue. Electronic grills, mechanical grills and steel doors minced the concrete corridors into sectioned cubes where a prisoners' line-up was pigeon-holed into a strict single file. Every few feet a prisoner was stopped by a door. Deviants and psychopaths were sent to different units of Bheesha to have their behaviour observed, corrected or punished. Or remedied. The thought of being 'remedied' in Bheesha was enough to sterilize any thought of resistance. Due to her case-history, Sunny had been forbidden to go near the 'pill lane' where medication was administered four times daily. Prolixin, valium, librium, thorazine injections and other chemicals handed out like gumdrops, prescribed for problem makers to make them sedate during their initial days in incarceration, till Bheesha slowly orchestrated their movements towards an urgency to do nothing. Till the most urgent thing became to decide to move or not to move. Already Sunny knew that the incessant clanging and opening of the iron gates in the unending corridors was something she would never forget. It simply went on and on and on. The persistent reverberation sent searing pain up her head till it throbbed and pounded ready to burst... The jail warden's torch washed over her halting its arc, verifying-examining-confirming-checking, preserving her like a specimen in amber.

Sunheri Kashyap. Prisoner number 0486, ward number 17.

Sunny Kashyap. Legendary director Vishnu Kashyap's daughter. Daughter of a whore. Occupation. Cock sucker.

A door opened. A well endowed woman walked in. The camera pursued her, spending a long time on the sway of her buttocks. She wore a clinging low-cut satin dress which struggled to contain her. The film was black and white but he knew the costume was red in colour. After all, he had bought it for her.

A flickering close-up magnified a devastatingly beautiful face with disturbing golden eyes. Tabu's face. Her easy unsettling unabashed sexuality challenged and provoked and disturbed. Vishnu felt sick and nauseous for he knew what would follow; he had seen the tape too many times. The full body shot lingered on every inch of her body, quick bounces from mouth to bosom to buttocks. Shoddy but perversely magical. For hadn't she come back to life? Smiling and beckoning—immortality conceived in light and shadow. Vishnu wanted to yank her out of the screen, pull her back in time, rescue her. Of course he did none of those things. His heart thundering, he sat frozen in the seat. The camera got close to her. His dead wife licked her lips and her white wet teeth glistened. She bent forwards, hand stroking her breasts exhibiting, clearly that she was enjoying being centre-stage.

'Darling keep it centre—I want to see everything—everything—'

He heard the strange doctor's thick voice. He switched it off.

Vishnu Kashyap could never watch the old tape beyond this point. He wished he could switch off the bitter memories too. But it had all come exploding back. The bitterness. The scandal. The vicious accusations. The pitiless half-truths. It had all come back with a big blast of ugliness. The morbid past mingled with the macabre present. He stared at the newspaper, pictures of his condemned daughter splashed by the callous media with ghastly details of her crime. She looked very fragile. But then she had always been fragile. Even when she was born and he had seen her sleeping contently in Tabu's arms. The tinier of the twins. Almost twins. Sunheri was born fifteen minutes after Suhana. He was so worried she would break like a brittle crumbly egg shell if he dared touch her. She was lighter than her sister and had golden eyes and Tabu named her Sunheri, the golden one. He feared if he touched her he would lose her.

When did he start losing her?

Vishnu Kashyap thought bleakly. He was her father. He should have shielded her. Protected her. But she never gave him a chance. He had been losing her for the last twenty-two years. Like he had lost her mother, he reflected grimly. Vishnu desolately stared at a laughing three year old Sunny...his Sunheri...caught and framed in happier times. In the distance, dogs howled and he could hear some singing and loud voices and merriment from somewhere nearby. He walked across the narrow corridor to Sunny's old room left exactly the way it was since she had left home. It was clean but the walls had a mossy mouldy feeling, the kinds you find in ancient houses with old memories. The limpid watery moonlight cut into little slices by the long window, fell as feeble stripy shadows on Sunny's bed. He was scared to breathe. Vishnu hurriedly bolted the room and ran to the dark and cold verandah. He avoided looking at the sharp edges and cornices of the towering film hoardings etched up overnight. Almost covering the night sky—Dream Star's latest film, starring Prince Sulaiman Capure and Avani Malan. He could not stand the gloomy quiet. After pacing the veranda restlessly, he returned to the living room and switched on the television. There she was, blazing on the screen. Her life a blank canvas for the world to paint its dirtiest fantasies. *'Out of control', 'ticking', 'party girl', 'cold hearted murderess', 'remorseless' 'just like her mother'...* was how the world described his daughter. But then Sunny had been 'that girl' for a long time now. The girl whose 'bold pictures' were on the net. The girl who did 'dirty dances'. The girl who brought disrepute to their family name with undisguised insolence. Provocative and foul mouthed when she wanted to be, Sunny had inherited Tabu's seductive easy charm. Magnificently feral when aroused, dripping innocence in repose. Exactly the same words had been used to describe her mother long, long ago. Her affairs, her addictions, her chaotic choices in life, and, in death.

"Tramp...like her mother—"

Kala's hostile face stared at him from the TV. His ex-wife was again on one of the channels. The woman who devastated his life for so many years with her unreasonable hatred, now barking grisly curses at his daughters.

"They are all horrrring murdererss—"

Kala's dead eyes stared at the camera sinisterly as she rambled on incoherently with old fury and sharp venom. The TV switched off abruptly and Vishnu found himself staring at his own gaunt face.

'Oh God! What is this? Why are you watching that beast?' Suhana said angrily.

'She has so much hatred. So much hatred even now...this woman—' Vishnu mumbled softly, unaffected by his daughter's anger.

'The woman YOU brought into our lives, papa,' she said harshly, regretting her comment when she caught sight of her father's crumpled face.

'I am sorry. I did not mean what I said.'

'That's—fine. How did the auditions go? Who are you taping now for the leads?' he asked without any real interest.

'Bizarre to not-so-bad, the script is taut—it's panning out—lots of talks happening, dad—I think you should rest now,' she replied softly.

'I too have an idea for a film—wanted to discuss about it with you. Wanted to befo—before this thing with Sunny—but now we have to get her out—we have to get her out—' He looked lost like a child.

'It's going to be okay. I will get Sunny...your Sunheri back...Papa. And yes, tell me your ideas.'

'I just want to rest now...you must carry on with your work, don't ever stop that. That's the only thing that remains with you. Your work. Don't ever stop your work. All this—this—will be sorted.' Vishnu said tiredly, closing his eyes as if wishing the ghosts away.

'Yes dad. Just take your medicines, and lie down.' She looked across at the withered shell of a man in front of her. Suhana did not have the heart to be angry at her father. She felt a mixture of pity and love for the man in front of her, the once darkly handsome 'legendary director' reduced to a virtual wreck after the terrible accident, shaking and shrunken. Abandoned by the industry and condemned to the margins of filmmaking. The great Vishnu Kashyap, newspapers said. The adage had been true but long ago. Very long ago. Much before his pathetic attempt at directorial comeback...some randomly sliced footage of shrivelled has-been stars past their prime who had agreed to work for zero budget in a bid to relive their golden days. His swansong. An embarrassing end to a blazing career. Suhana knew it had taken her father very long to realise that no one was interested in his ideas, his style of filmmaking anymore. Like it had taken him very very long to accept that his darling Sunheri was not interested in his kind of cinema. Suhana never forgot the terrible fight between her father and sister when tabloids reported Sunny debuting in a raunchy item number.

{'You want to be a nautch girl? You don't want to be part of decent cinema? A Kashyap girl will now become industry ki bar girl? Third-class directors like Jerome will make you wait in ante rooms forever—' Suhana had never seen Vishnu this furious with Sunny.

'So?' Sunny had yelled.

'Besharam ladki *what is this two reeler dirty film you are doing? Don't you care about our standing, our family respect in the industry?'*

'No,' Maybe it was Sunny's indifference that set him on edge that day.

'That haraamzaada Kalidas with whom you waste time... you know that he is a pimp, is he your agent? Am I dead? Are you in your senses? He is a pimp. A dalaal. Now he is getting you nautanki roles?' Vishnu was infuriated. 'Do you believe the rubbish that wretched Kalidas fills your head with? Or is it the drugs?'

'Mr Kashyap!' she addressed him by his surname whenever they fought, 'It's none of your business.' Sunny had saluted mockingly, which incensed him further. And Suhana could only stare.

'Time is never wasted when you are wasted all the time, Sir. But why not mention dear mother, Mr Kashyap? The 'respectable' Mrs Kashyap number one! Or is she taboo? They still talk about your wifey number one, you know, but of course you do know,

prancing naked to the party on a horse...shhhh! Taboo too right. Talking about mummy? Why she killed herself? Why she—'

He should not have slapped her. Sunny ran out screaming I hate you...I hate your wife...they don't see me. They only see her... her... HER. They see only mother.'}

Their mother. Their beautiful mother. While still a child, she remembered the wondrous glamour and fairytale aura around Tabu, but which was always tinged with a mixture of yearning and resentment, and finally disappointment and hurriedly hidden yellowing magazines laced with embarrassing tabloid tattle. Suhana hated her mother for killing herself. Even after so many years the accusations had not died, the whispers of the old scandal had never really stopped, just hushed when their family entered the room. And it was happening all over again. Her father looked scattered and, utterly tired and frail. His hands shook terribly, the result of a horrific accident years ago. But it was his tormented gaze which unnerved her. He stared into air as if he was watching a spectre come to life. A man caught between the ghosts of his past and a hellish present.

EARLY DROUGHT

He stared at Bombay's glittering skyline as if trying to see through the soul of a wily seductress. It had to be out there. The soul which had been sucked out of him. They should not have married. She should always have been unattainable, a mystery, an ache. But then he had been in love. And now that he had her, he simply did not know what to do with her. His out-of-control dazzling child-bride with her disturbing beauty. Each time he made love to her he felt emptied and drained and went into a void state. She was distractingly attractive to men who were drawn to her in hordes. He tried to control his possessive streak. To stay by the side of his new bride, he even refused a plum project which required him to travel around the world away from her. He was a helpless onlooker, watching himself getting sucked into Tabu's world. When she complained of missing the scent of washed veranda walls, he instantly commissioned a lovely garden as a gift to please her. He gave her her own garden to match the spectacular one at Bina's. Tabu's 'Eden', as she called it, was always laden with heady smells of rare flowers and exotic fauna. She kept the ground soft and damp, and pumped it with special khaad from Ganges. How she managed to procure the puffy black soil remained a mystery to Vishnu. But Tabu's Eden grew thicker and sweeter under its mistress's care. The garden smelled musky to sweet to odious depending on which shrub was flowering, marigold, petunias, bogunvillas, hibiscuses, bluebells, crocuses and daffodils bloomed in the stunning garden she had created on the terracotta walls of the patio. Creeping plants bursting with sunset colours coiled around trellises fixed to the wall, spilling on the floor, specially the money plant, for good luck, she told him. The garden flourished under her incessant care. Countless trips to the nearby farmhouse to get the special seeds, which she would plant and nurture with her own hands. She nursed the plants with a lover's caress...her hands encrusted with dirt. She was horrified when he suggested she employ a gardener.

'...What! But they are mine!' It was sacrilege to her to think that she would allow some foreign hands to touch her beautiful babies. No way. Talkative sparrows and noisy mynas, bulbuls, an occasional cuckoo...some wrens and robins and tewits flitted and hopped and tumbled through Tabu's little forest. They had got used to her beauty and she to theirs. They flew in and out relentlessly without fear, their eyes cocky while they shat on her patio without care and nibbled at her flowers. When they got too close to the fruits she would shoo them away, but they were never scared of her. They had started treating her as one of them. The garden became Tabu's favourite place.

And then one morning, when the flowers and the birds were wallowing under Tabu's attention, Vishnu woke up differently. Like a spell had broken. In a burst of clarity, Vishnu realised that since their union he had stopped complete communication with his craft. The director was swamped with guilt pangs that his talent lay wasted, his skills discarded and fruitless. When she tried to comfort him, for the first time, Vishnu felt petrified of her spell. He saw her unearthly beauty, as a thing outside her own control, waiting to guzzle him up, suck out his gifts. He felt himself hardening towards her, she who had turned him away from his work and made a useless, impractical man out of him. Vishnu turned with a vengeance towards his work. He promised himself he would not be swayed by Tabu's beauty and neglect his profession. Sitaara Matinee welcomed him back and Vishnu could not wait to start, and headed straight to the studios to begin work on his new film which was a hit at the marquee. A huge expense account and a complimentary posh apartment in upscale Marine Drive followed. It was a matter of time before Vishnu's compelling films had Bollywood hailing him as a path-breaking director and he signed a record multi-film deal with Sitaara Matinee, by now the biggest and grandest studio in Bollywood. Vishnu was happy he was no more simply a one-film wonder or simply Bina's son-in-law or worse, Tabu's trophy husband. Every hero and heroine wanted to work with him. Many for free. A couple of hits later, he was declared the new sensation.

Initially, Tabu enjoyed playing the great director's glamorous wife to the hilt. Tabu's charm, wit and impeccable pedigree did for Vishnu what his academic film school credentials didn't. It won him friends and admirers and an entry into the most elite clique of Bollywood. Tabu loved him completely, and in all truth, her life would have turned out happier had success not happened to Vishnu in such great measures, and had she been content posturing as the superstar director's mate. What he did not realise was that childlike and needy as she was, Tabu perhaps understood better than him, that their marriage was fast becoming one of convenience. His convenience. Success quarantined him from her. Being the superstar director made him inaccessible and insulated him from his wife in the most complete way which scared Tabu. Hailed as a visionary, Vishnu was being feted by the mighty and had the world at his feet, the world which was crowding a bewildered Tabu out of his life, leaving her forlorn and isolated. Did he deliberately not see through her pain and loneliness? Or had he misjudged her? For the famous Vishnu Kashyap, it was easier to go through life pretending that the truth did not matter.

It was a special day. She had decorated the house on their anniversary. They had missed the last anniversary since Vishnu had been on an out-station shoot. But this year, plagued by guilt for abandoning his wife, Vishnu made special plans for the day. He called her to tell her that they would spend the day together. She promised he won't be disappointed. With whatever she could find in the house, at such short notice, she decorated it in the best way she could. A huge bunch of concertina streamers and balloons stood instead of a glittering chandelier, silk saris on windows instead of silk curtains, she borrowed some lamps from neighbours and covered them with some of her expensive silk scarves. She thought of everything—his favourite drinks, his favourite music and his favourite food—and waited excitedly. But Vishnu did not turn up that night. Or for the next five nights. He had gone on an outstation trip as usual without informing her, with only a small one-line scribbled message on a piece of paper which his AD had forgotten to carry home. Tabu did not react at all. She quietly proceeded to remove the balloons and all traces of celebrations which had hung in the air for five whole days waiting for their moment of bliss. Their forsaken mistress consoled herself with remembrances of past happiness and new loneliness. Soon the room was as bare of gaiety as before and bereft of all colour. Tabu seemed to have shrunk a little, caged and prisoned in her own house. After five long lonely nights, that night alone in the house, she felt utterly suffocated and lonely and abandoned. Tabu Kashyap ran away from home for the first time. Maybe he should have understood the deeper malaise.

Did he deliberately turn a blind eye to the beginning of her madness?

11

DIGITAL DOLLY

Dressed in a simple white A-line dress, Digital Dolly gyrated and twirled seductively to loud lewd lyrics. The words of the song were decipherable but who was listening. Don, the popular icon of middle age machismo, aimed popped cherries, grapes, and raw baby papayas at the item girl's darkened navel. The lower and closer camera pans followed Digital Dolly's frenzied turnstile moves, till out of breath, she perched on a charpoy stroking Don's hairy chest, biting her lips in sexual anticipation. Don gritted his teeth with brutal anxiety, as if trying to keep a climax of herculean proportions at bay. Digital Dolly turned on her full seduction powers making love directly to the camera.

'Give me animal, Digital! Give me fire—' Dance Madame Chand Bibi whistled in appreciaion. 'By God! *tu phaad degi saari kutrina-futtrinaaon ki*!' The girl rushed and touched Chand Bibi's feet before resuming to take her position on the charpoy. She turned on her full seduction powers making love directly to the camera. Still swaying to the song, she unhooked her shimmery corset to reveal a golden brassiere. Don bent down and kissed her thigh and she gasped as if her bones had turned into fragrant vapors. And when he put her fingers in his mouth, her lips formed a small 'o'. Two cameras doggedly followed Digital Dolly's exploration of Don's body and lingered on a dragon with a snake tattoo on his heavy dark arms. A thick black snake which seemed to be throbbing with life. The camera tilted down to take in their entwined bodies.

'STOP! *Don ki gaand se camera hataao*—did I not warn you to avoid Don's hips and feet—got it? Bhenchodd cannot dance,' screamed Chand Bibi. For the next three sequences, the camera scrupulously avoided close-ups of Don's feet while devotedly recording each heave and pant and grunt of Digital Dolly.

'I don't know but yaar there is no mazaa-factor in this sequence. I want virile voluptuous carnal rustic coarse not fucking dance India dance—there is no sex in it...no fire.' Dance madame Chand Bibi said petulantly.

'We will fire it up with South Indian lyrics—rambha menaka urvashi type you know very Khajurao—Godavalli get me that tune—' At this song director Godavalli turned up the volume to full blast.

Heyy maangaa maangaa rendu maangaa–heyy mumbaiiyya poorilaalaakku dol dappi maa—heyy—

'What the fuck is this? What does it mean?' the girl asked.

'Who cares!' Chand Bibi sucked in her lips. 'We will premier it on youtube—the film will sell like hotcakes—they will run after you—*phaad dogee*!'

Some said Digital Dolly's real name was Patralekha Parihar and she was a smut actress from Bihar. No clarification was ever advocated and few who had dared to ask had suffered an abusive tongue-lash so the matter was mostly left at that. She was known as Digital Dolly and had built an illustrious career on her ability to simulate orgasms. She ruled the dim yellow light lit world of Z-grade sex films. She hit big time when one of her countless porn films shot to unforeseen, overnight notoriety: her film *Digital Dolly* ran to packed theatres in seedy single screen night theatres and the unedited versions went viral on the net. It was actually a simple film shot in a bedroom with a home video camera. The picture had her dancing with two men and a woman simultaneously in such fashion that it raised temperatures even in the freezing winter, and made her a sensation overnight. Over the years, the name Digital stuck to her and she was flooded with ménage de trois offers on reel. Never one to let go of profitable business proposals, she spent most of the next twelve months in bed and launched scores of raunchy reelers. She looked like a top of the line Barbie doll, except lately, Digital Dolly was getting a taste of the fickle nature of interest. She had been replaced by a much younger girl as the face of bold. And worse, none of her songs and dances had trended for the last three months. The novelty of *being* Digital Dolly had started wearing off.

But maybe it was not too late. What she desperately needed was an expensive rehabilitation programme. She knew her finances were drained after her breast augmentation surgery and nose job. Now she craved serious cash to raise her arse, tighten her crotch, maybe lift her eyelids and remove the slight tell-tale veins from her hands and perhaps another nose job would not really harm. She had hoped to make lots of money with Salem Hassan's Dubai shows. Except her plans were derailed by the murder. And now the police were on her sets to talk to her. No. She didn't want to 'merely chat' or 'just talk' or 'have a dialogue' or 'make a statement' about that night.

No. She would definitely not get involved in the bitch's shit. Getting involved would only lead to trouble, she told herself.

Digital Dolly sighed and entered the room marked 'Star' where the police officers were waiting for her. A servant entered carrying a special chair for her followed by food and soup. A trolley carrying her dresses was wheeled in and she started inspecting the wigs and the makeup-cosmetics, almost ceremonially. Finally satisfied she settled on a whorish pink what? smelling of cheap scent and turned her attention to the police officers. At that point, dance madame Chand Bibi also entered the room and swiftly planted herself on a vacant chair keeping a proprietary eye on her lead star.

'Cola for saabs!' staring at ACP Kabir Bhonsle Digital Dolly exclaimed, 'My God! You do look like Singham! Ajay Devgan type. Deadly-sheadly eyes *haan*. Chand Bibi, my dance madam here, saw you on television and I thought she was kidding but very solid *haan*?'

Shinde smirked and Kabir sighed. TV news had made his face most recognisable in Mumbai.

'I have never seen a fit police officer till now...what body-shody! Chulbul Pandey's body and Singham's eyes! You know in Mumbai we only get to see these *dheele dhaale* stomach-hanging-out-types. But you have restored our faith Mr Singham. You are not so bad yourself. Not as good as Mr Singham though,' said Chand Bibi smiling coquettishly at Shinde.

'Thank you. But if you want to stay here, you will have to be quiet. As noiseless as possible for Mr Singha—I mean Saab.' Shinde warned Chand Bibi. The dance madame shrank back into her chair but made no attempt to leave the room.

'Did you Google me? You know I have my own Facebook page!' Digital Dolly announced and Shinde rolled his eyes.

'She will soon have her own blog—are you on Whatsapp? I will Whatsapp you her—' Chand Bibi trailed off abruptly catching the policaman's stare.

'Uh—all sorts of cracks on the net—a hundred-rupee whore with fake boobs—that's what a jealous bitch has put about me on FB—!! These two babies—totally natural god-given!' The item girl proudly jiggled her mammoth twin assets in his face for proof and Shinde's eyes bulged out of his sockets.

Fact was Digital Dolly did not know what to make of the stern looking officer sitting opposite her. He had not once eyed her ample assets and that made her feel extremely unsure and uncertain on where she stood with him. For Digital Dolly, her sexuality was the supreme and valid currency when it came to dealing with men. But the ACP seemed annoyingly remote and unresponsive to her obvious charms.

'Ms Dolly I do not believe most of the things out on the net. Where shall we be then?! And I do not Google my witnesses. About the night—'

'Call me Digital naah—', she interrupted with a cutesy pout. 'You know, I am all shook up. Some cheapster has uploaded a morphed video of me kissing Chand Bibi! Imagine. She is my guru my, bhagwan. You know, I'm not the kind of person who will go for cheap publicity but this—industry is full of jealous people. I almost died of shock when I saw it. I plan to settle and marry and have kids in future,' the girl said. Chand Bibi's lips split in a sly smirk but kept shut.

'Going back to the night of murder—your three friends—'

'Digital Dolly has no friends in the industry,' assuming a third person the item girl hastily butted in. 'Digital is all self-made. My only friends are my darlings. Here. This is my lil Zebbie and Debbie!' She said brightly, pointing her painted talons at her enormous fish tank. Kabir's eyes rested wonderingly on a big aquarium housing over-fed bloated fish with dramatic stripes and a pair of oddly ballooned platinum coloured fish.

'Zebbie and Debbi are Chinese zebras... plecto—a plect—no wait its frigging Plecto-sto-mus! Cost a bomb, you know. I got them as a gift from—a fan! Part of my salary goes in feeding my babies, they are my only true pals. Don't shit don't smoke no smelly smells they don't take the place apart and no noise—They are so erotic. ...I can see your boy looking at my lipstick—this is called Ba'laue, it's made from batshit. It costs 900 dollars a gram. Just last month I got this Maca root powder, it enhances the desire to have sex. Did I tell you Zebbie and Debbie can fuck any time of the day from multiple orifices and with multiple partners!! These girls are made for pleasure I say—' She exchanged a knowing look with Chand Bibi. ACP Kabir Bhonsle had had enough of the item girl's fish and fuck obsession.

'Miss Dolly please save your titty and fishy tattle for your fans. AND—' he lifted a finger in warning, 'I do not care about who you have fucked, will fuck or won't fuck. Just get this. I am the person who you don't fuck with. NOW. Talk about that night. You, Nargis and Daisy and Sunny and KD. What happened in the room before you and your friends left Sunny behind with KD?'

'Puleeze don't call them my friends. We are just buisness colleagues. Professionals. No friendbaazi !? That Nargis Khaled is a cheap Lahori slut. Daisy Katta—hello—is too junior. And that Sunny is a doped out bitch—all girls call her that—creating problems for everyone—' Digital pouted churlishly.

'Your fingerprints have been found all over the place, in fact, we have recovered prints of Kalidas...I mean KD... from your dress too—and the lipstick is also yours—you could be in shit load of trouble.' The stern-looking police officer did not look as if he was bluffing and Digital's face rapidly clouded.

'WhaaaTT?! That can't be true! I met him several times but only job-wise...only work-wise! I don't send my dresses to the washer everyday, they can only be dry-cleaned—and the lipstick I told the police I left it behind by mistake—we were shoved out of the room—by KD—you can check with Nargis and Daisy—' she wailed.

'I am sure you are speaking the truth. Look at Shinde here. He is a fan! I know you will find it hard to believe but we are your best friends right now. But there are many people who think you are lying—that Sunny must have had some help. But who? Who helped her? They desperately want you in the station for questioning! If that happens I don't want you to worry, I will leave police constables to look after your Zebbie and Debbie. Of course they are not trained in fancy fish-sitting so if something were to happen to your two girls—'

Bhonsle pointed at the fishes and hit a nerve. Dolly was terrified. She looked around nervously and screeched at her maid.

'*Aiiiieee. Jaaao.* Get my glass. Go Go. Stupid *ullu ki patthee kaheen ki.* Standing here guzzling my hard-earned money,' and then suddenly she made up her mind.

'Mr. Singhamji I am not even involved. This is not my fault. Sunny created a tamasha at the farmhouse during the dance. It's all her fault. Doped out bitch. Bicholorides barbiturates benzederine amphetamines qualludes she was into everything. All at the same time. I have even seen her guzzling eu de cologne too!! She would pack her bags and leave without telling anyone before a show, and then come back without warning, bruised and groggy not remembering what she did or where she was. That was her pattern,' the girl hesitated and paused to take a deep swig of whatever was in her glass.

'Of course KD would get mad at her. Hooked onto all those pain-killers...this apart from her regular uppers. You know amphetamines controlled her even if she gotta sleep or shit. KD still did that bitch a favour. Got her dance gigs and stuff. Butyou know she would act as if she was doing a favour by going on assignments, after signing contracts!! Diva bitch from this star khandaan—always acting so superior!'

'You think this is all Sunny's fault?' Kabir asked.

'Stupid bitch, her airs got us in this trouble. Won't do this, won't dance like that...*fir aayee kyon*?! *Mera toh Dubai pucca tha*...it was all set and then she goes crazy...I hope she gets what she deserves. I hope she hangs for what she did,'she said.

'What did she do?' Shinde finally seemed to have found his voice.

'You should have seen her with...with Salem...such a big big man! She started screaming at him—by the way—I am sure she was acting up and jealous because he was eyeing me—'

'What did this Salem Hassan do?'

'Do what? Nothing. Just asked for a private dance. Not open copulation! C'mon, if you are that rich you are allowed to have your fetishes...she made such a big shit about it in front of everyone...he had paid for the dance show. Besides, she had led him on,' Rani said dryly.

'How?'

'Every girl knows,' Digital Dolly said in exasperation, 'if a man wines and dines you, then all he wants is breakfast in bed.

She flipped out with him. Madam Sunheri Kashyap suddenly stopped her act—she abused Salem and I think spat on him or something! Can you imagine? We are performers. Artists cannot ever lose control like this, however our fans behave!'

'Spat? He must have been very angry. Why is Salem such an important guest?'

'If you call owning whole frigging theatres and scores of entertainment companies and organized events in the Middle East and London nothing well then yes...he is NOT important!!' she said dramatically, 'It was all set! We were all going to Dubai—KD had a lot of money coming to him. You know Mr. Singhamji so much greed, hatred, violence... I am now going to do a movie where I will be a nun—I want to bring world peace—'

'From where?'

'Huh??'

'You said he had lots of money coming to him—from where?'

'How do I know?? I am not his manager... he is mine—I mean was mine—I can't do this, I am feeling dizzy now—' Chand Bibi reached her instantly and enveloped her in her ample bosom.

'Shhhh baby. There there...shhhh darling. Does baby want juicy?!' Chand Bibi cooed into Dolly's ears soothingly and barked at the maid, '*Aieee ladki jaa—juice laa.*'

'Please police saab, I need my artist to be in the right mood for the next dance sequence...she is looking so tired now. Where is the water? Shhhh baby girl. We will need a minute here baby are you okay—'

'No we are done—for now. By the way Miss Dolly, I think your Zebbie could be suffering from some liver disorder—I think the Malawi bloat disorder. Happens when they eat their own shit. Better get them checked.' Kabir Bhonsle commented as he left the room followed by Shinde. Digital Dolly flushed angrily and flung herself out of her seat sending the sofa rolling back with so much force that Chand Bibi crashed to the floor. The maid rushed in at the sound.

'*Aiieee ullu ki patthee.* Keep it here. Help madam get up. And go close the door, you dumbass.'

The maid trudged to the door after the inspector and shut it with a bang and a muffled curse.

'*Saali* Digital *kuttree.*'

'What did you say? I heard that, *ullu ki patthee...*' the women hollered simultaneously.

12

'We need an item.'

'I cannot have an item bang in the middle of this scene!'

'Ideally, I want three. A hot Lavni for the single screen front bencher, a mast Mujra for the multiplex babu. But you know what we simply have to do—? A Ho Ho Monny item. Do it.' Biddoo Bhojwani talked to Suhana like a man used to getting his way.

'Biddoo this film operates at two levels—' Suhana mouthed each word slowly as one does to a particularly dim child, 'a reality and a sub-reality. Right now my actors are in the psych ward and their world is shifting into a strange fight club! What I really need is a fight instructor maybe from Korea to do the action sequences—I do not need a dance master!'

'But that's my worry. I feel MCMM is turning out to be too anti-family. Remember we need to sell TV rights, no channel is going to buy it if the content is so dark. Besides, *kya karegee national award lekar*?' Biddoo said churlishly. 'I think we should also have a smutty item dance. Dirty pungent women in the tightest of blouses and petticoats....I had Daisy Katta in mind for this item with Sumraan. I have talked to Ho Ho. He is making a HIT song for us,' Biddoo said excitedly.

'Whhhat?!' Suhana looked stunned.

'Ho Ho Monny songs are THE formula for success. Everyone wants a piece of him. Think comm-er-cial.' Biddoo snapped his fingers.

'Biddoo don't snap on my face. And are we talking MCMM here because if we are then you must be fucking shitting me?' Suhana was furious.

What the hell was going on? Her sister was detained with a murder rap on her head. Her vengeful stepmom was gunning for them. Superbitch Jerome was bad mouthing her to half the industry. And now she was being sidelined from her own film. Worse still, her film, her baby, was being mangled and twisted and distorted. And she was expected to stand and watch! No way!

'Suhana I am not fucking shitting you. By the way, Ho Ho is fine with Daisy.'

'Ohhhh! Is that right! Who the fuck is Ho Ho Monny to decide?? I can't believe we are even discussing these characters. No way if I am directing this film.'

'Do not fuck with my commerce Suhana. I have run a test on her.' Biddoo shot back.

'You have—*you have? WHAT?!! WHEN?!!* And when were you planning on letting me in on it?'

'C'mon Suhana, don't make such a big deal. You had the court thingie to handle—the murder charge—'

'So? It's not fair that you call the shots behind my back! And by the way, it's only a charge. Nothing has been proven. And it will not be. She didn't do it. Wait a minute...w-what's happening here??? Is my sister's case the issue?! I understand the publicity is bad—

'Of course not. ALL publicity is good. No offence meant,' said Biddoo.

'None taken. Because you won't know any better would you? Biddoo, number one, Sunny was at the wrong place at the wrong time. The matter is sub-judice. Besides, I am handling it. And number two, the case has nothing...NOTHING AT ALL...to do with this film—I have worked my ass off for this film—do not treat me like a 'little lady' on the sets Biddoo—' Suhana shot back.

'I don't know what you are talking about, didn't we hire the cinematographer of your choice? The actor Sumraan was your idea—I wanted Prince—in any case, we thought with Sunny in jail you would be too caught up—

'Really now! I have never let my work suffer. Never. I never let my private and professional life mix... And what do you mean by WE?? Just who exactly falls under 'we'? As far as I know, I am still in charge of this project—' Suhana struggled to keep her voice calm.

'We were just trying to let you be with your family—'

'Don't say 'we', Biddoo. You cannot make decisions like this and not keep me in the loop—I have been working on this for the last eight months.'

'You cannot fuck with commerce.'Biddoo was adamant.

Typical, she thought. Mighty male, thinking he knows the market better than a woman. Or had Nisha Poddar's piece on her miffed off his little ego. *Suhana: totally in control of MCMM, despite the family tragedy. Suhana: the real 'man' behind Noir's new opus.* That must have hurt him bad. Stupid Biddoo. Pathetic man with the IQ of a twelve year old and the ego of a giant whale. MCMM was her one remaining joy to get her mind off from Sunny's dreaded ordeal. And it killed

Suhana to see her project being taken away from her. Now that the project was in control and looking magnificent, the Noir head honcho suddenly wanted to play Mr Big Man on the sets. Wanted to be at the helm of affairs, insisting that he knew what the audience wanted and cutting out some of her definitive scenes. Too non-commercial, he called her! Stupid self-important pompous dickhead. Suhana was trying hard to not to get disenchanted with the business side of filmmaking.

'But you know its an all-male cast.' Suhana said.

'Fine. The item girl would be the only female in the all male MCMM. By the way, we need to work on Sumraan's ending. The hero cannot die, Suhana!' Biddoo cribbed.

'How many times do I tell you? There is NO hero in this film. The plot is the hero—'

'Yaa yaa, I know that. The camera is the hero. The cinematographer is the hero. The lightman is the hero. But the hero is not the hero!!?? Listen....what's the point of making a 50-crore film where everyone dies?' Biddoo was caustic.

Right then she wished she could shoot Biddoo. For her the hero of the film was Iyer's brash and irreverent camera work, perfect for the visceral portrayal of Mumbai and her characters seeking revenge and redemption. Now if only dickhead Biddoo would get off her back with the item number chant.

'Sometimes, you have to go with these sort of things. You know how it works. It's business. Hey what do you know, you may just get the keys to a spanking new Mercedes car by the end of the shoot. Smile, girl! Beside your film is looking too pessimistic,' Biddoo spoke to her as if to a ten-year-old.

'MCMM a harrowing account of the darker, realistic side of man. It's bordering nihilistic, yes, but that's what we had discussed, that's how the feel of the film is. It's something we haven't tried in Bollywood before. And now bang in the middle you want an item number??' Suhana pushed one more time.

'We simply want to take it a notch higher.'

'Biddoo...the hero...Sumraan is supposed to be a rough, street-bred character—he does not do *gaana waana*. He represents the soul of the city. Edgy and restless and tough and merciless. Now you suddenly want him to sing and dance?'

'Yes. Don't be so harsh. Audience *desi hai*. Even our toughies have a heart.' She was being left with no choice but to shut up and obey.

'Have you seen the barnyard animals dance—it's viral on youtube!' Biddoo suddenly asked Suhana.

'What?'

'No hear me out—Ho Ho Monny saw this amazing dance on movement of barnyard animals! Like the Duck Waddle, Horse Trot, Kangaroo Hop, Squirrel, Chicken Scratch, Turkey Trot, and Grizzly Bear—the the—fox...fox...'

'The foxtrot Biddoo.' Suhana said tiredly.

'See, now you are getting it. We are on same page now—no choreography, simply moving to the beat of the music and—erratic dance mostly performed by ravers...come I will show you—Bela you come, come here girl!—give me your hand—couple moves together arm-in-arm—what happened Bela? Loosen up girl! Exaggerated hip movements. You know it's a sex pantomime which displays the man having a sensual, aggressive attitude—you know you are right, Daisy may not suit our film well—may not be good for this—too desi—I want someone chic—seriously—just one little thing favour?'

'What '*one little favour*' Biddoo?

'I was thinking—if Sunny is released—on bail—she can do an item for us. What do you think? A huge Friday 'superbang' and box office hallelujah all at one go?' Biddoo was all shiny eyed.

Suhana stared at the producer disbelievingly, not sure she had heard right.

'C'mon...don't look so scandalized. When is Sunny out on bail? I am sure we can work out something—' Suhana realized he was not kidding.

'No point in wasting time thinking up 'ubercool' ideas, when you have real stuff at home. Baby remember your Noir audience's *mentality wohi hai*! You will ask Sunny haan, Suhanaaa please at least ask her—'

Suhana got up and walked out of the sets in disgust. Maybe she would head to the beach, she thought. To clear her head and calm down sufficiently before the court hearing. As she revved up her car, her assistant Bela ran out waving her appointment sheet at her. But Suhana could not bother with any more appointments today. Let the toad Biddoo handle it. Let him do the shitty sweaty jobs too. Play the big man to his heart's content. Bela's yell that she had an evening appointment with ACP Bhonsle was lost in the engine roar of her silver SUV.

13

DAISY KATTA

'You are a fucking arsehole, Silky Mehta! Huh! No you are not open-minded. You are...you're just bisexual and a big mouth—' Daisy Katta raged at the top of her voice on the phone.

'I have already shot the item number. Even if that *chutiya* producer drops the item you have to see to it that he pays me my complete fee—you are my manager—I pay you 30 percent—you work the phone lines and get me another item. That crack-whore you are giving the role to—you really think I didn't know? She will only give you herpes in return and that too if you are lucky, *chutiye*—shut up! You listen to me...if I don't get my money I—hello I will bumboo you so badly it will hurt you more than your hamsters and ducktape and staples and epoxyresins. You are a blight! Bloody terminal illness *se marega*! Jeejus is watching you fucker!'

Daisy slammed down her phone. She still had the sexiest body in B-town—a certain dewy sweetness of an old film movie-star—pouting lips, a sexily bulging stomach, a delicious voluptuous sexpot. Having never quite cut it as an actress who could 'act', Daisy Katta was fast finding her abysmal 'acting' career fading away even before it could start. With younger actresses arriving on the scene regularly, plum movie offers were just not coming her way. Besides, every top actress, with or without the body, was willing to strip down to her skivvies. She wasn't even the number five choice when it came to 'bold' roles anymore. It was the 'wait' for roles she couldn't stand. Like waiting for Biddoo of Noir Studios to tell her...did he want or not want her for the MCMM item?

Fuccckkkk! After all the things that she had let him do with her. The bastard Ho Ho Monny had said she was a shoo-in for the job.

Fuckkking men. All the same.

And her manager Silky was proving to be of no help.

'I have had it with this frigging town. This is it. I am quitting. I am moving to Milan to be a full-time model, but before that, I am going to tell the truth about the big so-called pillars of Bollywood,' Daisy ranted breathlessly in front of ACP Bhonsle.

'Everyone wants to expose someone,' Shinde muttered.

'I am not a cheap item. That's so demeaning. I am an actress. A dream girl. People come to see me dance. They don't want rona shona. I make a shot red hot. This industry is filled with lechers who treat women like a piece of meat who give us a bad name. Everyone wants a piece but *upar se 'respectable' rehna hai.* New age shit! I have some *hazaar* horny respectable daddies. I can screw their *izzat.* But first I am going nude. Yes. NUDE,' Daisy chuckled at the effect her declaration was having on the police officers.

'But why does Daisy Katta want to go nude?' Holkar asked matter of factly.

'For a very noble cause. No, not animals. Someone has already done that. I want to get Mumbai's drains cleaned.'

'Uh.'

'Don't be surprised. I know you must be thinking why a girl would do something as scandalous as taking off all her clothes, but it's not for cheap publicity. I want to give the boys at the MCB some incentive—you don't know the MCBs??!! The Municipal Corporation of Mumbai baba...the boys want incentive. I am not like whatever-her-name-item who is taking off her clothes for cricketers. Puleeze! I have more class. I am doing it for a noble cause. Not for some silly sport.' Daisy revealed her grand plans excitedly. She wore a sheer top and no bra, the darkness of her nipples showed through the filmy fabric. Bhonsle tried not to stare.

'Just a second, I have to make pee pee..!' the item girl ran out leaving the officer open-mouthed. Sitting on the commode, flushing, washing hands...her conversation continued...

'You know in Lingaswamy's film I was offered that part first. The one which Sunny is starring in. That *Scent of Love.* But...Oh gawd! Aahhh!' *The noise of hot piss...*

'He was more interested in having the tart on his dessert plate, no guarantees, if you know what I mean.' *The commode flushed twice.*

'But KD got her in...you know it's sick, these managers have no respect for any actress here.' *She came out with crumpled tissue in her hand.*

'You were not happy with KD?' Holkar asked as she stepped on the treadmill refusing to be still.

'KD was my—manager—secy whatever, *panautee thaa*— and a thief. You know, he pocketed some of my expensive gifts for himself. I did not even know I had got a car as a gift for my last gig!! Can you imagine what a robber! Got his just desserts if you ask me...Jeejus is watching, isn't he? Dolly said he was investing in real estate in Dubai or Goa...*arrey par mera paisa kahan hai*??'

'You were registered there—at KD and Silky's company—'

'*Toh kya?* I still am represented by them. But I am not going to pay this Silky Mehta a single penny. He took 30 percent admission fee and what have they got me? No films. No talking roles. Just one crummy sister of the hero part. Hero *ki behen* and I will not even get raped or something!! C'mon... Do I look like a choot?'

'Of course not,' Kabir said quietly.

'And what production company are you talking about? They were running into huge losses. Silky blamed KD for almost packing up his company—KD laughed and called Silky a weasel! He used to taunt him pop goes the weasel! It was so funny! But it made silky very angry—pop goes the weasel... he used to hate it!

'KD had money and he held out help to Silky only on the condition that he sell him the company. Dirt cheap. Changed the name too. Silky Velvet became Kaydee Productions. KD pissed him off. But that's what's going to happen to every fucker, they will get fucked.'

'But wasn't KD already with the Bawlas. He made enough dough there—'

'There is nothing like too thin...or too rich. But I don't know about the Bawlas—'

'Did KD ever mention any problem with the Bawlas??'

'Jeejus!!! Why do you think I know?' Daisy was tearful. 'I am just a girl trying to make a living. I have a sick mother to look after,' she clammed up and no amount of coaxing would make her open her mouth on the matter.

Kabir had the file on Daisy. The daughter of a yesteryears actress, Resham Rani, who had seen her time under the sun, the stunningly fresh-faced Daisy Katta was one of the more beautiful item girls in Bollywood. But she had a history. At fourteen she became a full-blown heroin addict who needed work to fuel her craving for drugs. Her debut, a rock-bottom porn flick, had gone viral and registered 28000 hits before her mother got it removed by calling in a favour. She was then secretly shipped off to a rehab facility in Los Angeles, and hated her mother forever for that, but as they say, old habits die hard. She was back to her old ways in a week. She was soon reduced to a shaking shivering wreck of a girl with scarcely hidden needle jabs and virtually incapable of coherent speech. Her mother washed her hands off her when she found her in her vanity van in a drugged stupor sitting in a pool of her own urine. That was a turning point in Daisy's life. She reckoned that though she hated her mother, she knew that with her own tattered reputation, if producers still let her in their ante rooms, it was only because of the goodwill of her mother. At that point fate intervened in the form of Silky and Kalidas. And the world of adult films and item numbers opened up for her. The saving grace was that she still had most of her looks intact which made her a highly in-demand item girl, but Daisy still harboured celluloid dreams of making it big in Bollywood, just like her mother had. She was angry at not getting the right opportunities.

'You know mere talent doesn't help you sail through. Even girls like me have it tough. There are very few opportunities—'

'And that night...was an opportunity ?' Shinde asked.

'Yes KD had promised Salem Hassan's shows and concerts. It was a very very big deal. Many many countries. The money was very good. And he was heavily investing in films. I could have got so much more work. I heard he invested in at least three blockbusters last year. His men bought distribution rights and exhibition rights of whichever film he placed a finger on. Of course many were sad turkeys which didn't make to Thanksgiving. But he didn't care. He just had one interest. Heroines, actresses, item girls. They were all item-girls for him anyway...serial item-iser!' Daisy was tickled with the word and smiled. 'Item-iser,' she said again.

'Did he threaten you or anyone else?'

'No. No. It was the way he is built. He was like I mean supposed to be really big you know like...I mean you know—'

'No I don't know.' Kabir said.

'When happy, KD could be very generous. But when he's angry, he could be a son of a bitch. He would cancel shows and gigs and concerts and tours across the Middle East, for as simple a reason as like if he felt slighted... or if some actress did not do *salaam*...or some actor did not come to his party... or worst if he was in town and not invited. He could be very mean and the only way anyone could get to him was through his libi—I mean—he is a horny hound dog. Rumour has it he had once crushed a girl in passion. He bit off a girls breast and the other one still has painful stitches you know. Raakhsas monster.' Daisy took a deep swig of her iced tea. 'Last time he had sex with a girl she—she was discovered almost out of her mind from pain. She was carried to the hospital, screaming insanely tied on the very bed on which she was lying. She went into a coma from infection in a ruptured bladder.' Daisy turned pale remembering what she had seen. 'Not only he, his bastard bodyguards had also had her—she was out of her mind she—just a little girl. A model and so fresh.This place was not for her.'

'Where is she?'

'Left. Went back to Nagpur, with Mumbai's gift to her. Veneral disease. Last time in Dubai, some of his bodyguards got really aggressive. Thinking we are item girls *toh free maal hai*! Lewd bastards sent me countless lewd messages and graphic MMS's of their private parts. I always kept my distance—'

'But you did want to do his shows.'

'Show me a girl in the industry who minds an Arab paying for her jewellery and knickers and I will show you a slutty liar. Jeejus..! It was just a dance. The money was really good. Besides, there were four of us. Safety in numbers and all that. Sunny did not want to come at all. At first.'

'So what changed her mind ? Was it KD?'

'They had a strange relation. You know, one night she called me screaming hysterically that he would kill her. But when I reached her pad with a couple of girls she acted like nothing had happened and she and KD were the best of pals. And I felt so stupid standing there. She used to hide bruises and black eyes, but I was like dude...don't you ever come crying to me. You want him and you got him.'

'Why would she want to hang on with someone like KD?'

'She needed the powders and the pills. You haven't figured that out? She was broke—is broke. God knows where her money goes...but if uncle KD was handling her account *toh bhaiyya* say ta ta! She would never go to her high-flying sister for money. Was pissed off with her father too. A few loose marbles in that pretty head if you ask me. Really messed up and a full-blown addict. When sober, KD had her on short leash. But I think Salem had specially asked for her item dance performance. KD wanted us to make a good impression, after all, he was offering to sponsor our international gigs...lots of money...lots of Bollywood shows...I really wanted to go to Turkey...but this murder blew it up for all of us–' Daisy Katta's lower lip trembled in emotion.

'I mean she screwed it up for all of us that night. I needed the money, I really needed the dough.'

'Achha I should be on channels by now. Sshhh there–I AM ON TV!!! Heyyy that's not me... Uhhhh! It's that Lahori Nargis!!'

ACP Kabir Bhonsle could not believe what he was watching on TV. His witness number three, Nargis Khaled, was on TV zipping around like a stoned canary. The cameras followed Nargis's manic run outside a fashion studio pursued by some social activists waving flags and brandishing sticks. The astonishing drama was being played out in full presence of the media.

'Pakistani model and Bollywood item girl Nargis was beaten in Mumbai on Monday evening by some unknown social activists in full camera view, for a controversial photo-shoot she did a few days back—

'Oh god it was that cheap shoot she did with the flag. Sacrilegious,' screamed Daisy agitatedly.

Suddenly Nargis swerved crazily back towards the cameras and screamed.

'Stop hitting me...stop stop! I will reveal the truth about everyone—' Nargis screeched waving a little black diary even as two bulky activists got hold of her and unceremoniously bundled her into a car and out of the venue to some undisclosed destination—

'This is a re-run boss. Apparently it's been running all day. This happened yesterday!' While Shinde's eyes looked as if they were ready to burst off their sockets, a visibly stunned Daisy Katta struggled to regain composure.

'How come we missed it?'

'We were with Daisy Katta sir. Before that, Digital Dolly' Shinde stopped short when the television screen went frantic with shots of paramedics carrying Nargis in an ambulance to the hospital.

JUST IN: ITEM GIRL NARGIS RUSHED TO HOSPITAL
JUST IN: NARGIS ATTEMPTS SLITTING WRISTS
JUST IN: MYSTERIOUS CALL ALERTED HOSPITAL

'Didn't I tell you she will do anything? How cheap! How desperate can you get? Even I didn't think of this! Ohhh Jeejus.' ACP Kabir left Daisy Katta wringing her hands in misery.

14

Life in Mumbai could turn you crazy-loony-mad. If that didn't do you, then looking at the glittering happy people from your shitty angle could edge you to the psycho level. He had been there. An outsider looking in from out side with his nose pressed to the window of the party where everyone was invited except him. But today everyone wanted an *in* into his party.

Sitting in his plush office, Munjal Bawla took in the scene around him. A group of distributors, cinema owners and producers were waiting patiently to see him. Like any other day. They all wanted something from him. Like any other day. Protection and power.

His younger brother Chotta Bawla was reading from a newspaper.

'Last night a massive cyclone in Darjeeling destroyed DS Studios' expensive sets erected for the film Metal Man—'

'*Bhenchod!* This has become out of control. What should we do?' The white-faced senior executive from Dream Star Studios sweared nervously.

Chotta continued reading loudly.

'The force of the cyclone caused a twenty-feet light tower to break, killing three unit members—charred by overhead cables—several seriously injured—'

'How did it get out so soon?' Munjal rasped. 'You make it difficult for us to contain this now.'

'Dream Star is willing to pay.'

'That your Dhanna Seth will!! Chotta...check if the dead ones are registered with us? I want all the details on their years of service, dependants, insurance, relatives-everything,' Munjal signalled to his younger brother Chotta Bawla. Built like a monstrous bull with the temper to match, at six-feet nine-inches Chotta Bawla completely dwarfed his lean and slender elder brother.

'You know what's the greatest pleasure of my life?' Munjal said thoughtfully, '—the greatest pleasure is reading the sports section of the newspapers in my garden while eating my breakfast. Chotta reads only real estate and crime. That *chutiya* there reads the Bollywood section—they have so many supplements—it's a *bhenchod* shopping mall!!' Munjal looked astounded.

'It's a different world,' said the DS guy sagely.

'Same world. Different toys. But you know...same shit.' Munjal was cryptic.

'I saw on TV haan...so bad what happened to KD bhai–all over the news—'

'*Tera saga-wala thaa*?' Chotta Bawla said darkly, 'what do you care *chootiye*, you will get fucked either way.'

'The press—what are you saying to the press? About *your* dead?' Munjal asked caustically.

'Same shit...Uhh...that Dream Star Studios is extremely distressed by last night's cyclone and our only concern is for our colleagues who were hurt badly on the set.'

'Why badly injured?? Say 'hurt'. Say 'minor injury'. Don't make stupid statements. If the thing explodes it's your arse... HA HAA Chotta, look at him. He is shitting bricks.'

'What about the families of the dead artists? They will also—press for huge damages—' The DS executive wanted to know.

'Settle *kar dengey maamla.* But tell me...your film '*Metal Man* is what...a spy film naa?? I have a party, wants to invest big in production. Anonymous. Does not want name on poster also. Seventy crores. But ready to go upto your balls will blow to hundred Cs! Of course wants fifty percent on all profits, music, satellite, overseas, desi. But cash *mein dengey* eighty percent!! But tell Dhanna Seth this time Munjal wants fifteen percent. Paperless *hoga,*' Munjal asked.

'I don't know—'

'Of course you don't know. You are just a small arsehole. Your job is to get the message across—*Abbey* I can call also. But who knows *saala* nowadays all phones are tapped. Tomorrow if your film becomes a blockbuster you will hold me to same shitty 10 percent. This is Bawla's final offer. Tell your Dhanna Seth.'

They called themselves Munjal Bawla's army, or simply the Bawlas. Everyone in the film industry was aware of them, in awe of their ruthless clout. Their official job was to look out for the rights of innumerable faceless voiceless 'backroom professionals' and workers employed by the powerful studios in Bandra and Napean Sea to tiny production houses operating out of hired makeshift garages in Powai and Malad. Except it was the least-kept secret in the industry. That they had no qualms about striking under the table deals with the same studios when it suited them.

There were lots of theories on how the Bawlas came into being. Some said the Bawlas crept in through the cracks between the lifestyles of the industry elite and the teeming faceless masses on whose brow-beaten shoulders the industry stood. If the studios had recognized worker rights and not been so aggressively anti-labour there would have been no gaps for the Bawlas to enter. IF. Fact was Munjal Bawla with the help of his carefully picked men had already entered and had firmly ensconced himself and his army in crucial levels of the industry.The Bawlas functioned like an army with heads appointed for different areas. They collected knowledge from an army of informers, including item girls, star managers, coordinators, high-class hookers to out of work stars, and journos and junior artists, stuntmen, trolley men, unit hands, grips, stagehands, makeup and hairstylists, and projectionists. *A shoot had to be stopped?* The Bawlas headed by Munjal and Chotta, who some called professional mischief-makers, were experts at galvanising groups of wayward craftsmen whose primary task was to collect crowds within minutes to disrupt work. *Accident on sets?* The Bawlas reached before the police to determine the compensation amounts. Like when the set in Multan Studios collapsed due to old mine workings under it, or when the scaffolding collapsed resulting in three workers and a child being crushed to death, or when a fire broke out in Gangaram Balani's film set which scarred eight junior artists, it was the Bawlas who decided the compensation. Increasingly it was a lot cheaper and time-effective, to deal with the Bawlas.

The seat vacated by the DS studio executive was soon occupied by well-known producer Tunti Shah.

'Munjal...what's happening?' Complained Tunti Shah. 'We are paying the registration fee, even then your men come and ask for more money every day. They shout and scare our foreign technicians. Half of the foreign crew wants to go back.'

'But you are giving all the work to the *goras??* We have to redress labour issues,' Chotta retorted sagely and Munjal smirked.

'How much?' Tunti asked.

'Fifteen per cent. Costs have gone up.'

'Fifteen per cent is too much. *Nanga karoge kya*? What will I get? Eighty percent will go on overheads.'

'You dare to argue with Munjal motherfucker? Have you forgotten who you are talking to?' Chotta got up with such strength that Tunti was alarmed.

'Now now...you listen to me.' Tunti held out his hand in front of his face as if pre-empting a physical strike.

'Chotta...Chotta! Beta relax! Calm down Tunti Seth, these young boys—their blood boils in a minute...my brother means no harm! But Seth, I think you underestimate yourself.' Angrily Chotta passed Munjal sheets stapled together which read estimated overseas earnings. 'Your last film. I have the figures. 15 crores in UK, 20 crores in USA, in China...in Taiwan. In the Middle East. *Waah*! Mota Seth, is your CA not telling you something? Increase our overseas on this film. You have my guarantee, my men will not bother you in future. And you know what? We will get your *firangees* for you...*pakad pakad ke laayenge*!'

'But how is that possible? I will become *nanga*. What will I get? The overheads budget is a nightmare, the cost of hiring studios, the stars, the bloody stars take a cool forty per cent. Best is you please kill me then. Kill me,' The fat producer's face was suffused with a dangerous red colour.

'Tunti has become emotional. Haa haa! *Arrey Mota Seth ke liye AC tez chalaao.* Why do you want to take that 40 per cent star? Leave him for the big studios. I suggest you take Suman

Malvade and Bhavesh Daborkar. Take Digital Dolly for your item number. They are registered with us. You can give us fourteen percent and the rest we'll get from Suman Bhavesh and Digital. *Manzoor*??'

'I can take Raja Koppikar for comedy—but I have already canned with Nargis Khaled—'

'Tunti did you see what that bitch has gone and said about Sulaiman? You know Sulaiman is our boy. OK *naa tera naa mera.* Let's deal at thirteen per cent. FINAL.'

'—Munjal you demand too much—'

'We demand the fees because people like you hire artists from private agencies who are not registered with us. This leaves our people without jobs,' Munjal said menacingly. 'We have warned directors and producers many times that we would not tolerate this. Only if you would listen.'

In fifteen minutes Mota Seth walked out of the office wiping his sweaty forehead with a huge white hanky trailed by his army of harried looking ADs and CAs.

'Thirteen percent! Are they mad? I will be destroyed,' said Tunti Shah.

'Sir, we will cut costs. Take a mid-type heroine. Add two more item songs and a rape-shape! The backroom staff, juniors artists, slash their budget. Now that Bawla has his cut, he would look the other way. We can't mess with the Bawlas.'

Mota Seth stared hard at his CA and wondered who he worked for. But he had little choice. Mota Seth and hundreds of producers and filmmakers like him had little choice. Everyone had heard stories about what happened if you refused to deal with the Bawlas.

◆

'I don't think Tunti Seth is keen on settling. *Nahin karega.*' Chotta Bawla said.

'*Tau marega*–and then we will shit on him. Who is next?' Munjal Bawla's smile did not reach his eyes.

{Mumbai fucked you like no other place in the world. It was the place where millions came with stars in their eyes. Mumbai swallowed them whole. Made stars of a few chosen ones, and the rest she shat out. In Munjal Bawla's eyes, they were all the same. He had made millions off both of them, and intended to continue doing so. Munjal was one of those chosen few who fucked back. And hard. And tinsel-town spread her legs and welcomed Munjal. To get fucked. Again and again. Munjal Bawla remembered the time when he first came to Mumbai. He was terrified that the city would swallow him up whole and shit him from the other end. To be fair, Munjal had never dreamed that he would become a feared man and rule over Mumbai. To be fair, Munjal had never expected to live this long. He never wanted to come to maximum city. He was born in a poor suburb on the outskirts of Navi Mumbai. Beaten within an inch of his life on false charges of theft, he had been lucky to escape from a mob who wanted his blood for daring to rob a rich chawl owner. Actually, he had gone to the house to fuck the landlord's daughter, some nth time. This time, he had taken his Chotta along who had eyes set on the luscious younger sister. The two dreamt of getting the sisters in bed at the same time. The girls had finally agreed and the excited brothers waited for the men of the household to leave for their daily business. But in their excitement, the stupid girls had forgotten that there was a sick ten-year-old brother left at home, who was shocked when he went to investigate the muffled noises and creaking coming from the unused attic room. Munjal's face deep inside his younger sister's breasts and Chotta's hands milking the older sister, the

four bodies were totally naked and in utter bliss. The two were on their way out of the window when they ran into the returning landlord and the other men of the house. Munjal and Chotta ran the fastest race of their lives, chased by the men who swelled into a mob, straight to the bus stand and got onto the first bus which brought them to Mumbai. They had landed in Mumbai with just the shirts they were in and virtually lived in them for weeks. The brothers stayed in a nondescript chawl for a long time. Observing, assessing, planning and soon, launched into a life of petty crimes like blackmailing, theft, beating, hustling and bootlegging. It was only after a couple of years that they became known as the Bawlas. But Munjal Bawla was not satisfied with small-time hustling. He had plans for himself. It was a matter of time before Munjal graduated to the bigger game and married a small-time producer's daughter. His father-in-law taught him everything about the unorganized film industry. After two years of playing the good son-in-law and taking over the production house, Munjal dumped wifey and moved on with her goods to the real game. Bollywood. Where frauds, big and small, were a natural part of everyday life. He had made Bollywood his. Thrived on her deceits and scams and frauds. Munjal Bawla had broken every rule in the game and set up his own rules to create his empire protected by his devoted Bawlas. For them information was everything. Of course, and loyalty.}

15

NARGIS KHALED

Nargis woke up in the hospital room to the sound of the shrill intercom ringer. She was alone, but not for long. The voice on the intercom informed her that guests were on their way up. Nargis's throat was parched and she would have sold her soul for her favourite drink—rum, brown sugar, eggs and cream, and Benedictine all mixed together in the blender, and amyl-nitrate poppers added just at the right moment. Just thinking about it was giving her an orgasm. The cloying smell of the chlorine disinfectant made her sit up as she groggily removed the lace sleep mask stuck in her hair. The lights had been on all night, she was on suicide watch. Nargis reached for the orange juice on the table and groaned aloud. Her hand was sore from the tell-tale injury on her wrist. She attempted to step out of the bed but felt too weak and collapsed back. She reached for her bedside table and picked up a bottle of Vitamin E pills. She took out a safety pin and pierced the pill and wished there was some glycerine around to mix in it. It was the best and the cheapest softener for her non-existent eye-wrinkles. She dabbed the Vitamin E oil straight from the pill under her eyes, and stared at herself and smiled. Yes she still looked stunning despite all she had been through in her short career in Bollywood.

Nargis became Miss Lahore at the age of fifteen. Her real name was Waheeda Khaled Momani and she had lied to the pageant organizers about her age and name. Her conservative parents disowned her when she had not only refused to marry a 45-something business-man in Islamabad, but had posed in a skimpy outfit for the pageant, with a 'Miss Sexy' crown sitting pretty on her head. Waheeda Khaled Momani had other dreams. Dreams of Bollywood. She ran away from home, dropped out of school and started living with the smitten judge of the beauty contest, Mr. Soz. The young girl,with her brandy brown eyes, curly black hair and doe-like eyes had an irresistible charm which made grown men turn into boys. But being the next Mrs. Soz was not Waheeda's goal, so she grabbed all the money she could lay her hands on, dumped the huge silver candlesticks and expensive silks and shawls in the extra large fake Louis Vuitton bag Mr Soz had bought for their honeymoon, and copped it by sneakily changing her destination and flight time to Mumbai. She had to pay a small fine but that was okay. Waheeda was on the ride of her life. The first thing she did when she reached Mumbai was find out the address of a doctor who would give her bigger tits. Getting the boob size 34 B became an obsession with her and life got easier when the doctor, sensing her desperate-but-hard-on-cash status, asked her to sleep with him. She obliged readily. Her reward was the biggest and most beautiful pair of tits. She then changed her name to Nargis, got herself a PR-secy-manager-coordinator rolled into one who, impressed by her boobs, first slept with her, then happily supplied the eager girl to horny actors and producers who promised her the world in exchange for a fuck. With an equally smart head on her shoulders, Nargis saw to it that her toils and exertions got her closer to her goal. Within a year, Nargis was an in-demand party girl, had her own site with a choc-a-bloc date diary and three hit item numbers and innumerable little talking and walking roles to boast of. But the big break which would have made all the difference to her career evaded her with alarming regularity. At least five really important film offers of huge consequence slipped out of her hands almost overnight. And she knew why. Nargis had taken a hard look at her life and decided that some people would have to come through on their promises and fast.

'Come in,' she said. The door opened and the familiar looking police officer came in. ACP Kabir looked at Nargis sitting up on her bed in the nursing home, her stunning eyes rimmed in red, wrists swathed in rolls of bandage.

'No wonder you look so familiar. I see you every day on TV. You are famous!' she grinned.

'Not as famous as you ma'am,' Kabir said. Nargis had the grace to blush.

'Raped fucked screwed banged rodgered for five years. By Mumbai. And now on this hospital bed. All alone,' she said with a wry smile.

'How are you feeling? Doc said just a scratch—you are ready to be discharged—'

'I am not okay. It was an accident—'

'Good that the ambulance had already been alerted—'

'Are you implying that I called the hospital—that this—this all is drama?? Why will I do a publicity stunt. Nobody would mess with their face for publicity. I hurt my jawline and my forehead—'

'I am not here to question that hypothesis. At least not this time.'

'I know who is behind all this—my life could be in danger. I have noted everything in my black diary—I am lodging a police complaint against Prince Sulaiman and Chaman.'

'The Prince Sulaiman? Superstar Prince??' Kabir asked incredulously.

'Yes. And what '*Prince*'? His real name is Sulaiman Ali. And '*Capure*' is not even his father's surname. It's just a figment of that megalomaniac's imagination.'

'He is casting some other girl for the role he had promised me in his new film. For years he has been promising me a heroine's role! But now I am just an item girl for him! Not good enough to be heroine material for Prince Sulaiman?? I was good enough when he was raping me *haan?* I will demand justice, I am going to file a police case against these scumbags. But that's for later. What I really want to say is do check out my film *Banjaran Kairi,* its preview is happening soon—I'll send you complimentary passes for it—I may be from Lahore but I understand Indian culture very well. I want to show people what real sex appeal is all about.'

'Sure. Shinde please set a reminder—But tell me Miss Daisy, you must have scared a few people with your habit of keeping details... and secrets and little black diaries!!'

'Let me tell you. When you are in Bollywood, not only who you know, but what you know helps. And it's a man's world so we girls need to keep ourselves armed. I don't mean knives,' Nargis said.

'Let me tell you. I am a simple *gharelu* girl from Lahore. I had been warned about the casting couch in this film industry but I never believed it till Sulaiman stripped naked in front of me, asking me to have sex with him in his office right there and then. This was when I went for an audition for Fullhouse, five years back. I screamed but then what had to happen happened. Who am I? Who will believe me? But I have proof—I am waiting for the right time—I am an actress not just a cheap type girl—I had acted in several films in Lahore, I was a beauty queen—'

'How well did you know Sunheri?'

'Sunheri—? You mean Sunny—uhh no one called her Sunheri except her family I think! When I first saw Sunny I thought she was a big heroine or some big shit. *Khandaani hai*, I heard. But there is something...like an almost a self-destructive quality...in her. She wanted to make it as a heroine you know, but she really did not have it in her to act. I am not lying. I have seen Sunny acting. It is embarrassingly bad. Real *bakwaas* acting. Acts like a sleepwalker. But dances like a dream. There is something about her that the camera loves when she moves. As long as she does not say anything! She got the best item numbers—but would act pricey, sometimes disappear suddenly—KD used to literally stuff her with dope just to keep her in one place. Once when she called me bawling uncontrollably I tried to tell her to check herself into rehab, but she stomped out cursing me...back on the road...and popping pills and barbits on the move. We would meet at shows and she would be all graceful and sweet and smiling and calm. And with KD again. Of course she would never talk about going to her sister for help—let me tell you she wore the Kashyap surname like a thorny crown. But she never played the victim. She had the goods and was up for sale. The story is the same with every girl.'

'KD knew about your secret black diary habit?' asked Shinde.

'Huh!! Are you joking? KD himself gave me most of the details. He loved bragging that he had half of film he had half the film industry's daddies and mommies by their balls and snatches. He would flaunt his Bawla connection—and I think that's why people were scared of him. He had a lot of insider dope on people, used to use it to get money. He angered a lot of people—overstepped his limits too—just recently there was some—some Johnny D'Souza—KD was furious—'

'Who Johnny D'Souza?'

'I mean he did not voluntarily tell me. I stumbled on his name accidently it was written on some piece of paper—asked him who was Johnny D'Souza, just a casual question and you should have seen his reaction—*chootiya* started abusing me—threw me out in my bra—arsehole low-life schmuck—'

Now...who the fuck is Johnny D'Souza?

'Hmmm right. But really...uh...who is Johnny D'Souza?'

'Like do you think I care?!! After he threw me out like that. *Chootiya aadmi.* I would act all hazed and zonked out during our sessions and note each and every detail about each and every hero, heroine, producer, director—it was my ticket, you know some day—some day if I got stuck in a jam I could always dip into my treasure and call in a...what you say...a friendly favour!'

'Did something...anything strike you as odd, that night—'

'It was all odd. But the usual odd. Salem was—fixated on the topic of sex. With whom we had done it. How we liked it. If we would like to do it with him. Just getting his kicks and cheap thrills. Even while we were doing our mujra dance act, he would shout out lewd questions. He even asked how many abortions I had had. I didn't want to annoy anyone. I tried to tell myself that he was testing me to see if I reacted badly. But Sunny flew off the handle. She shouldn't have come. She was acting up even before the show, and KD crammed her with barbits and locked her in the loo, and let her out only just before the dance. She was not in the shape to handle this shit—she—she started yelling—and Salem got furious—and she jumped on him...started tearing off his clothes, her laughter got hysterical and weird, and she started wailing like a baby and...and then she pissed on him—that was funny you know...I also started laughing seeing his face—Salem was going mad—it was chaos—'

'Dolly said Sunny spat on Salem. '

'No she pissed on him. I saw it. And—'

'And?'

'She was always far too beautiful, attracting attention of the really demented and far-off kind. But herself, she was not predatory like that bitch Dolly or Daisy.... Look what you want to know is what happened. She attacked KD, that's obvious. When he barged into our hotel room, frankly it was very scary. I really don't know what happened between them that night after I left. How could I have known? I left, remember?' She said extra brightly.

'Are you sure you are not hiding something? Or is this one of those things you will add in your little diary—for a rainy day??'

'Officer, in Bollywood everyday is a rainy day. I have learnt one thing about this industry—you are not allowed to fail in this city—I don't make a mess for myself and I don't create a mess for others.'

'For your sake I hope you are telling the truth. There is something we found there. In the room. We know it belongs to you—'

'I am not ashamed of my sexuality. That sex toy is mine. It's the latest version of a simple vibrator. I am not ashamed,' Nargis said. 'Just a little something I got to show the girls. Big deal? You know it's strange and sexist that in today's modern times anyone should question why a girl carries a vibrator or has condoms in her purse and that she should be expected to feel embarrassed by it. I bought it in Italy and it's battery operated. It is red and shaped like a banana but is ribbed to enhance pleasure. The 'pinky banana' is a popular brand!' She ended with proprietary pride.

'No crime right?' she asked.

'No. No crime.' Kabir replied.

16

'*A dead body has been recovered off Marine Bay, suspected to be that of actress Dannie—*' Kala stared at the yellowed newspaper cutting she always kept in her purse. Of course it had not been Dannie. And every time a body was discovered in Marine Bay, twenty-one bodies in seven years, it was not Dannie. Seven years ago when her daughter vanished into thin air, Kala got to know of it from TV three days after she went missing from her boat. No one had bothered to tell her. Jumped or fell, they had asked the question a million times.

'*The twenty-year-old actress either jumped or fell to her death from the second level of the luxury boat*' The lines were ingrained in Kala's mind, as was the video. The retrieved CCTV footage showed Dannie going over to the deck and then a quick flash of her fall from the two level red and black boat. Kala remembered each detail. The stunning red luxury boat presented to Dannie by Dream Star studios after her first superhit. The crew had noticed that Dannie had been missing since morning and when she couldn't be found, the CCTV footage was consulted. The hazy recording showed her jumping or falling, it could never be concluded, from the deck of the boat. A total of twenty-one bodies were recovered from the spot, six miles off the Marine Drive Lighthouse, over seven years. It was never her daughter. And then the police gave up and closed the file. Kala clutched the yellowed paper, looking up at the court deliberations only when Sunny's name was mentioned.

Her beautiful daughter. Rotting in the soil somewhere while Tabu's daughters were alive. Kala's blood boiled with age old rancour. She would make them rot. Kala could not understand why every person she cared for was snatched away from her. Her husband Vishnu. Her brother KD. Her daughter Dannie. It had started right from her favourite aunt, Bina, the superstar. As a child Kala had stared at her movies, convinced that Aunt Bina was a fairy goddess. She felt special when Bina visited their house in her star car and with her army of servants to shower her sister's children with expensive gifts. Why did Aunt Bina stop loving her after her bastard daughter Tabu was born? Not only did Kala loose a doting aunt, even her own mother became partial to Aunt Bina's stunning daughter. Overnight, Kala, handsome in her own right, became the plain-looking elder sister, introduced eternally as an afterthought, or mostly not at all. Everyone loved Tabu first.But Kala's world had come crashing when, her first crush, the young Vishnu who she had wanted for herself, also fell in love with Tabu. Kala Kashyap knew that she had been shat upon by fate. And it was time to shit back.

Time had set Kala's features hard and reduced her already thin mouth to a straight gash. With plucked eyebrows pencilled in a high arch and a look of permanent disapproval on her face, she stared at the young girl in front of her malevolently. Sunny's golden eyes reminded her of the one woman she had truly hated all her life. Even after Tabu's death, her golden eyes mocked her from countless tabloids and gossip shows on TV. Tabu was alive even after death through her seed, Kala thought with growing hostility, whereas all that remained of her brother and daughter were putrid bones and decomposing memories. Her eyes met Vishnu's for a split-second and they stared at each other. Kala looked at the desolate father in smug victory. For Kala it didn't matter whether Sunny was guilty of this crime or not. In Kala's eyes, Sunny was guilty of a bigger crime. She was Tabu's daughter. And she looked diabolically like her.

'Not the sort of daughter anyone wants. She is a brazen hussy. SHE is an expert at playing the demure bitch and the devious seductress. Prowling around men for momentary satisfaction. Sexually she is out of control.' Kala's righteous tone rang out in the court as she took stand. The day's hearing was punctured by her continuous spitting of venom.

'KD gone Dannie gone KD gone Dannie gone Sunny going going gone going going gone,' she hummed to herself.

{She should never have agreed to marry Vishnu when Tabu died. But Aunt Bina had insisted and a part of her was elated at the chance fate had offered her. Of course she had made a great show of sacrifice of marrying Vishnu only for the sake of the two motherless daughters. It had backfired horribly. Though she too bore him a daughter, Vishnu never became her husband. He remained Tabu's husband. And she, Kala, became her daughters' keeper. She had dragged herself to court despite the pain in her crumbling bones, a cruel sentence passed on her by time. Kala would not have missed this day, or any of the hearing for anything. She remembered the last time she had seen him in court. When she had charged him with abandonment. Abandoned by him for his daughters. And now he stood condemned through his daughter. Kala wanted revenge. From Vishnu and his two daughters, and from Tabu. Mostly from Tabu. Her dear ex-husband's first wife. The wife he drove to death. The wife he loved to death.}

The prosecution lawyer showed the court autopsy pictures of more than forty wounds on Kalidas's body to prove the severity of the murder. The photos and summation presented by the prosecutor described Sunny as a 'she devil', a 'danger to humanity'. The prosecution was demanding the severest punishment for her. Shocked by the gruesome photographs most of the jurors looked away in disgust.

'Will you let the perpetrator of this crime go scot free?' The prosecutor hollered dramatically at the jury.

'I was always scared. Warned her father that she was the sort you know will end up dead in a toilet with a gut full of pills and a needle jabbed in her arm. Debauched...perverted... you should have seen the girls who came to her house...all painted trollops! We are asking for justice,' Kala raged and had to be warned by the court to keep her emotions in check.

{Consigned to a loveless frigid married life by parents who were happy to get the plain and dowdy Kala off their hands. She had known for a long time that Vishnu had never lost his love for Tabu. His consuming love, and afterwards, hatred for his first wife, had left him utterly incapable of love. She had understood the truth about the man she had given her life to, too late. And by then she was scared to come to terms with the truth, as acceptance would have been recognition of her uselessness in Vishnu's life as a wife. He had only wanted her as a mother for his two girls. She was merely his children's keeper. And the futility of her wasted life twisted her heart.}

'KD gone Dannie gone KD gone Dannie gone Sunny going going gone going going gone,' Kala hissed softly at Vishnu sitting two rows away.

'Your daughters will die too. ROT!! It's Sunny's turn now.'

'I don't want to speak to you,' he gasped at her extreme hatred, his thin face shrinking an extra inch in tension.

'KD gone Dannie gone KD gone Dannie gone Sunny gone Sunny gone,' she took up the chant crazily. 'Mark my words your end is coming soon,' Kala said, her features grotesquely distorted with bitterness.

'Dannie was my daughter too,' Vishnu turned around and said with a lingering sadness, 'You call yourself her mother? You knew nothing about her.'

'Your slutty wife started it. Your slut produced sluts.'

'Shut up, psycho,' and he walked off trembling.

Kala's mad rage culminated in a spine chilling screech, 'And your seed will rot with you. As you sow, so shall you reap sooo will you reap—' A crafty smile lurked on her lips, her eyes seemed to hide a guilty secret. She would see to it that Sunny's youth would rot in the cell. Revenge for the life she had been consigned to, by the one man whose love she had craved for. Kala wanted revenge from Tabu who stood before her in court today condemned. She would punish Sunny. Punish the Kashyap women.

'KD gone Dannie gone KD gone Dannie gone Sunny going going gone going going gone,' she chanted, smiling in triumph. Her empty eyes mocking the world, privy to a guilty secret locked up tightly in the innermost recesses of her mind.

MISSHAPPEN MOON

'I think you are a very sad isolated person,' she had told him forlornly when she came back from rehab the first time.

'What do you mean?'

'We are together but only physically. Mentally you are the most remote person I have ever seen. I think you want to be lonely and detached all the time,' she said.

'That's rubbish.'

'Why do you hate me?'

'I don't hate you. I hate desperate people,' Vishnu was exasperated.

Tabu was only seventeen at the time she got married, and was obviously not ready for the responsibilities of marriage. Her acting career fizzled out even before it had started but then, she had never seemed serious about it. That her own husband refused to cast her in his films dented her fragile self-esteem further. It was sometime then that she developed an addiction to crystal meth, which soon became her sole purpose in life till she blacked out at a party. Getting her to rehab was the easy part.

'It took this to get you back to me. You loathe me. You find me repugnant. You look for reasons to stay away from home.'

'Tabu, you have too much on your mind. Stop being so self-absorbed. Distract yourself. Get a hobby for god's sake.'

'There is something within you I can't reach. And you won't let me,' she had said, before he left to travel the world to attend several international festivals. And then one night, when he was on location in Turkey, an agitated Bina called to say Tabu was pregnant. With twins.

'What have you done to my baby? Why is she looking so wretched and desolate?!' Bina lamented. 'I thought you would put her in your films. Instead she is having babies at this age! She is eighteen! What a waste!' Bina did not hide that she rued Tabu's early marriage and motherhood. She was convinced her daughter was suffering from severe depression, and was in fact in no shape to take care of herself, let alone the twins.

'I can't believe you can talk like that—I am sorry you have to accept that she just does not have it in her to be in films or have a career—' Vishnu remained unruffled.

'She is not the girl she used to be,' Bina bemoaned loudly.

'—most girls grow up, you know Bina. You should tell Tabu to grow up fast—'

'My god! What a heartless sod you are! You people are so—her education had been more progressive. I thought you saw that. I regret I let her get married to you. She needs to get out. She needs attention. To socialize. Meet people. She is just not the girl she was.'

'Well then Bina, seeing that you understand your daughter better than I understand my wife, the heartless sod that I am, why don't you do something about it? I have never stopped Tabu from being the girl she was—and excuse me but I have a film to direct—' It was Vishnu's most successful year. He had given three back-to-back hits and superstars were queuing up to work with him. The reigning heroines were ready to do virtually anything to be in his films. And the tabloids lost no time in linking Vishnu

with his heroines. He had not visited home for almost six months and Bina took matters into her own hands to get her daughter out of depression.

He could not identify exactly when she had started having her affairs. He remembered that she had started looking frightened and happy without reason and he had been startled. Tabu's increased stoicism and acceptance of his long absences took him by surprise. He suspected that was hiding something from him when he spotted her sneaking in and out at times but he did not suspect anything odd. A part of him was relieved that she had something to occupy her, maybe a hobby. Vishnu was relieved she was off meth, and left her mostly alone. The girls, adorable little cherubs, were delightful company and it was with them he preferred to spend the precious little time he had left for his family. And then it came out in a tabloid. Several others followed, with pictures and proof. Her little outing in a famous nude artist's farmhouse and some intimate pictures. He would have ignored it for tattle had it not been for the tell-tale pictures. And then her rendezvous with the doctor. The doctor who had been giving the tired and emotional Tabu treatment of the most intimate kind for her nerves. This consisted of giving an entirely naked Tabu a nightly rub up and down in the privacy of her house. Vishnu felt violated, his world compensated. Tabu was making more headlines than him. Tabloids splashed when the captain, in whose company she was seen often, said Tabu had been a 'surprisingly easy conquest'. Lurid details of their love affair were published and became the talk of the town. Then there was the celebrated author and then another. He got to know of her affairs from the tabloids.

When he found out about her shame, he went on for many days as if he knew nothing. He never showed any sign of whether anything was different. But he had stopped sleeping. He became withdrawn perhaps, but Tabu didn't know the difference. He would stay awake staring at her till late night getting more and more contaminated with anxiety. His angry solitude progressed to an insomniac's delirium and coherent communication between Vishnu and Tabu became almost impossible. As she withdrew even more, he was confined irrevocably to a permanent state of virulent anger, sometimes prepared to go to any extent to stop what he thought was his complete humiliation. He found her presence abhorrent and did not make any attempt to hide his repugnance. Unable to withstand the prolonged maddening hostility, the ugly verbal assault and lengthy interrogations, Tabu lost the strength to live. Vishnu forbade Tabu all communications with the outside world and decreed complete ban on her movements. Tabu lost whatever remaining cheer was left in her, became morose and continued on a downward mental spiral into bottomless darkness, bitter and isolated, with fading fantasies of long lost tender moments as her only refuge. Her girls and her garden suffered neglect.

Then one fine day when she was watering her plants, Vishnu burst. Shouting like a man possessed, his eyes dark with despair, Vishnu pitilessly smashed to pieces her favourite flowering pots, tore up her garden. He dragged her ruthlessly from one corner of the garden to another and threw her callously on her well- tended flower beds, his faced etched with implacable decision. And in front of her eyes he cold-heartedly and systematically began uprooting her garden, all she had tended with care and prized and cherished. Not content with mere uprooting, he plowed, ransacked, smashed and broke every single pot painstakingly planted by Tabu, all the time screaming invectives, hurling abuses till he started frothing from the mouth. Suhana and Sunheri came running to the patio and ran to their mother lying shrunk in a corner. Vishnu caught hold of the frightened girls who cowered and trembled in fear from their father who seemed transformed that day into something ugly and infinitely scary. They could not understand why their father was screaming bad things at their mother. Vishnu dragged the twins away from their mother with a warning that this was the last she was ever going to see the girls.

Something broke inside Tabu that day forever. She spent the next week vomiting every night, as if her body too was rebelling against its mistress. Vishnu took the girls to his new apartment—an unfortunate act he would rue for years to come. He still remembered the fateful night with horror and dread. His friends had gathered, distinguished members of the media and critics, and it was an intimate soiree with scripts being discussed when Tabu entered unannounced. She looked flushed and Vishnu should have read the warning signs. But when he told her to leave, he golden eyes crackled with such contempt and disdain he was rooted to the floor. He had never seen her so sure of herself and he did not want to create a scene in front of the crowd. Vishnu gave her his hand and led her in, and his friends gathered around his beautiful wife. And then Tabu calmly removed the huge coat she was wearing and stunned the gathering. Tabu, Mrs. Vishnu Kashyap, his wife, the mother of his children, was utterly and totally nude. In high heels and with a wine glass in her hand. Tabu then proceeded to straddle a horse dummy and posed naked even as the media clicked away. Vishnu turned to stone. He had no control over this woman. This was a stranger who Vishnu had never seen before. Finally, one of the guests threw a stole on her and took her out of the room, but not before she had been rendered infamous for posterity. Vishnu realized the extent of her madness. But it was too late. Tabu's paranoia drove her to leave her home and live on the streets for a few days. After several days of living on the streets, she was discovered hiding in the toilet of Bioscope Studios. She had cut her hair short in an effort to disguise herself and the caretakers mistook her for a homeless woman. She had spent a lot of time living in cardboard boxes and smoking crack pipes. One of the bums tried to rape her, kicking her in the stomach when she resisted, hitting her in the face and dislodging the caps on her front teeth. After being missing from home for four months, she was discovered covered in lice and filth and shit. This was the last time Tabu ran away from home. No one would see her alive again.

17

Not bad he thought. Not bad at all. Prince Sulaiman Capure regarded his image reflected on the long rococo gilt mirror in the sixteenth century castle set. A piercing gaze which flashed steel over the aquiline nose and a strong sexy mouth. Prince remembered the time when as a young hungry model he had to wait on horny producers, eager for a part, any part, in their productions. At five-feet eleven-inches with a perennially sexy tanned complexion, he was much in demand after the shoots had wrapped for the day. And he had made the most of it. What he thought he lacked in looks he made up in charisma and total lack of inhibition. It paid for his expensive tastes and soon he got his first two-line part in a film. A dying cop's role. Thankfully the film tanked and he was discovered by Dream Star.

Prince Sulaiman Capure considered the arched ceilings of the hallway, the fiery burnt brick fireplace was stunningly reminiscent of a quintessential castle dining hall. The richly adorned wallpaper, wall candles, and medieval-era paintings, down to the art deco bathroom walls—the set director Mithila had kept every little detail in mind. He was not exactly a fan of medieval architecture, but this time he was impressed. Mithila had really outdone herself. Her film-set designing course in

France University had done wonders. He would know, he had paid for it, or at least that's what he told her. All he had to do was to make a call—after all, they wanted him to accept an honorary fellowship. It was a win-win exchange. Prince got excited thinking of what all he had made Mithila do for that one favour. Her tight butt and slim breasts were a change from the over-endowed women he had been humping. There was a time when they could just not be big enough. When he loved nothing more than to dive deep into the milky mountains after a pack-up. But his tastes had changed drastically after Sunny with her perfectly formed body. He had become more discerning.

'Should I do a film with an item girl as my heroine? The prince of hearts, a superstar, walking into the sunset with a B-grade dancer?' he asked lolling on the deliciously un-made silk bed which Mithila had kept rumpled artistically for the shoot.

'You cannot let it go for a snatch even if it's fur lined!' The shifting studio lights caught Mithila's face and he decided she was mean looking.

'This is what your heroine is wearing—if you hold her from the waist like this...the split see goes up all the way up to the thighs.'

'I am all for risque darling—what about a live demo?'

Without blinking an eye, Mithila hitched up her skirt to the thighs and posed.

'That's all the risqué you will get from this item darling—Now be a good boy and try out your costumes—'

And then he saw the men. Prince's face abruptly darkened. Chamanji had informed him the special team from Dream Stars would be on the sets from today. But he had not expected them to land on the sets so swiftly. Fact was he did not want them on the sets at all, but he could not do a thing about it. They were minders sent by Dream Star to keep an eye on him. So that he did not get into any trouble, Chamanji had tried to placate him. But he only had himself to blame for the bloody mess. It started with a simple habit of switching between pills for weight loss and drinks to control his nerves and drugs for the creative shot. Within no time, he had taken to gorging on cocaine dunked in quaaludes and uppers to prolong the drug haze. And then it happened. He was careless about hiding his addiction. Someone mailed Nisha Poddar a few candid shots of him, unshaved, unattractive, tottering in a daze covering his face with a hand—all taken from a high-powered telephoto lens. Nisha's scathing special on drugs and Bollywood stars did the rest. She had hinted in the article that a huge exposé would follow. And he knew she meant his unmorphed photos. A furious Prince had almost beaten up the hack when he crossed paths with her at a party. The situation that threatened to destroy Prince's career was contained when the Dream Star honcho took matters in his hands and complained to the owner of *Bollywood Truths.* Nisha was severely reprimanded for running a potentially lawsuit-inviting story based on unsubstantiated facts. Of course, Chamanji with a hound-dog's instinct carried out a stringent investigation and with the help of a Bawla insider on the sets managed to hunt down the mole. Turned out that the stylist, sore with his long hours and pathetic pay, had copped out about the going-ons in the superstar's vanity van to the inquisitive hack. Prince exploded in fury. He snapped at his hairstylist under the pretext of messing up his gel and dislocated the hairdresser's jaw. But from then on, the shaken studio management, desperate to avoid any repetition of the unpleasant incident, had placed innocuous minders and enforcers on the sets to keep an eye on their star. They had to protect their prime asset. The minders took their job seriously. He just had to remember to be careful. He grinned. But the smile did not reach his eyes. Someone had kept a *Bollywood Truths* copy in his van, neatly folded. His gaze froze on Nisha Poddar's new column.

'In *Indiawala Hero,* Prince's character suffers from a case of galloping self-aggrandisement exceeding that of the superstar!! Stinks of old wine in new bottle!!'

Poddar went on to write:

'Suhana Kashyap: the most promising new age director.'

The superstar's face suffused with rage after what he read next. The columnist had hinted in not so many words that Prince Capure had been desperate to star in MCMM but had been rejected as

'The talented Suhana Kashyap who is at the helm of affairs, felt that Prince Capure did not match her vision for *Mumbai City Mein Maut.*'

Cunt Suhana. Sister of that whore.

He recalled she had looked right through him at the producer's party. Like he was dirt. Slut probably had cement between her legs, he thought as he dialed Chamanji's number.

'Chamanji, I still don't have it! Where is the MCMM script?? What happened to the AD you were talking to?'

'They are absolutely secretive about the script. I have never seen anything like this before. All my scouts have hit on nothing. Nil. Zero. I think no one knows the next scene. I think she sleeps with it. '

'For god's sake, it's just a script. It must be typed somewhere. Printed somewhere. It will be on someone's hard-drive. Has to be somewhere...the story of MCMM! That Nisha has almost called it a fucking *Sholay.*'

'I know, I know. I have seen her article. Forget the bitch. I have spoken to Munjal—there is a way to—are you listening?—listen there are other ways to get back at all of them. I have had a word with Munjal. He is expecting your call.' Prince listened carefully to what Chamanji had to say. The star felt hot under the collar and his fingers pounded a familiar number.

'There is a film being shot at white woods—'

'Hmm—'

'Disrupt it. Interrupt it. Stop it.'

'Time bound?'

'Yes. There are some foreign crew members on the sets of MCMM—just fuck them up. I need you to create a hungama at that new studio, Noir's shoot—I want you to frighten that Suhana Kashyap—shake her up a bit—tell her she can't shoot in Mumbai or something—

'Hmmmm.'

'Don't even ask for the permissions. They have all the papers. Just break some chairs, damage lights, do *hallabaazi*—scare the *goras,* and scream and shout slogans against them—remember, the shooting should be stopped. Scare the living daylights off them. Fuck them up—!'

18

Rains brought new life. And insects and mosquitoes. And weird looking silvery-white and pink cockroaches, the type she had often seen at home, when she was a kid. She remembered Vishnu telling her they were albinos, just like the colourless twins in her neighbourhood who would peel to lobster red if they stayed out in the sun for more than twenty minutes. She was scared to death they would dissolve in front of her into flesh and blood. She often wondered if their blood too was colourless. Sunny stared at the cockroaches coldly peeking out from the basin drain above her with their creepy pinkish eyes. She hoped they would not be adventurous enough to jump down on her. Soon there would be hordes of them. They were being flooded out in multitudes with the rain water flooding their cold dark quarters. She was sure they hated her as much as she hated them. She remembered a line from a book...or was it some Tarantino film?

We are worms, biting your skin, digging holes in your flesh, eating our way into your brains.

Sunny tried to move her hands but failed. They were stone heavy. She lay there limply on the floor. She had been lying there lifelessly for more than three hours now, too scared to move a muscle. At first she thought she was having a terrifying nightmare, when rough hands had grabbed her in her sleep and blindfolded her, all the time abusing her, viciously kneading her breasts. Two stinging slaps on her face made her realize it was happening for real. She fought one hand loose, finally got a nail in and ripped downwards as she met flesh. Someone screamed and she felt a heart-stopping slap on her breast. She felt brutal pain shooting in her head. And then someone's wetness groped her lewdly, and she fell backwards. She lay sprawled on the floor panting and sobbing as more voices mouthed lewd obscenities in her ears.

'If you don't shut-up Sunny-honey we will stuff and jam you inside your toilet after we have shat in it...!'someone laughed. Handcuffed with a plastic rope and blindfolded, she was made to kneel for an hour in the boiling hot night.

'*Saali zor se mat kar. Marr-warr gayee toh?*

'Heroine ji, having fun? Sunnny-honney??'

'Please–'

'You have been to many Bollywood parties. Now this is your welcome party okay. Just relax have fun–'

She felt hands touching her breasts intimately. She choked with terror when a wet mouth kissed her on the lips and a tongue plunged inside her. A muffled deep voice asked her to shut-up and stay still.

'*Aaj hi saara karegi*?? Let's leave some for next time.'

'If you tell anyone about this...we will do this to you every night. Someone cruelly pinched her on her thighs. A hoarse voice whispering obscenities in her ears ordered her to lie on her stomach. Fearing the worst, whimpering Sunny did as she was told, just as suddenly the assault stopped. The rough hands undid her blindfold.

'Keep your eyes closed till we leave cunt. Remember you can't prove a thing. And if you open your mouth then—'

She had tightly shut her eyes till they smarted and stung with unshed tears. But she dared not move even hours after they had removed the blindfold and untied her. She lay in the same place, crunched in a foetal position, as dark changed to dawn. In between she drifted and came back, but she dared not move even when guards banged their wooden mallets against the steel bars outside every cell in the morning, pausing a little more in front of hers.

She knew she was the latest tourist attraction at the Bheesha Jail. Since the time she had been lodged in her cell, everybody from inmates to staff to guards had been peeking in at odd times. She had around nine to ten peekers every half an hour. Everybody wanted to see the Bollywood starlet in jail. She had become numb to the stares which stripped her bare while she slept, shat, ate or bathed in the group showers every morning, seven girls at a time. She had been told the suicide rate at the Bheesha was five times the rate in the general population. Hope was shunned at Bheesha. And so was loose conversation. An inmate warned her about Bheesha 'eyes' and 'ears'. Devices like small parabolic mikes picked up chats and banter in the hallways, cell blocks and mess hall. No one wanted to know another's shit. They were all too deep in their own. Too traumatised after the incident, Sunny did not report the attack. She did not react to the whistling and catcalls and deliberate touching and the expletives thrown at her during breakfast, especially by bar dancer Manchali who was covered in lice which she loved to take out and squish in front of Sunny's lunch plate. Manchali had a track record of vile and aggressive behaviour. A regular on the pills line in Bheesha,

Manchali was addicted to prolixin, but after her intake was cut off, she alternated between suicidal behaviour and aggressive rage.She had already been to solitary for two separate assaults on jailhouse roommates. Bheesha had dealt with Manchali like they did with rebellious prisoners at Bheesha.

Step#1: Complete severing of family contact.

Step#2: Intimidation of relatives of prisoners bordering on humiliation.

Step#3: Presenting a brutish, bestial, and 'sociopathic' image of the prisoner causing near-complete alienation.

Step#4: And then there were the brutal beatings of rebellious inmates with the loudspeaker on. Manchali had not yet reached that stage. But Salma had. After five years of going through the offences-punishment cycle repeatedly, she became the living example of what Bheesha could do to its prisoners. Salma's deterioration into her skeleton, the decay and death which surrounded her, was enough to terrify the most hardened inmates. Except Manchali.

'Oye item! *Tera woh nanga video thaa naa*?' Manchali goaded her again. Sunny, her body sore and aching from the brutal hurt, looked down at her food plate and mechanically put another bite of the tasteless dal in her mouth.

'*Randichod. Hamse better hai kya?* I can dance better than you madamejee!' Raucous voices hooted and whistled.Cracking lewd jokes, the younger inmates broke into a lusty jig to the lyrics of a hit item number, lifting their shirts to reveal their breasts and pulling down each other's salwars singing to Sunny.

'Heroine jee hai, ab toh ṭattee bhi hamaare saath hi dhoyegee.'

'Arrey show us your figure naa. We are not boys. Maybe that's the problem. No men. No show?'

'We have already seen everything in your DVD, baby jee your cunt is on the net. *Main toh isske kapde niklaaloongee...'*

'Sati Savitri's mummy was also red hot item...' Manchali kicked her feet in the air in front of her face and waved her hands in front of her breasts. Sunny glimpsed the fresh wound on Manchali's neck, the slash of nails—

A gurgling roaring sound—the only thing Sunny could think of was a black cesspool overflowing from deep inside her. She picked up the steel glass, drew her arm back, and threw it at Manchali with her full force. As if that was not enough, Sunny flew across the room in rage and hit the girl on her face. She hit Manchali with her big stainless steel plate. She struck repeatedly, smashing Manchali's nose into a rosy pulp till she had to be forcibly peeled off the screaming terrified girl by four guards. The prison hall erupted in anger.

'Haraamzaadee...'

'Kuthree yeh kya kiya rey?'

'Break her bones. We will break her bones.' Manchali's nose had been broken for good.

Punishment was swift. Sunny was confined to solitary after being reprimanded severely. Her calls were stopped with immediate effect. Stunned at the sentence with no chance for appeal, Sunny submitted meekly when she was shifted to her new cell, barely wider than the thin, dirty mattress that covered the floor. Behind a low concrete wall was a squat toilet, the stench from which there was no escape in the windowless room. The rough concrete walls deterred idle leaning; the constant overhead light inhibited sleep. The delivery of food through a low slit in the door, the only way of marking time, divided day from night. But she was not scared of being numb, she did not want to feel anything. To remember anything. But with no pills to fog her mind that had already become difficult. The memories were a constant now.

{'Sunny Kashyap. Legendary director Vishnu Kashyap's daughter. Profession. Item girl. Occupation. Cock sucker.' Standing in little knots drunk men at the party nailed her with their leery gazes and lewd comments watching her frenzied dance.

-jungle-mein-aaj-mangal-hoga/bhookhe-shero-se-khelungi-mai-

'I wanna eat a candy bar out of her cooch right now.'

She listened numbly to the words. A voyeur of her chaos. The air was suffused with the stench of her shame, the scent of their scorn mixed with drugs and smoke and sweat assailed her senses, still not deadened by the pills which KD had crammed down her throat before leaving the girls to perform for Sulaiman's private guests at his farmhouse.

-i-am-a-hunter-she-wannta-see-my-gun/when-I-take-it-out-women-wannta-run-

'See my gun...see my gun,' someone shouted in chorus.

'—don't worry Sunny honey. I am getting you a film after this. I am a financier you know!'

She attempted to move away but her legs mechanically thrusting to some demonic beat were not her own anymore. Thick greedy hands kneaded her thighs in the middle of her dance performance.

'Please ssstop—' she tried to utter but her tongue felt jammed.

'Arrey Chamanji relax. You are happily married with two kids.'

'We are all happily married with two kids. Very fulfilled life. So what?' he said eyeballing her with glazed eyes. 'I don't need fulfillment, just to fire my creative juices flowing. Waise bhi sab aag toh isski jholi mein hain?' *Sulaiman's secy Chamanji had often raised a toast to her between his snorts of grade A cocaine at parties.*

-malaa-zaao-de-malaa-zaao-de-

'Stop stop STOPP IT!' she managed to whisper groggily, trying to fight the haze and the hands. Strong hands caught hold of her by her neck. She found herself staring into Salem's colourless watery eyes.

'Zaao de? Kahan zaao de? *O womaniyaa this is a dance show right—so shake your booties cunts—for our distinguished guests,' he yelled and the other girls resumed their act.*

-iknowyou-want it-butyonev- gonnagetit- tere haath kabhi na-aani-

'Whatever you say, I grant you she is damn hot beauty! Just like her mother, chip of the old block! These frigging item girls, they suck so much dick to make their way up and suddenly they want to detox. But yaar, most fuckable piece I have seen...' She recognized Sulaiman's close friend and big time distributor's voice, hoarse from years of amphetamines addiction.

-chaar-botal-vodka-kaam-mera-roz-ka-

'Vodka...Vodka! C'maaon whore sit on my lap.' The rich sheikh from the middle East had suddenly joined the party.

'—immm not a whore—' While trying to escape the sheikh's brutal embrace, Sunny caught hold of Sulaiman's silk jacket. The actor leaned forward and pushed her to the wall, striking her cheek with a stinging blow with the flat of his hand. His contempt for her pervaded the dusky, dim lit room like some sick malady.

-maine-honto-se-lagaayee-tau-hungama-ho-gaya-

'Do not wrinkle my jacket! Did you hear, the cunt-shop here took my name!! What is this? You are gundd– O god I hope she is not in love with me. Ishk vishk? Shiiiit! Be nice to these girls and they want to play wifey.' His soft voice sliced the air. *'Be ambitious. Be a whore. At least a whore gets paid,'* he said and doffed a neat bundle in her direction, before slamming the door behind him.

'I think angel face here does not want the film role. I am hurt! you know I am biiig man. Biiig money. Doesn't that excite you? C'maaon be bold honey, show me your fire, show us your animal like you do in your items' Salem hissed trying to grope Sunny. *'Go and sit on her lap. Go be nice to her. Consider this your audition. Put everything you have in it. Think of it as a business fuck,'* Salem pointed at a leery well-built woman drooling over Sunny.

-no-no-no-maine-pee-nahin-hai-maine-pee-nahin-hai-

'Okay. Get me a contract. Give me a two-minute blowjob and that item number is yours.'

'Two minutes? Tera timing toh mere kutte se bhi kam hai—'

'That's because your dog's bitches are in heat. This one's cold as a cucumber man—Not like her red hot mammy'

-ringringringaringringringa--ringringringaringringringa-

'—STOP...STOP...STOP' But no words had come out of her paralyzed mouth. She wanted someone to intervene. Shut the clowns up. Her head was swimming. The sweat which had gathered at the nape of her neck from her overheated body now dribbled down her back into the crack of her bum. She vaguely saw the sheikh move towards her. Things got worse when someone pulled off her top and asked her to dance on Salem's lap. Sunny realized something was drastically wrong when her body stopped obeying her. Her hands were moving ludicrously

slowly, and words of protest froze on her lips and she knew that her body was unable to fight the strong amphetamines gushing through her blood. She felt rough hands all over her body and in an effort to avoid them she fell clumsily on the floor with the sheikh thrusting himself on top of her. Her world was collapsing and she could not move a muscle. She stopped listening to him and suddenly he left. She just wanted the pain to go. She was dizzy and nauseous, and hot urine soaked her crotch and went streaming down her leg. She had no control on her bladder any more. She sat down on all fours with a table cloth to wipe the urine. The sheikh and his men were livid and were yelling and she could not understand. Her head was throbbing by now. She was hazing out.

-oooowomaniya-womaniya-womaniya-

-oooowomaniyawomaniyawomaniya-

The party was over. She and the other girls were roughly shoved out of the room. Another room. Room number 909.

And the nightmare just would not end. She saw a bloody mutilated KD clawing his way towards her as she cowered in fear. How did he get so bloodied? How did the knife get in her hand? She had woken up hours later with high fever, still groggy from the effect of the strong drugs, her throat on fire. Nothing made sense. Had the world gone mad? The police handcuffing her, the noisy reporters, the screaming crowds. They had all left one by one, leaving her behind in her little patch of dirt and mud and piss. She slumped to the floor and let out a loud piercing wail, finally diminishing into moans and sobs of comprehended tragedy.}

She heard the cell door close on her private hell. It had a new number. Cell number 36. Sunny Kashyap lay down on the floor of her cell and licked the fresh mud off the floor.

19

Built in an area of two thousand acres on the outskirts of Bavasa, the Anattā ashram belonged to a sacrosanct order of sisters founded way back in 1968. The sacred sisters of Anattā lived a simple life. They propounded the theory of the non-self, the owner-less. The sisters believed it was their undertaking to unite the sex with the soul. Their beliefs and philosophies were inviolable. Untouchable. Sacred. The strictly solitary society disallowed orthodoxy, banned belief in the trinity and prohibited the search of salvation through faith in some unknown god. They rejected the conventional occult sciences and forbade alchemy, tarot, cabala, scientology and astrology. They believed the ownerless state could be achieved by being constantly and relentlessly occupied with simple work.

On a normal day you could predict the hour by the noises you heard. A clackety clack march at 6 a.m. sharp for morning prayers, a conch shell at 8 a.m. meant the start of breakfast—thick curd, two chapattis and boiled potatoes, all sourced from the ashram's vast tracks of gardens. Wood being cut and water being transferred in big copper vessels to the kitchen from the ashram's well meant it was 1 p.m. Till then, the clackety clack of Sister Daya's sandals as she worked in the garden was a constant. She loved her garden which was beautiful but not as outstanding as Sister Sachcha's breathtaking garden, Daya thought wistfully.

Today Sister Daya was trying hard to stay calm. Water had flooded Sachcha's garden and there was no sign of her anywhere. To make matters worse, hens from her quarter of the farm had escaped. It had taken Daya all morning and a half to get them back in their enclosure. Sister Daya frowned, picked up a wooden dong and hit the cow bell. It gave off a dull clunk, a signal for Sachcha to come to her barn from wherever she was. Daya waited for forty-five minutes, beating on the cow bell again and again in vain. The barnyard clatter was increasing with every minute as the animals bounced and squealed and churned up their smells and kicked the dust in hunger. The chickens and ducks and sheep were upset and the bleating goats got so loud they almost drowned every other sound. Daya decided to feed the animals first and then head out to search for Sachcha. Leaning against the fence posts, she tossed grains into the yard and watched the assorted birds scramble in noisy frenzied clucks. She then fed the goats and the cats and dogs who were Sachcha's particular favourites. Daya was by now sure that even the dogs had not been fed properly or at all. This was very unlike Sachcha, who was devoted passionately to her garden and even more to the animals, and till now had never been lack-a-daisal about her work. Sister Daya headed towards the meditation hut to have a word with her. The sun was high in the sky, it was almost 3 p.m., the time when Sister Sachcha practised the most rigorous tenets of the Anattā life, the jhāna and dhyāna and had reached a state of strong concentration focused on a single physical sensation rūpa jhāna. Because it was Wednesday, and on this day every week, the sisters of this isolated sect prayed to keep the Yakkhas still. Yakkha: One of a special class of powerful non-human human beings—murderous and cruel—corresponding roughly to the ogres of fairy tales. A thorough search of the meditation hut revealed no sign of Sister Sachcha. Before making a formal call for Sachcha Sister, Daya decided to head towards the communication room, the one place where the reticent sister was least likely to be. For the last seven years since she had joined the sect, Sister Sachcha had been most stubbornly averse to all forms of communication with the outside world. No newspapers. No computers. No television. No magazines. Maybe she should try her hut again, Sachcha could sometimes lie there happily for hours without talking to anyone. Maybe something was troubling her, for Sister Daya could swear that for the last seven years Sachcha had not broken a single rule of the sect and had become the most obedient and exemplary sister of the Anattā order. Or maybe she had met with an accident? Sister Daya paled to think of the possibility, which however remote was quite real, especially if Sachcha had gone over to the slippery and swamp- filled western side to look for the shrubs she wanted for her kitchen garden. Alarmed, Sister Daya almost missed going to the communication room when she spotted Sister Sachcha's pale face staring at something. Daya almost sprinted inside the TV room where happily all seemed well. No one was watching what they shouldn't and she felt ashamed at having doubted her. Before Daya could ask her about her health, Sachcha's expression stopped her in her tracks. The mild-mannered sweet sister looked as if she had seen a ghost. Sister Sachcha suddenly got up and walked out of the room oddly, almost rudely pushing her out of the way. Sister Daya gasped in shock and called out to the sister who walked on ignoring her calls. Daya stared at her receding back. Sister Sachcha walked fast, almost ran till she reached her garden, on the other side of the ashram. In spite of the cool clear mountain air, her cheeks were burning and sweat was dripping from her forehead, she felt clammy and her head just would not stop throbbing. She laid her head against the trees, looking oddly comfortable against the scaly rough bark. Sister Sachchca felt nauseous and suddenly bent to vomit. Daya watched her with rising concern.

EVIL SEASON

That morning began as an ordinary morning. The brilliant yellow sun gave no inkling of the raging horror which was to unfold. Vishnu was eck-deep in the production schedule of his new film with Sitaara Matinees, Dildaar, a doomed love story with the biggest star line-up he had ever worked with. He had not been home for weeks. He heard about it on the radio.

'—Tabu Kashyap, wife of famous film director Vishnu Kashyap, seriously hurt in fire accident—Police quoted eyewitness claiming the victim doused herself with an inflammable substance before setting herself on fire. The former actress recently separated from her director husband Vishnu Kashyap who was away at the time of the incident'

Vishnu rushed home. Of course it was all over by then.

When he entered the house, a deathly vacuum engulfed him, sucked out his air, till he could not breathe. The house was impregnated with a sick spirit and despite the gathering crowds, an unnerving silence pervaded. News travelled fast. He could see some tabloid reporters talking to the milkman, scribbling on their pads. Photographers discussed the best angles and asked someone if the window could be opened for better light. Some odd relatives with swollen eyes were huddled up beside the dazed twins. At the time of the incident Bina was on her way back from America.

She had urgently summoned some of her close friends to watch over her grandchildren till she reached.

'Is mummy going to die?'

'Why is she covered in white cloth?'

'Shhhh.' An old woman in mouldy chiffon, Bina's friend, struggled to console the girls in between her hushed conversation with someone, all staring gloomily at the remnants of a ruined family. Three-year-old Sunny was the first to see him.

'Papa! Aunty said papa was going to punish mama, because mamma dated strange bad men so she killed herself—' Sunny's baby voice broke the silence, shocking everyone. The startled journalists stopped their conversation mid-way, watching his reaction intently.

'Daddyy daddyy daddyy. Don't you hurt my daddy.' Sunny shouted at the media her face crunched in anger, hugging her favourite doll. He stood there indifferent to the child's question, not bothering about the stares. They could write what they wanted to. Running away was the first thought which struck him. And then, nothing. It was as if his mind had suddenly emptied of everything. He knew that for him, normal life had been suspended forever.

He walked limply to the room where it had happened. The burnt out AC was removed and it was evilly hot inside. He felt sweat trickle down the back of his ears. The dark stone floor, still greasy from the sarson ka tel spilled during her daily poojas, had a singed odour. A whirring sound made him start and he looked over his shoulder with a shudder. It was just a big fat moth, with a gorged inflated stomach, getting ready to settle down on a wall which had turned white with heat. The blinds of the room were drawn tight, but he could see that the heavy stone floor had cracked into pieces from the blaze, the windows black with soot. The fan and the photo framed had twisted out of shape, the photographs were charred. The wall had peeled off in portions where it had been hosed with water, revealing blistered layers. In the centre of the room, the earth had split open due to the heat. That was the place where they had found Tabu. Like a burnt out rag, not scrunched in a foetal position like most burnt victims, but legs splayed out like she was embracing the fire. The air was charged with anguished violence. Clusters of small insects whirred and hovered over something juicy and dead. His hands gripped the lone chair dumped in the corner, which surprisingly had escaped the blaze. A dark oily haze settled on his shoulders, the air stung his eyes, entered every orifice. He felt a rush of madness beyond the realms of logic and reason. And then his heart choked with remorse and anguish and rage...and...pain... mostly pain and immense desolation and a deep-gnawing guilt that crippled him. He felt nauseous and clammy. He wanted to vomit but could not. His tongue felt thick and furry and tarred. He walked now like a man in the grip of a raging nightmare stumbling across the room unaware of what he stepped on in a hurry to get away. He could not breathe. But his legs betrayed him. There was a brackish smell about the place from the several washings and a smell of dead fish lingered, from the burning stones. Suddenly he bent over and retched his guts out. He vomited for long till there was nothing left to vomit. When he finally joined the mourners he seemed to be carrying a burden of baffled sadness in him, the part inside which should have been alive was dead. From then on, a darkness remained in his heart from which everyone, even his own daughters, were forever excluded.

Bina made no attempt to hide her anger and publicly accused him of driving her daughter to death. Things reached a breaking point when a heartbroken Bina refused to hand over the girls to him. She threatened to destroy him and see to it that he never ever got any work in the industry unless he handed over the custody of the twins to her. Vishnu refused and an angry Bina slapped a case of wilfully causing suicide and managed to get him behind bars for three weeks. But the police could not find evidence to stick the charge on him. A revengeful Bina refused to hand over the twins to him, threatening to involve him in a costly custody battle.

Perhaps he should have ignored the summons from Sitaara Matinee to be back on the sets. But the start-to-finish schedule at an outstation location with an absentee director was costing the studios too much money. Vishnu was desperate to get back to the girls, to restart his life, but in his numb and haunted state he was in no condition to work. It was a disaster waiting to happen. His reflexes were not fast enough. Vishnu did not see the truck coming from the other side. A horrible car accident wrecked his health and sent him to the ICU for a week. Vishnu suffered horrible injuries to his neck and back and the strong drugs left his mind muddled and useless for anything creative. He was dropped by the studios. Sitaara Matinee replaced him with a young director from the south who was hungry enough to finish Vishnu's incomplete projects for a token fee. In a much publicised gesture of magnanimity, Sitaara Studios did not ask him to return his signing amount. But between money on his treatment and the court case, Vishnu Kashyap was soon close to bankruptcy. His two children shunted between one set of hostile relatives to another, as he and Bina fought it out for the best part of a year. The twins, overwhelmed by the happenings, crushed by their memories, stumbled in a daze through a universe of grief and pain. The children were subjected to the merciless compassion of insufferably polite relatives and the incessant media glare.

Condescending smiles, snide remarks and suspicious remarks greeted the children wherever they went.

—unfortunate orphans! Kha gaya Tabu ko bastard!

—do you think he killed her because he got to know about her affair?

—now we must feed them. But we owe it to Tabu.

If they were dented and bruised from the intense cruelty and unflinching scrutiny, the twins did not show it, at least not openly. The ageing Bina, finally wised up and saw the bitter truth of what was happening to her adored grand-daughters, and finally agreed to let the girls go back to their father on the condition that he marry her niece Kala, who would supervise the well-being of the children. Vishnu agreed but it was already too late. He got back his daughters, but they now seemed different from before from not expressing their pain for so long. Suhana became aloof and quiet, and Sunny's aggression turned inwards. Kala who had jumped at the opportunity to lead the glamorous life of Mrs Kashyap, soon found to her dismay that the man whose love she was seeking was already lost. He had nothing to give to her or to his craft or to the industry, and the industry had nothing to offer. Vishnu Kashyap made two sad attempts at a comeback before a losing battle with health forced him into retirement. Sitaara Matinee turned its back on him and he suffered a nervous breakdown. Vishnu Kashyap was confined to the fringes of Bollywood in no time.

❖

20

It was a striking set. The biggest set of the biggest studio in the industry. Bollywood's first permanent set created at the sprawling locations of the Dream Star or DS Studios. Owned by Dhanna Seth, DS studios was one of the oldest and grandest studios of the industry which had started as the modest Sitara Matinee and had now evolved into one of the most well-equipped modern studios. Claiming to be the first fully prepared studio ready to switch to high definition, the Dream Star film sets were built at a huge undisclosed figure, ostensibly running into hundreds of crores. The studio earned the distinction of enabling the shoot of a full-length commercial Bollywood film on a start-to finish schedule in just thirty days. Intended to be a permanent set, great attention was paid to the exteriors and interiors to carve out several streets complete with cobbles and trees and pavement, lined by a discotheque, a *shamshaan ghat*, a garage, a boxing ring. One of the streets seemed to have been chalked straight out of the seventies' retro look with terraced houses at one end, and a corner shop at the other. The lead actors were given their own dressing rooms which they had to occupy during the course of the shoot so that the production house knew about their whereabouts at all times while they were on the sets.

Luck was the keyword when it came to Dhanna Seth's productions. And Prince had been lucky for his studio, spewing big grossers with clockwork regularity. That's why the actor was on the verge of being offered another three-film deal by the studio, and understandably, Prince Sulaiman Capure was a very happy man.

At DS Studios, on the sets of the film *Metal man* Prince had just been given the news that gutka baron Subhash Veerani had bought the distribution rights of his film at a huge undisclosed amount. Veerani had also put in enormous amounts in event management and was excited about organising his first Film Awards.

'It's all the same shit. But at least you get to see Kareena Katrina here. That's my greed,' Veerani said to Prince.

'QUIET ON THE SETS!'

'CELLS OFF OR WILL BE CONFISCATED. And no newspapers.'

'AND...ACTION!'

Prince Sulaiman's scene required him to rescue from ruffians his lead heroine's best friend played by Daisy Katta. The ruffian now lay dead, garrotted by the hero who was looking for his kidnapped love. A painful death awaited any villain who stood in the path of the hero and his rightful love. At the sound of the clap, Prince moved towards the girl who was lying unconscious her clothes in tatters. He winced and his face hardened...but the eyes had a far-away look.

'TAKE!!' Film director Jerome Mangwani, specially roped in to direct the fight scenes, boomed on the microphone.

'The stunt coordinator wants a copy of the script.'

'Shut up. Fuckball. Why the fuck does he need a script for a fight scene? I will throw up if I see a choreographed fight. You know, every director is like hey you can't shoot the intensive action scenes in 10 days, you need 25 days. And I told them, why do you need 25 days? To jerk each other off?' Jerome was indignant.

'Also Prince, you will need a scar on your face. To always remind you of the *maadachod* who fucked your sister—makeup Annie, Prince's flesh has to hang haan? Let's damage your duplicate.'

'Hey you know I've also heard about a guy who put gun powder in his chewing gum and blew off his jaw—'

'That's great! Punch in the scene. Let the hero take his chewing gum and fill it with gun powder, make the villain chew it at gun point and BANGG! The damage has to look has to look pretty severe, and the bleeding, muscle destruction. Very brutal and visceral. *Abbey* duplicate don't grin. You won't get to dance with Daisy Katta. You are the punching bag here. Probably a broken jaw? At the very least, he should almost certainly lose some teeth? Let the knife go through the hero's open mouth and through his cheek and let him rip it out and slash the villain haan? I don't want a specific fight technique. Prince will be grabbed and pulled and punched and kicked at the same time. Some knife fighting, sword and stick fighting, multiple opponents coming at him like a pack of wolves, and some one-on-ones. Anything goes. This is going to be the best fighting scene ever—'

'Give me a minute. I have something to attend to.'

Prince dismissed the director and sauntered casually towards item girl Daisy Katta engaged in a deep conversation with Subhash Veerani.

'You are such a rockstar, Prince. I am your number one fan,' Daisy simpered and jutted out her slim long legs clad in stockings and the shortest of shorts. Veerani stared goggle-eyed.

'Is this what you are wearing for our song?' Prince stroked her legs lazily with his eyes. 'Yes. You like?' Daisy's smile widened.

'Wearing a bra?' Prince asked.

'What?' Daisy was not sure she had heard right.

'I said are you wearing a bra? A brassiere? For the song.'

'Show me your stomach,' Prince demanded.

'Huh?' Daisy reddened.

'*Arrey* girl. I want to see is your navel pierced?'

Daisy Katta lifted her t-shirt allowing Prince to inspect her navel.

'Nice. And tattoo?'

'On my thigh.'

'Show me,' he commanded.

'It's...it's...near my bikini line,' Daisy said with nervous excitement.

'You won't be showing me anything I haven't seen like a million times before. Show me. *Kuch toh chemistry dikhao.*'

Daisy Katta took off her shorts with one swift movement to reveal her tiny white panties resting snugly on her crotch. She lifted one leg and placed it on Prince's thighs.

'This will surely bring on a holy shower of bliss,' Subhash Veerani looked slyly at Prince.

'That is entirely in my hands,' Prince replied without missing a beat.

As Prince Sulaiman settled to inspect Daisy Katta's thigh

tattoos, his place was taken by his duplicate for the strenuous fight scenes ahead.

'Mr. Rockstar, let's not keep the press waiting shall we?' Chamanji interrupted, 'We break now for your press meet. Lots of interviews lined up. Prince, we need to talk before the press briefing–!'

'In a minute Chamanji. Wait for me in my room,' Prince called out to Chamanji's receding back, ignored him and smiled at Subhash Veerani.

'Veeraniji come to point. *Award shaward dilwaa rahe ho ya nahi?*'

'Best actor or best film?' Veerani asked.

'You are talking like those dumbass *chutiya* film critics. If they want me to marshal their New York parade, I need more than one. Critics and popular-shopular. I want both,' Prince said with finality. If he had to talk to the press, then he might as well promote his new look, he thought, mussing up his hair rakishly. It brought out his fresh tanned-rugged look. Maybe he should change into a Calvin Klein shirt, a blue silk scarf and khaki linen slacks. He knew he was looking good. He hoped that girl from X-channel who always seemed to be in vapid awe of stars would be there, she always asked nice questions and did not try to fuck his happiness.

'No no NO! Absolutely not! Sir please! It's a tight schedule today! Not a minute to spare. SP saab said you'd come tomorrow. When did we shift this appointment for today? I am not aware–' Chamanji was arguing with a well-built police officer.

'We din't–just thought we would take a chance. If you could give us a minute or two–' The voice was rough and no-nonsense.

'Why so much noise?' Prince asked and the two policemen turned to gape at the superstar.

'The police wants to chitchat about that...crime. You know the Sunny thing,' Chamanji said. Prince smiled thinly.

'I have a very very busy sched—besides, Chamanji handles all my appointments—'

'We can come tomorrow if you want. This will not take long though—'

'Sorry—Sir, it's not possible,' Chamanji said, stealing a glance at Prince.

'Okay. Let's do it. Tell me how can I help you?' Prince flashed his famous pearly dimpled grin.'We must cooperate with the policein any and every way possible.' Prince said generously and Chamanji, threw up his hands in mock surrender.

'We want to talk to you alone. I am ACP Kabir,' the well-built officer informed Prince in a matter of fact tone.

'But I don't see any need to—' Chamanji interrupted.

'Chamanji...chill. ACP, you can't force me to send my secy away. But I am always there to help the law. Chamanji please. I...am...entirely at your service now, right ACP?' Chamanji swallowed his annoyance and glowered at the policemen for a few seconds before walking away stiffly.

'Don't mind him. He worries too much about me. Keeps me out of trouble,' Prince winked conspiratorially, 'I presume you are here to talk to me about my so-called *relation* with Sunny? Tell me ACP, do you take your investigation leads from tabloids,' Prince ventured cheekily.

'Only when we are doing Bollywood murders,' Kabir answered with a smile.

'That's very dangerous,' Prince looked at Kabir intently.

'Yes. Some people would find that very dangerous...for them.'

'Like this so-called journalist Nisha writes about me, *an ageing playboy with an ill-fitting toupee perched on his head,* just imagine...this is my real hair. One hundred percent real. Not even weaved. But we stars learn to ignore these hurtful digs,' he said grandly. ACP Kabir Bhonsle's smile did not reach his eyes.

'This is a very violent town. What exactly do you want to know officer?'

'It's ACP Kabir Bhonsle. I want to know how well you knew Sunny?'

'I was not in a relationship with her offi—ACP. If that's what you are asking. I knew her—know her only slightly.'

'The pictures of both of you at parties look slightly more than friends to me.'

'She is a pretty girl. What can I say? You make it sound like casting couch or something...she was pretty amenable. It's one of those things...you can't believe the tabloids, they see a superstar walking out of a party, and a girl also chooses to leave the party at the same time—bingo they are a pair, the girl says something and bingo they are seeing each other, bingo they have a scoop!'

'Nargis Khaled says—'

'Please. I don't know what that lady's compulsions are. I just know the truth. So yeah, maybe I bought her a beer or gave her a lift to the pub but will you sue me for that? You are nice to a girl, they want your help. So you are sweet, do a favour, recommend them—I don't like to break their hearts, you buy them a beer, something nice, and then they start reading too much into it...and then you are in an awkward situation. And you tell them to not call you and they take it personally! It's like you can't be nice to people. And when they can't get what they want from you, they start screaming casting couch—'

'Witnesses claim Sunny was molested at the party by your guests—

'Not my guests as you put it. They are all respectable people. With families. I didn't even know she was there. I am a superstar, ACP. It was a party for my films, everyone was in high spirits. Something may have happened. I don't know, I had left—if something happened, it happened after I had left. I cannot verify, that's for you to find out ACP. Though I have heard that she was mostly on drugs so you really cannot say about a girl like her—'

'What about KD?'

'What about him?' The actor asked with lucid blank eyes.

'You had cast a lot of models from his agency?'

'But I don't handle all that! The casting etc. is not my thing. The studios handle that.'

'Why do you think he was murdered?'

'He was a cruel bitch and his time had come!! I could say that if I knew him...ha haa...joking. He obviously had angered someone enough to kill him! Not me! I am not the killing kind... all these scenes you see in films...I can't stand blood, I hate fights. I didn't like him or hate him for the simple reason that I did not know him well enough—Oh here come my minders, the studio...Dream Star Studios have thoughtfully provided these wonderful men who look after me—they take care of me, see that I don't get into any trouble,you know. I am an asset. If you had that much of your money riding on me...you too would protect me—'

As the police were escorted out, Prince shouted out to the ACP.

'Please officer! Sunny must get justice!'

'It's my intention Mr. Prince Sulaiman Capure. That's exactly my intention.'

Prince watched at the beefy police officer walking out when a noisy commotion broke out at the studios' gate number 4. The star walked frowning. Some men had barged into the sets of the film from the back gate.

'Shooting roko! Stop the shooting bbey!'

The Bawlas had descended, led by the burly Chotta. The film's Spanish stunt coordinator had been *gheraoed* and the Bawlas were demanding either his services be discontinued or three times his fees be paid as penalty to them. Within minutes, the foreigners present for the dream dance routine were also rounded up.

'Haay haay! Wapas jaao! Mumbai chodo waapas jaao! We will not allow foreigners to shoot for a Hindi movie.'

'Do you know who you are shitting with?'

'Fuck you. Do *you* know who is shitting with you? I am Chotta. And that's where your problem starts.'

'Listen, this is Prince Sulaiman Capure's set—you cannot do this!' a hapless production controller tried to control the situation.

'I said I don't fucking—'

'Shut up benchod—' Prince butted in furiously, 'ARE YOU MAD? ARE YOU FREAKING MAD? I don't believe this! Why are you here on my sets?' the actor screamed at the indifferent Bawlas.

'You idiots do you hear me? You are supposed to go to the next studio. In White-Wood Studios. This is White-Forest Studios. This is my shoot. Get out. Get out now–'

Looking confused for the first time, Chotta abruptly stopped the sloganeering and after consulting with someone on his phone he asked his astounded men to wrap and leave the sets.

'Sir, misunderstanding *ho gaya.* The boys are new,' Chotta said, looking not in the least bit penitent.

'You are lunatics! All of you!'

'Let it go naa boss. This is Chotta's personal request. The boys mistook white forest and white woods? What do they know–'

'GO–'

'Shall we go to the other studio–'

'GET LOST–'

'We will reach there in fifteen minutes–'

'The bitch has packed up. You bloody fool. Get your *haraamzaadas* off my set. Now.'

21

She woke up at 4.15 a.m. with a pounding headache and a searing sense of loss. She tossed and turned in a state of gloom for what seemed like hours. The birds struck their ribald chorus, a bike revved noisily, followed by the raucous barking of dogs. The noises sounded trite and common and pathetic. She put the pillow on her ears to snuff out the noise of the passing vehicles. The milkman dumped the milk at the door and then someone's car door slammed hard, a baby cried. Familiar sounds seemed alien and unfamiliar today. Suhana wanted to go through the morning trying not to panic about the trial or think of Sunny in jail. She had not visited the sets of MCMM for the last three days. and no one had called her. Not even to gossip about the commotion created by the Bawlas at the sets of Prince Sulaiman's biggie *Metal man.* No calls from her secy, a deathly silence from her production staff and not a peep from Biddoo. After months and months of living through the chaos of MCMM, she found the silence unnatural. To hell with it. She dragged herself from her bed to perform her routine, going through the motions mechanically. It all finally sank in suddenly when she broke an egg. Her body started trembling and the first pangs of guilt, anger and desperation ripped through her. The egg broke and missed the pan by a mile. The stone floor was spattered with the ochre yellow of the yolk surrounded by veiny viscous fluid like putrid memories. She stood frozen for a full minute, scared to breathe. With a scream she finally ran out to the garden, hoping it would take the kinks out of her throbbing head. A sweet smell of decay, the kind given off by rotting vegetables, greeted her. The garden had gone to dust. The plants were rotting alive. There was dust on the petunias, the leafy cholius was dry and dead, the money-plant was drooping limply, cobwebs hang from the fountain which had turned a sickly grimy yellow, its floor alive with insects. The ants and termites and cockroaches had already marked their territories and were carrying on doggedly with their daily affairs, confident in the doomed fate of the garden. Suhana felt guilty at constantly postponing her plan of renovating her mother's garden, but then she was not Sunny. She glimpsed a police car entering the driveway and skidding dustily to a halt. A well-built man in uniform stepped out and walked towards her briskly. Suhana sighed. The meeting with ACP Kabir at home was her idea. She did not want to go to the sets with her family issues. Introductions were dispensed with curtly and Suhana did not feel like to hiding her annoyance.

'What do you really want to know?' she began brusquely.

'Excuse me?' ACP Kabir was caught off guard by Suhana's direct gaze and rude tone. He hurriedly corrected his expression, regarding her with puzzlement.

'You obviously already think that she is guilty, don't you?'

'Wh–wo! Wait a minute!!' he said incredulously.

'Please officer. You think that we Bollywood types are all alike, right. That we are sinfully rich, lead debauched lives indulging in immoral activities! Right? And so we deserve all the pain we get.' Suhana's eyes blazed in resentment.

'Hold on! Hello. How can you be so sure that you even have a clue as to what I am thinking?' he said disbelievingly.

'It's written all over your face,' she said indignantly.

'What is written all over my face?' Kabir was mystified.

'That we Bollywood types are deadbeats on drugs twenty-four by seven. And we deserve this shit.'

Kabir regarded her anger with bafflement. The TV had done no justice to Suhana Kashyap's looks. Though she did not have the smouldering sensuality of her sister, what she had was completely her own, and uniquely appealing. Suhana's short bob accentuated her heart-shaped face, perfectly proportioned mouth and a pert provocative nose. She had the deepest darkest eyes he had ever seen outlined by thick black lashes. And a way of looking at you as if you were the only person in her world. And a figure which gave boys horny dreams. She gave him a look which indicated that she knew exactly what was going on in his head. Kabir refused to blush.

'I think you are presuming too much,' he ventured valiantly.

'There is so much hate and jealousy just because girls like my sister are bold enough to lead the lives they live. Reckless and stupid girls, but better than being stuck in boring dead-end nine-to-fivers—everyone wants to punish them for the lives they themselves could not lead,' Suhana said.

'Are you implying my job is a shitty boring dead-end job and I will make celebrities pay for my boring life?' Kabir laughed disbelievingly.

'Who wants to be another statistic,' she ignored Kabir's incredulous expression. 'In any case, what's a decent job these days?' Suhana finally offered token truce with a tired smile and a cup of hot coffee. Of course there was still no apology.

'Let me tell you, this is great industry to be in. But then we also have dirtbags who screw it all up give the industry a bad name—since I was a child I have loved this crazy industry with colourful talented artists wearing the most fantastic clothes and painted faces like a fantastic comic opera. An imaginary make-believe world of fantasy yet so real unlike any other because we make people laugh and cry and hope and kiss and dream. Sunny was—is a dreamer—she had—has gone through so much. But Sunny is no killer. You police officers and the press, they are already pronouncing her guilt... have you seen the trash on TV? What utter crap! You don't know my sister like I do.' She said.

'Tell me about her,' Kabir sipped the bitter coffee and thought he could hear her talk all day.

'This garden...was beautiful once. Full of life. Alive. Tended by her. Sunny has a way with plants you know,' she pointed to the wasted garden around. 'No person who can grow a tree like her can be a killer.' She walked with Kabir through the dreary, cheerless garden, her feet sounding brittle and hard on the scratchy shabby grass.

'This garden had the softest grass and the slightest wind would bring about its beauty. There was a white rocking bench, with a beautiful snap-dragon painted on it. And there were lilies, snap-dragons planted in the shape of a heart, roses, and lilacs everywhere and wild roses too. They were her favourite.' The police officer looked at the dead garden around him trying hard to imagine what it must have looked like once and failed.

'That heart-shaped thing was Dannie's idea. Dannie...my step-sister. Tragedies have a way of finding this family,' she said softly.

'It must have been difficult when Dannie disappeared. We tried our best—to find her body.'

'I don't blame the police for that. It's not possible to solve every mystery,' she said with surprising generosity.

'Dad always felt that Dannie was the one who truly suffered from neglect. He felt guilty for her. He used to say that Sunny's beauty could not hold a candle to Dannie's talent! He always said Dannie had it in her to be a great actress. That made Sunny furious. He was right I guess, but Sunny felt betrayed. Always wanted to prove him wrong. If only dad had—but then if only my mother had—too many if onlys—come I will show you our room,' she said leading him into a small room with very huge windows.

'These huge French windows were Sunny's idea—she wanted them really big—like she wanted all the light in all the world to fill her room—'A four-poster bed sat in the centre, canopied and covered with pink satin and lace edged quilting. 'The cleaners do it every week—Papa never lost hope—he believed Sunny would come back. That she would eventually get tired of the slutty items and the crazy gang she hung with—and look where she is now. Except Dad has still not given up hope.'

A huge glossy black blow-up of David Bowie's 'Ziggy Stardust and the Spider from Mars' almost covered one wall. The edgy poster had coal-eyed David smoking a cigarette, the flame from which seemed to have engulfed his head.

'Sunny's first love. She wanted to be David Bowie's bride.' Against the opposite wall was a chest of drawers with perfume bottles and a tortoise shell comb and brush set with matching manicure tools and lipsticks, nail-polishes and glass figurines.

'Her room. Just the way she left it,' Suhana smiled to hide her sadness.

'The press puts us as *estranged sisters*, the tabloids love to say *a family divided* or *not on speaking terms*. She hasn't been here for a long time. Two years and nine months.'

'Any specific reason?'

'Only one reason. Kalidas—KD. I did not like her going out with Kala's brother—'

'Why did you dislike your uncle so much?'

'He was NEVER my uncle. He was the shitty brother of the beastly woman my father married, Kala.'

'You disapproved of KD?'

'Disapproved is a very trivial, mild word. I hated Kalidas or KD as he called himself. I despised, abhorred, loathed him. What he did to Sunny, the crowd he got her into. I curse the day he became a part of our family. I curse every second Sunny spent with him. I abhorred him from the bottom of my heart—and to put it on record I am very very happy that he is dead. What officer? So will you suspect me now? Whoever murdered him did the world a favour. But Sunny is innocent.' Suhana's eyes blazed in anger.

'That is for the court to decide but do you have anything else by way of real proof? Do you have something which can support your statement, something more than mere belief? You know sometimes the hardest thing for a family is to accept that their own blood could be involved with a crime, but every criminal has a family.'

'You say *mere belief*? Belief is everything! Sunny is not guilty.'

'The evidence is stacked against her. There are witnesses.'

'Well, your evidence is wrong. And your witnesses are

lying. They only saw her attacking him. In anger. But not killing him.' Suhana shuddered at the memory of Kalidas's mutilated body. Bhonsle stopped when he saw a black and white picture. He picked up the old frame and stared intently. It was a picture of little Dannie with the twins, Suhana and Sunheri. The grainy picture showed Dannie standing on a slab- top to the backdrop of the Taj Mahal, flanked by Suhana on one side and Sunheri on the other. Dannie's hand was on her step-sisters' hair, which she was mischievously mussing up with a girlish grin. The three were smiling warmly at the camera, an easy camaraderie between the three children. A perfect picture of the perfect family. Signed lyrically, *To the sexiest girls in the world. From the one and only super-duper king of the world. Me...*

'That *Me* is KD—his gift to Dannie. When Kala took her away she had wanted a remembrance, a keepsake—KD took this photo to please Dannie. She was already a child star by that time. She was a star since age three. Later she left us, went away to live with her. With Mrs. Kala Kashyap in her big art-filled mansion. You know, Kala stuffed her house with art.' Suhana said. 'I hate her stifling arty house and her hushed walls. So many canvases crucified in her suffocating festering rooms gasping for air...' Suhana paused to take a long drag of her cigarette, wondering why she was revealing so much to a man she had just met, that too a policeman. But grief does strange things to people she thought. And talking about her fears somehow made it all tolerable. She rubbed her forehead with her long slim fingers as if physically trying to smoothen the snarls in her head.

'You know, Sunny hated Dannie's room. When she stayed with us I mean. She had a nice clean room. And it was huge.

We were angry that she got her own big room while Sunny and I had to share our tiny room. Sunny got back childishly by putting huge cockroaches inside her room. Dannie was shit scared of cockroaches. That was obnoxious, now that I think of it, because she was never mean to us. You know she was so scared of Kala that she would only invite us to her room when Kala was away. Like we were taboo or something. That used to really hurt you know.' Kabir took a deep swig of the coffee and realised the mug was empty. He kept it carefully next to the picture of three girls.

'I was in love with her room. The walls were plastered with posters of Billy Jean and David Bowie and Jimi Hendrix. And then she had these dolls which Kala used to get for her from her trips abroad. Little Bisque dolls...so beautiful....so fragile... with matching gowns and bonnets and chemises and booties and its own cradles–Sunny was crazy about them. I used to steal Dannie's dolls' clothes so that she would throw them and I could get the dolls–I used to hate that we had nothing except the school timetable on our room wall for décor. She had muscular sword-wielding monsters on one side, goblins and gremlins filled her attic. A computer sat on her desk. That was the only time I really hated her. She got a computer. But then she let me use it so often that all was forgiven. I gave her some of my *bhangaar*, you know, old DC comic books of Batman, Superman..and some old old phantom and Tarzan comics. It was really funny to see her mooning on that *kabaad*, you know, torn comics for days.' Suhana's voice had become a soft whisper as if she was talking to herself.

'She was the first big star amongst us kids. Even when she was a child she was a superstar. Celebrity since age three. But I never felt jealous, infact I felt bad for her. Dannie was like a little girl, pasty faced, so clean and she had no sexual dimension whatsoever, if you know what I mean. I remember Kala used to really push her. She wanted Dannie to be *the* biggest star of the family. Kalidas, I mean KD, got her film offers when she was a kid. Sunny got very pissed, after all, she had been told she was the true beauty of the family. Sunny would try to grab KD's attention, try to show off her beauty. That used to upset Dad. If only—I wish I had been more firm, but I think she lost patience with what she called my moral policing! Fuck... let me show you something—'

Suhana returned with a disfigured picture of herself: her eyes had been gouged out.

'This is what KD presented me when I had him thrown out of our house—when I discovered what he had got Sunny hooked on to—*To the biggest bitch in the world. May all your nightmares come true. And all the goblins and gremlins you dream of come and feast on you. Uncle KD is watching you bitch*—he wrote that on my picture. His last words to me.'

By the time Kabir Bhonsle got around to asking his next question she was already uninterested. She picked up a glass of cranberry juice and some canapés, swapped her shoes for a comfy pair of slippers which revealed shapely ankles and settled down with a book—it was clear their meeting was over as far as she was concerned. He turned to say goodbye... He shouldn't have bothered. She was busy on her phone.

'Yes Bela. No I will not come today.'

'No tell Tony—what's happened? WHAT? Okay I am on my way—

Suhana turned to look out Kabir walking at and thought there was something attractive about him. Infact he was the first man she had seen in a long time whose easy masculinity struck her. She had had only two kinds of men till now—the gym brutes and the manicured metrosexuals. And the users, who she could tell from a mile off and avoided like the plague. This was definitely a new category. Her phone rang again and her first impulse was to ignore it. Then she saw the SMS from P.K. Dang.

SUNNY IN JAIL-FIGHT. SHE BROKE INMATE NOSE. SENT TO SOLITARY.

◆

Carefully keeping Suhana's disfigured picture in a plastic bag Kabir walked out, his heavy boots impaling the rough soil. The sad worn-down fountain stood with dirty water stains where crystal clear water must have gushed out once, today choked with dirt and strange wild flowers shooting upwards from the soil. A sad and sorry sight the garden—ravaged and dull, with a strange ugly life of its own. She was right about one thing though. About his job being shitty. And the pay was even worse. She would not know that. There was no romance in working long hours. He had not wanted to be a police officer. It was expected of him. His father was one, his grandfather had been in the force. His uncle was one. And it was expected from him to become one. And he would like his son if or when he had one to be one. What else could he do? But after n years in the force it was getting to him. After n number of years of pounding the slime street nothing had changed. The roaches always came back much fatter and with stronger hides. Kabir was in awe of the cockroaches. In the event of a nuclear war it been vouched that they would be the sole survivors. Their ability to adapt to the most stringent conditions was awe-inspiring. Then there were human cockroaches. Kabir called them human-roaches.The indestructibles. The human roaches were divided into king-roaches, the criminals, and hunter-roaches, the police. At the other end of the spectrum you had the roach bait. A roach bait was one who could swing either way. But as a rule they got screwed from both the ends. The king roaches did not do anything themselves. They had a vast army of devoted slave roaches who looted, killed, raped, blackmailed and kidnapped for them. One rule held sway in roach kingdom. You could not cross a king-roach and hope to live. It was a damned lucky roach who would survive such an attempt. Mumbai's night life was bursting at the seams with such roaches. ACP Kabir Bhonsle sat in his car and started making notes. He was known for his detailed reports and he wanted to make sure he did not miss a thing. The best way was to put it down when it was fresh in memory. On the face of it, it was a simple case. An item girl attacking her manager. But things were just not tying up. Like who else was in the hotel room apart from Sunny, because it was now clear that whether she had killed KD or not, more people were involved. There were just too many coincidences Kabir's liking. He was now unwilling to totally rule out a connection to Dannie's death, however remote, and the men were not happy with reorganising Dannie's 'dead-case' file.

'Pure scutwork! Bollywood has severe allergy to truth or wwwhaaat? I wore out my phone ears but *no one* really remembered Dannie—*no one* knew anything much about the Bawlas—and this Johnny D'Souza again *no one* has seemed to have heard of him...' Shinde said driving the car.

'Bank? Hospital?'

'No birth records, no phone listings, the address in the bank is fake—actually the bank is the first place his name shows up—it's like the *benchodd* has not even existed before that—

The simple open-and-shut case was not turning out to be simple. A new murder, some old connections and some unfolded stories. The strands were tangled even as they were knitted. And he was no closer to finding out the truth about what really happened with KD that night. Bhonsle was pissed. Why was KD scared to utter Johnny D'Souza's name? What had he done to earn his wrath? KD's locker had disclosed bank details of the mysterious man. But about the man himself, barring a fake address and a photo of an untraceable grave looking bespectacled man, probably bogus again, there was no clue to his real identity. There was one puzzling fact though – Johnny D'Souza's account had been abruptly closed just a week back, a few days before KD's death.

'I stoked my source at the bank and the tax department says there was hardly much money in his registered event management business with Silky, barely a thirty-forty thousand a month, and being on the Bawlas' rolls must have hardly been profiting unless he was making money on the sides—'

'What's this KD Silky business really?'

'Say producers and event managers—on the face of it doing stage shows, India, Dubai and some other countries and handling the accounts of lots of small-time models and artists but really a cover for making explicit films—who knows?'

'He could be making money there—or the side business... maybe someone blew his cover—'

The real clincher was that the origin of the mysterious money trail leading to KD's account was proving impossible to decipher, for the simple reason that the account was routed through Dubai. Somewhere in this puzzle was an answer and he fully intended to find out what it was.

He walked into a commotion when he reached the station. Holkar holding a piece of paper was sprinting breathlessly towards him. It was discovered in Johnny D'Souza's locker. The note was typed on a simple white sheet.

It was Silky Mehta's suicide note!

'Whattafuck is this?'

'A suicide note. Of a man who is alive!'

Suicide note of a man who was very much alive! What the fuck were you planning Johnny D'Souza and why was KD so scared of you? And just where the fuck are you hiding?

22

Psychedelic Swarovski crystals perched daintily on noses, deep vermilion gashed their heads a provocative red. Drippy lips moistened by scarlet tongues matched the blood-coloured *aaltas* splashed on their feet like war paint. The item number audition resembled a battle-zone.

aal g bai aala g bai aala g
aala aala aala aala
padala pikalaai aamba

Girls and women of different ages wearing glitzy vivid shimmering nine-yard saris practised the exuberant *chhakkad* and *junnar lavanito* the beats of *tuntuna* and *manjira* and dholki. Waiting for her audition to start at the Velvet Red Studios, Nargis Khaled tried not to stare at the competition. The search was for three hot new faces for a lavni item in a big budget multi-starrer.

'*Chalo stree party*—me Malai Malini. But for you 'Masterjee'. We are doing a *sangeet baarees.* Do you know *baithakichi lavani*? You have to sit in one place...and move your breasts and hands and eyes. Like this. *Gol gol.* Round and round.' The dance madam Malai Malini heaved her chest and showed each *adaa, nakhra* and *nautanki.*

'Only move upper body. Don't move your hips—the expression of your eyes should show your feelings. Very naughty and erotic....double meaning...cheap *nahin* sexy *lagna hai*!' Malai Malini demonstrated to the crowd which had divided into two clear groups, junior artists who ranged from 17-35, largely out numbering the young models mostly in their teens and early twenties.

'Hello you at the back—why are you showing your teeth? Is this a joke? *Lavni* has a history okay. Married woman's menstruation, soldier's amorous exploits, adulterous love, the intensity of adulterous passion are all themes of *Lavni.* Is this a *nautanki* for you? Don't do *jokebaazi haan? Chaliye...*one by one show me what you got.'

Today there were some new girls Nargis thought. Young and better looking, dressed in branded wear, in expensive heels, shades, designer purses dangling carelessly from their manicured nails. And incredibly thin.

'Look at those models,' hissed a plump junior artist sitting next to her spitting venom at the models. 'How is Munni here any different from them? Now these *modelniyaas* are taking our job.'

'Those girls look upper class?? From which angle? *Saali* they are decent and we are B grade? Bloody non-union models are taking our jobs. Napean Sea sluts.'

'Aaaayy shutt upp!' an incredibly thin girl sporting designer wear retorted loudly.

Nargis ignored the fight. She had her own shit to figure out. Three crappy weeks. Nothing had come her way. It was like she did not exist. Nargis hated the feeling. No shows no interviews no reality TV no walk-on parts. Zero. She felt like a big zero. After

Tunti was forced to chop her from Banjaran Kairi, *the word was out. She was blacklisted. And she knew who was behind it. To make matters intolerable, she had heard on the grapevine that Daisy Katta was getting the Metal man item, and Digital Dolly had been invited to popular reality show 'Biggest Tease'.*

'I said *they* are prostitutes—did I take her name now? What's her problem? Only she feels bad—why? Because the truth pinches *haan*?' the plump junior artist made fun of the thin model.

'The truth will come and pinch you in the arse if you don't zip your loose lip cunt—' the model screeched angrily.

'*Haan terey darwaaze par toh Salman khada hai naa... signing amount ke saath hain??*'

'They are here just to have fun,' the junior artist said bitterly. 'They want money to blow in discos. I need to pay bills.'

'Enough...shuttup! *Bhnchott!*' the place erupted when a junior artist lunged for the highly manicured model, pulled her by the hair and pinned her to the wall, 'Yeh shut up shut up *fir se bol!* Say it again—

'HEY HEY! This is not your whore house shut up everyone!'' Madame Malai Malini's formidable tenor boomed from her mike.

'Take your fight somewhere else—this is a professional place you motherfuckers.'

A sullen silence descended in the huge hall. This was the headquarters of the Artists Association where junior artists, TV-artists, extras, models, item girls, small time actors and hordes of people arrived with their Bollywood dreams. Extras, if they found work, made 800 rupees a day. They had to pay hefty membership fees to join the Junior Artists Association. But they were a desperate lot.

'You have some nerve. I am not a junior artist. I am an actor.' Thirty-year-old Prem Pandit, spelled as 'Prremm Pandeet', the son of a businessman, arrived six months ago from Jaipur. From an angle, he looked startlingly like Shahrukh Khan in his younger days. Every morning, armed with his head shots, he visited studios and producers. Assistants took his pictures, promising to summon him for auditions. Very few called back. But Prremm Pandeet was sure someone out there was going to give him a break.

'Here comes our junior Shahrukh! Master Prremm Pandeet! *Nehh Hiiiiinh....NehhHiiiiinh...*' the coordinator hammed in an exaggerated style and the hall erupted in laughter.

'You want something else, you end up some place else. With *lookkas* and *haramis. Sab ki pphhat jaati hai.* Hey cunt how is bizness?' Adjusting his bulky bag of portfolios on a seat, Prremm Pandeet teased the second female assistant of Malai Malini.

'Here comes the driest prick in Mumbai. Little boy, *apne jaise khambast item ko koi kami nahin!*' The young girl shot back uglily.

'Ha ha! Market is flooded with imported pussies, who is interested in your item now?' Prremm was clearly out to have fun.

'Shut up bandra gutter line...! *Saala!* I will see what this prick can do. *Kaun uljhaa?* Who fought first, who did *lafda?* Oye ...Hey...What's this *yeh kya hai*?'

'What are you staring at? Bloody dumbfuck loser bitch! Move back. Don't touch my bag!'

'Hey! There is a camera in his bag? Hidden camera? Why are you recording this...selling footage to some cheap news channel—how much are they paying you?

'The truth behind your item auditions—you have already taken Mink Mocovich for this *lavni* item. All of you! The producer has already cast the main dancer. They are only casting side dancers—

'Aaaakkkkk—Helllp get her off mee eeeek!!'

'*Naheen chodungee saali choo*!'

'WHAT THE FUCKK IS GOING ON??'

A commotion erupted which resulted in fisticuffs. Prrem Pandeet's camera was snatched away from him and the reel pulled out. All pandemonium broke loose and the auditions were abruptly stopped as Prrem Pandeet struggled to escape with his precious camera.

Nooo! This could not be happening to her now. Not at this stage.

Nargis was very scared. Was it over for her? She was scared of doing the rounds of two-bit producers again. But she had been told she stood a solid chance at the auditions... just show your face haan?

You are a shoo-in, it's just formality.

But a rapid plan was forming in Nargis's head. Her eyes glued on Prremm Pandeet and his camera, she felt her heart racing in excitement. She would shock them now. The limelight would be on her. They would pound her door for interviews.

Bastard, you'll get what's coming.

She was definitely not going to shut up. With a determined expression, she decided life for her would certainly be very different from then on. She had to speak to Suhana Kashyap. But first there was someone else she needed to speak to. Nargis dialled Nisha Poddar's number as she followed Prremm Pandeet stumbling out of the auditorium.

23

Silky stuffed a chunk of *ghutka* into his red mouth, leering at the model perched in front of him in the suffocatingly small lift. An out-of-work actress, he remembered her from a TV-commercial. Her stunning figure and spotless skin betrayed by the desperation in her eyes. The desperation he could always sniff from a mile off. He spat out the bitter betel and gobbled some pan masala and pressed the button to his rooftop office. Silky hated talent and beauty. But he needed talent and beauty, because all he was capable of was the 'deal'. But he was okay with that, because Bollywood was teeming with 'deals'. Hungry desperate deals in the form of these young girls, and lately, boys, flooding his office. Swarming like flies to tinsel-town hoping to be the next big bitch. A few hard-knocks and they were happy with even walk-on parts in some horny cheapo producer's quickie reeler. That is when they were not busy trying to be some C-grade actor's floozie or cursing their schmucky karma and envying the girl who made it. When their dreams started fading and after they had spent hundreds of nights on an empty promise and a fuck with no luck, they came to him. He was their big man. Their Santa Claus who made things happen. He liked the name. Silky had spent the majority of the last twelve years in Bollywood gorging on many such 'deals'. They were there at the bars, lounges, fashion parties, anywhere and everywhere, their hunger and desperation writ large on their faces. Problem was there were so many of them, small-town beauty queens, miss nice hair from Ballimaran, Bhojpuri miss nice lips, Agra sexy hips, Delhi miss white teeth. Everyone and their dog and his bitch wanted a slice of B-town. And now the bitches were flocking from overseas. Dubai, Lahore, Islamabad, Ukraine and countries whose names he could not even pronounce. Except that the one who was actually getting the big break was him.

Unless if you were a Kuttrina! No wonder they ALL wanted to be Kuttrina. And they all were looking for their own Sullmans, he thought in his head.

'Hey beautiful. How did it go?' Silky stared at Natasha, the model he had sent for a talking part at Bumboo Productions' new film.

'Sillkieee! The part was too short. Just had to pick up the pen and take it to the hero!' A buxomy girl in a tight pair of jeans and off-shoulder blood red top walked to him, complaining.

'What do you want? *Mughal-e-azam.* For that I will send this Anarkali.' He pointed at a pretty girl in a frock grinning vacuously.

'I told you it's a short part. Listen, why don't you do a portfolio shoot. Valentine Day type with a big red heart on your thighs. Okay and wear a bikini.'

'But Valentine's Day is so faar...it will look stupid.' Natasha pursed her scarlet lips petulantly.

'Shut up cunt. Who cares? *And* you need to tone up. Look at your body. *Baaprey! Yeh kya hai?* You have frigging craters in your thighs!' Silky lifted Natasha's skirt till her underwear showed and pointed at the riddled butt. The other girls tittered. Even some punkers with spiked orange and purple hair and no waists looked up.

'*Gym-wym nahin jaatee*?? You are looking like an auntie!! *Do bachchon ki mummy*!! No one will take you like this. Forget the bikini shoot—wear a see-through saaree and make it wet. Don't wear a blouse.' Natasha stared at her thighs tearfully.

'*Arrey* why are you sad—come to Santa Silky—give me a hug, now go. And send me my thirty percent darling,' he said pointedly.

'You charge tooo much Silkiee—but I need to talk to you. Alone.' He stared at the Cuff Parade chick in front of him. Bitch, he thought. They all were bitches. Silky hated Cuff Parade chicks and the Bandra babes, who according to him were not hungry enough. They expected him to 'talk' to them and pay for their manicure, their makeup, hair and clothes! And they were so stuck up they would open their legs only for the famous high fliers and power brokers.

'No heavy talk right now... Get my 30 percent in my account, or pay cash. Today.' He knew what she wanted to talk about. The ad film producer wanted to fuck her, and she was not sure whether it would be good for her career plans. She thought she was selling herself short. Gawd. That's why he loved the wannabes, the really despo trying-to-be's and the never-would-be's. He thought they were more grateful and caused least trouble. They never had stupid dreams of the big film contract or the TV show or the ad film or an item number. He offered them the chance they would never get. The offer to be up close and really intimate with the producers, the stars, and if they managed to swing a deal, well, good for them. Of course, not one of his girls had been able to swing a fuck into a fat deal yet. They got the little parts, the hanger-on roles, the side dancers, a couple of sad items in some Z-grade flicks, but nothing meaty. But they kept coming to him. Silky smiled and entered his garishly lit room. He had just settled down on his red leather sofa, when ACP Kabir walked in. Silky recognized him instantly from TV news. He got up nervously, staring unsurely at the police officer.

'Nice office.'

'Thank you. I er—I have been expecting you all day.'

'So this place is your company office?'

'Head office. We have branches. KD and I jointly run—ran it. Poor bastar—I mean poor man—he worked so hard, this company was mine but the ideas were all his. He was a genius—'

'You have changed the name to Purple Velvet—wasn't it KayDee productions originally?'

'I think clients are put off with death. Bad for business. No point reminding them of KD—poor man the way he died. I could not eat. I cannot believe—*arrey chotu, thanda laa*!...For Sir. Police *ke hain*.' He smiled nervously.

'Lots of youngsters come here?'

'I am just an errand boy. A social worker. I have always helped these young girls and boys who come to Bollywood with dreams and little else. Beautiful girls and talented boys pound the doors of indifferent studio houses. Get treated like yesterday's dirt by even the set hands. I look out for them. If it were not for me, half of them will in any case turn to the trade in some seedy place... *hain jee*! You know they start doing item numbers do stage shows get famous...I do this from the heart *hain jee*. I feel for these girls and boys. They call me their Santa. Santa Silky!'

'You have a family?'

'Never married! Mother died, no father, no family. All alone sir. But these kids are my family. Like my children. These kids you know, they arrive starry-eyed in Mumbai... *sone ki nagri* they think...hoping to make it big, some have huge ambitions but zero talents, some have a little bit of talent but no luck...and thousands in between. Few become famous, some make a little money, lose it even faster...get into wrong company and then they have nowhere to go. If it weren't for me, some of them would be in shitload of trouble. But they are not innocents lost in the woods. They know what they are getting into, most of them would do anything to get there. And I mean anything. This crowd outside...don't be fooled by their faces, I mean I am not kidding...that doll face who just left this room, you saw her? She is into heavy stuff,' Silky licked his lips and spoke to Kabir with a sideways glance.

'*A class apart.* She is talented but there is something about her which is destructive...like Sunny has that quality—in fact I restrain her...after all a girl has to survive beyond a film yes?'

'How well do you know Sunny?'

'She is from the Kashyap family. Nice family. Everyone knows about them *hain jee.* Her father famous director, *ab toh unka time achcha nahin chal raha. Unki mummy jee bhi...well sir sab hi jaantey*—I mean she was also very famous.'

'What about your friend and partner Kalidas—KD?'

'Sir *newswaalas* are spreading the wrong information. He was not my friend. Just business partner in my company. Nothing personal relation *jee.*'

'Your company?? I don't think that's true Silky?'

'—uh!' Silky's face withered in front of him. *So the information was true.*

'You have run into huge losses?'

'Ups and downs are part of business—it's temporary,' Silky bleated plaintively.

'But why are the Bawlas looking into your company's accounts?'

'It was all KD's fault. He was managing the accounts,' Silky said crestfallen, rubbing his hands in despair. 'It was that *haraamz*—uhh—He thought I knew fucking nothing—well lemme tell you I knew fucking all what he was upto—I was shocked when I got to know we had no money left in the company account—where was the money? We were suddenly bankrupt. I had borrowed heavily from people. I had loans to pay. We had no money!' Silky's nerve was ticking out of control.

'Correction Silky. You had no money. KD infact always had money didn't he? That must have hurt right? You doing all the hard work with the girls and boys, training them and yet you were broke. But KD mysteriously had all the money!! You were not even a little curious about the money he had?'

'Like he would tell me,' he said dully.

'Seems to be reason enough to be very angry with him?'

'Are you saying I had him killed? Haa you overestimate me! Bastard was a thief, made money on the side. Thought I did not know about the discrepancies in the accounts. He used to cheat the Bawlas too. Fleeced small-time producers on the side. He thought I had no idea about his mystery accounts, the phoney cheques siphoned off, the cosy nest-eggs under psuedo-names, the missing goodwill gifts which never reached the intended stars. The list went on and on. But would he give me a cut?? No. Just ten per cent?? To keep shut?? No. After all I did for the company, he said he was doing the hard work—said I had no right on the money!'

'That's unfair,' said Shinde.

'He had some boys working for him. Would use his image as a Bawla to earn money from so many people. I caught him taking bribes from independent producers who wanted studio backing. But he just laughed. Said it was Bawla work and I would not understand. I understood everything—'

'What else did he do?'

'I knew how he took a cut from single-screen distributors who concealed profits. Fixed books for them for a cut. I was mad at him, he just would not let me in. And then he wanted to go to Dubai. Bastard was defecting!' Silky said, his hands pounding the side of the table in fury.

'You were quite angry.'

'Of course, wouldn't you be? If your entire life's savings become shit's worth and—heyyyy are you suspecting me? I told the policemen that day I was at Jerome Mangwani's party. He wanted some models—you can check with him—I have an al-uhh-bye—rock solid al-uhh-bye—and I cannot even see blood without fainting, just ask these girls—Molina cut her hand the other day and I fainted—'

'He is breaking my heart,' Shinde said.

'But if Munjal got to know that KD was defecting, after committing so much fraud, he would throw a shit fit... you knew that...so you did not keep quiet, did you?'

'It was my conscience—and he thought I did not know about his cosy nest-eggs! Munjal Bawla looks after us. I could not stand it anymore. I did mention to Bawla so as to deter KD. They had a talk or something but KD never told me anything. I think he suspected me...in any case he stopped taking my calls.'

'Do you think the Bawlas had anything to do—'

'They are big people. I have no idea or information I can share with you and I know my rights. I am cooperating very well. Telling police everything then why—if you think—'

'I don't think anything, Shinde here thinks something... What do you think Shinde?'

'Mr. Loose Lip Weasel here snooped majorly, and ratted out KD's shit to someone. Who is Johnny D'Souza?' Kabir asked.

Silky froze and his eyes jumped out of their sockets at the question. Kabir was reminded of *Oggy and the Cockroach*, a cartoon his nephew was addicted to. Their eyes also always popped out like Silky's when they were shocked.

'Johnny—wh-who...?' Silky sank lower into his overstuffed velvet sofa and whimpered.

'You can refresh your memory—or we can refresh it for you at the station—but I don't think your clients outside will appreciate your little date with the police', Shinde said blandly, his smile barely reaching his eyes.

'But why are you harassing a poor man like me. I know nothing uhhh—I ...KD never even let me meet him! I happened to see some documents KD was filling and when I asked him about Johnny D'Souza he got very scared. Yes, for the first time, I saw him scared. I knew I was on to something. Imagine that *haramzaada* scared of someone! I thought maybe there were collectors after him—maybe he owed Johnny D'Souza money—'

'Why would Johnny D'Souza have your suicide note in his locker?'

'My wha-WHAT? My soo-eee-sydenote!! How is that possible?'

'That's what we want to know from you. Who is Johnny D'Souza and why would he have your suicide note in his locker? Why would he want you dead?'

'I..don't...know...I—my suicide note!' Silky looked as if he was going to pass out.

'Guys, sit down it's going to be a loonnng day.' Kabir sat down and stared grimly at the sulking event organiser.

'KD didn't like me asking him about Johnny D'Souza—made me swear I would not mention the name to anyone—said we both could get in serious trouble I've never seen him so scared—he even offered me money—' Silky said when he had calmed down.

'You took the money and still copped on KD?'

'Noooo! That's not the way it was. I did not even know who was Johnny D'Souza. Still don't know why KD was so terrified of me even mentioning Johnny D'Souza's name. I thought if I threw the name around a bit I will get something you know...I just did not know who to ask. So I mentioned it to couple of girls Digital...Nargis...who know everything...but nothing happened. Then some producers, nothing happened. That's it. I don't know why this Johnny person has *my suicide note*—you say?'

After the ACP left, Silky prowled around his room nervously. The newscaster was talking about the murder.

Why did Johnny D'Souza have his suicide letter? What the fuck was that about? Was he planning to kill him—but why... WHY! Made no sense!

Maybe the police was lying! Yes that made sense. Maybe they wanted him to say something which he would regret later—fuckers were lying they wrote the letter their-fucking-selves! Silky thought and heaved a sigh of relief.

Didn't the hound dogs have anything else to talk about? So who gave a fuck about KD? Why couldn't he have been crushed under a truck and gone into oblivion unnoticed.

Silky caught a glimpse of himself in the mirror. Dirty flat eyes with bulbous bags, limpy dyed hair and a mean scowl. There was a time when he had almost made it as an actor, crossed over to the other side. But a nasty rape charge by a junior artist did him in. He had gone blue in the face claiming it was consensual, which it was, but the bitch had turned on him when her TV serial role did not come through. Not only did he spend time in the slammer, he was out of work for almost five years. The prime years of his life had rotted away, and even now, after thirteen years, none of the big ones wanted to be associated with him. How KD lost no opportunity to throw it on his face. How sickened he felt to be ingratiated to him. And he had called him a bum and useless and a wimp and laughed at his face. He had caught cocky KD cheating hadn't he? Who was laughing now!

24

'*We are keeping a tab on each and every movement in Barrack 13 where Sunny has been kept.*' Bheesha Jail superintendent Manto Singh answered the queries of the media with practised ease.

'Please—dear media—one by one—wardens have been appointed in the barrack to ensure Sunheri Kashyap's safety in view of the attack on her a few days earlier. An inquiry panel is already looking into the attack, and let me assure you, the guilty will be found and brought to book—our jails are very safe—'

'I can't hear you—yes—Sunheri Kashyap has been given a health checkup and has been found to be stressed and weak—there is no special treatment...she has to use the barrack's common Indian style toilet and community bathroom. Sunheri would have to use the mat and the pillow provided by jail authorities, and also follow the routine set in the jail manual. Madam please let me finish answering—She gets up by 5:30 a.m., when the head count begins. She has breakfast in the common room—tea and bun/bread—followed by dal, roti, sabzi and rice for lunch and dinner. The barrack is equipped with fans and a TV set. All the inmates of Bheesha Jail keep their clothes beside their mats and eat out of utensils provided by authorities. She would get dinner at 7:30 p.m. sharp—'

ACP Kabir Bhonsle left the press and hurried down the jail premises to meet Sunny before her court appearance, her first after the jail skirmish. She greeted Kabir Bhonsle with a frank hello which was disconcerting enough as this was the most beautiful girl he had never seen. Her chopped hair made her look like a school girl, utterly helpless and frail. A tiny tattoo on the side of her neck was an S– a two-mouthed forked tongue snake. And then she smiled and there was a simple splendour around her. He stood transfixed for a second.

'So Suhana told you about me. You must have figured I am the feisty one. She's so idealistic,' she said softly. Kabir's heart missed a beat.

'*Memories, me and my partners in crime. Throwing up a thousand times. Pissing off the system, one cop at a time. Time is never wasted when you are wasted all the time*—you like the ditty? I made it. Unless you find the real author!' Sunny said.

'Are you sleeping well now?' He asked.

'No dreams...mmmm the bliss of undisturbed slumber! I think if I don't dream, the ghosts will not be able to stare back at me. It's their window, my dreams. I will shut the window... maybe...I think.'

She paused not looking as if she expected a reply.

'You know who I miss the most. Dannie. My half-sister. I always felt she understood me more than Suhana. Of course I hated Dannie when she was around. Hated her so terribly when Dad said she had talent and I did not. I was the beautiful one...but the talent...they all praised Dannie. Forgot me in front of her. They only remembered me when they talked about my mother. Like my face was a reminder of something shameful. Can you imagine living like that from the beginning?' her eyes did not betray her emotions.

'The funny thing is Kala hated that I got along so well with Dannie. The truth is she was unable to bond with her own daughter, I don't know. Maybe she was filled with so much hatred and anger. A child senses that. Even an infant. Dannie was a dark and skinny infant, needy and whiny and weak with a naturally withdrawn nature. She nursed poorly, cried for hours and vomited daily. Kala hated that her own child refused to make eye contact with her for two years, choosing to smile only when Dad or we visited her, which Kala found intolerable. She banned us from visiting Dannie and then Dad too, feeling sure we were poisoning her child against her. Dad's presence seemed to work wonders for Dannie. He could make her howl with laughter—he was like that with me once. Looong back!' she smiled gloriously and Kabir held his breath.

'But you know in a strange way she was like me. Dannie. Always trying to be someone else. I pretending like I *could* act. She pretending like she was *not* acting. But I knew...I knew. She was acting all the time—I stole her favourite dolls once. Her Bisque dolls. I didn't even like them. But I stole from her. She knew I had hidden them but she did not shout or anything. Just gave a sort of a look which was so tragic—man I really miss her.'

'You returned her dolls?' Kabir asked.

'Are you mad! They were just god-damned dolls. Whatever for?' she burst out, her eyes suddenly brittle, the spell broken. 'And what do you have to offer me today, Mister Officer?'

'I am sorry Sunny, I have little to offer for solace. As of now there is no factual evidence of your innocence. I am not here to ask about the jail attack that's being looked into—I want you to tell me why exactly did you attack your uncle?'

'I attacked him. I was angry. I think I blamed him for a number of things...it all came together...when he threatened me. I hated him—'

'What happened at the party—wasn't the party at Prince Sulaiman's farmhouse?' Kabir said. Sunny paled and looked away...

'I know from the other girls you had an altercation with one of Prince's guests—Salem Hassan—?'

She looked evasive, not wishing to tell him anything.

'—I am—we are performers. Not whores. They believe we are dead from up here—and maybe I am?' Sunny's voice trembled. He realized he was being stonewalled but refused to back off.

'You blame KD for that? Nargis said you were locked in the bathroom and beaten up by KD—why did you not want to go? Were you scared of Salem's reputation?' Kabir asked.

'Please don't waste time feeling bad for me. I don't feel anything. I am free of society's double standards, free of its hypocritical rules and its restraints. It was, is, good money. And I love to perform. There is nothing wrong in what I do. If the audience pays to see the hero they pay for us too. What's the difference? And I needed it—' she clamped up.

'—for your addiction?'

'Initially it wasn't. It wasn't always like that. The pills were just to relieve the pain.' Sunny sounded drained.

'That night—'

'KD was vile—I don't know what happened to me—like I suddenly became someone else...someone strong enough who could make it all stop—make him stop—so I let *her* take over and stop him—I hit him with whatever I found—I wanted him to feel the pain—he was very very hurt and I left him—I had to go away, my head was hurting. I hated him enough to have done it anytime anywhere. I am sure I could have killed him too because I am happy it happened. I am happy he is dead. I am happy he met his end the way he did. But whether I did it...I am blank I cannot...I just do not remember a thing.'

'Can you think of someone else who could have maybe done this?'

'No.'

'Everyone needs saving officer!' she shouted to his receding back.

'—everyone—needs—saving!' Sunny sat motionless for a long time after ACP Kabir Bhonsle left. She sat without moving on the cold stone floor of her new cell till the warden came to escort her for her bail hearing.

'The attacker banged KD's head against the wall, provoking injuries to the back of his head and then attempted to strangle him with a piece of lingerie. In a bid to cause maximum pain, almost half the scalp was left badly bruised and huge chunks of hair were pulled out from the roots in bunches.' In the court a blow-by-blow recreation of KD's murder was being created.

Sunny stared unaffected by the tumult of the press around her earlier or the surreal drama being enacted in the suffocating heat of the courtroom now. Confined behind a firm wall of separation between her and the world, Sunny felt like a tourist watching the chaos of her life from a distance. She could not resist the impulse to stare at her step-mother in her favourite crispy *tussars*, ballooning around her like a tent, her stiff petticoat grating behind her. Kala's face had twisted with a mean expression of implacable hostility. Despite the courtroom AC, Sunny broke into a cold sweat which mixed with the warm liquid dribbling down her thighs, a familiar childhood sensation because of her weak bladder.

On behalf of Sunny, P.K. Dang made a formal complaint against the fact that KD's pictures which were being heavily used in the appeals process had been released by the victim's sister to the media in a bid to bias public opinion against Sunny. He accused the prosecution of sinking to make a despicable personal attack on his client's character by labelling her a 'she-devil'. The defence argued that things had gotten out of control between Sunny and KD when she was molested at the party to which KD had sent her, crammed full of drugs.

'Fear was his power over her and her weakness. This is not a fear which can be explained as a peddler has over a user, but a much deeper fear—built over the years of living with him, if you can call the beatings, the abuse, being stuffed with drugs, as living. Sunny's uncle KD held such power over her that she had turned against her own family, her sister, her father. I want the court to just imagine a relationship so vicious and vile, where an uncle gets his own niece hooked to drugs of all sorts—for which the accused has already paid the price—she stands ruined in society's eyes—and has memories so terrible it will probably take her the rest of her life to get rid of them—'

Many present in the court stared at the fragile girl in the dock. Shorn of makeup, she looked too young to be out unescorted, let alone face the charge of a murder.

'Please imagine—from the age of ten the victim had been welcomed into her house by her father to look after the accused and her sister but what happened is cruel beyond imagination—' For the hundredth time since entering the courtroom that morning, Sunny found Kala staring at her. Eyes studying her intently, as a predator would look at its prey, her gaze seemed to bore into Sunny's flesh.

Sunny's counsel P.K. Dang argued that her attack on KD was not a pre-planned act but one taken in self-defense, under the influence of drugs she had been plied with by the victim himself. They argued that Sunny's manager had fraudulently exposed her to a potentially dangerous situation by forcing her to go for the dance party. Staring at Sunny from the other side of the court, Vishnu's face went white. Suhana gripped her father's hand firmly to stop it from shaking.

'Sunny—has seen brutality and cruelty beyond measure—she was in a physical state where she could be relieved of her sanity with just one piercing, invasive look—hate can drive you insane, but there is always reason in madness, just as love is madness in emotion.' The sunlight streamed in through a high window, illuminated the polished patina of the elegant wooden panels around him. It glanced off the bald head of the judge. This was the third time in far too many weeks that the prosecutor and P.K. Dang had locked horns on the latter's attempt to declare the suspect insane, and therefore unable to serve their time in prison.

'She was also far too intelligent, and worse yet, crafty for her own good. She is not insane—however badly Mr. Dang wants us to believe...'

Unperturbed by the comments, Dang, with a flair for the dramatic, walked on determinedly to the prosecutor's side, his coat slung over his arm.

'In my opinion, Sunheri Kashyap or Sunny is as much a danger to herself as to others and prison is probably not the best environment for her rehabilitation—' he smoothly rattled off, feeling a rush of self-satisfaction at the slowly forming acquiescent look in the judge's eye, and the suspicion he could see, unhidden, in the prosecutor's eyes. The latter proceeded derisively, 'Do you really think a girl who butchers a man doesn't belong in jail?' he challenged, eyes fixed on the jury's face searchingly.

'I would hardly have testified to that otherwise, would I, but that's not true.' Dang's voice was challenging and arrogantly dismissive, as the prosecutor stepped in front of him, blocking his path.

'You have a habit of declaring your clients insane and moving into your asylum,' he said softly, his voice dripping sarcasm.

'I have a habit of siding with truth,'retorted Dang.

'Are we going to allow this sham to go on? To let the accused make a mockery of the legal system? The case is going against the defendant when suddenly, Mr. Dang, a creature of habit, starts making penguin noises, pulling vegetables out from under the defendant's chair calling the witness's pet parrot to the stand to testify. Perhaps he's stalling for time while an associate tries to find the evidence to show the accused in good light or maybe he's finally just flipped under the strain of the case.' The court erupted and so did the defence attorney and the judge. In the complete commotion which followed, the judge's voice could be barely heard—

'To say—to say nothing of the high chance that you would be severely disciplined if not disbarred as soon as the nearest Bar Association ethics panel heard about it—'

'Stop smiling YOU WHORE!' There was complete silence in the court as Kala's shriek interrupted the proceedings, 'Look at her face. There is no shame. But then—your mother was a whore too, *randi ki aulaad*—'

'What's happening in this court?!'

Kala's outburst erupted the court into a commotion and the angry judge furiously ordered for her to be taken out of the court immediately. A soft voice broke the chaos, Sunny was smiling as she spoke.

'*—When she embraces, your heart turns to stone, she comes at night when you are all alone. And when she whispers, your blood shall run cold, you better hide before she finds you.*' In a chilling voice Sunny taunted Kala. Now there was complete commotion.

'You cannot talk like this—in the court!' The judge was apoplexic.

'Just look at the devil's daughter—jusssst lookkkk at herrr—she is that witch Tabbbuuuu—' Kala yelled, madness dribbling off her eyes, her face split by a thin red gash for a mouth. The court orderlies moved towards Kala but the crazed woman's reflexes proved too fast. She ran from them and lunged towards Sunny, knelt across before anyone could stop her and slapped her on her cheek. The noise of the slap ricocheted across the court corridor. Sunny's face froze at the dark purple welt spread across her face. A shrill unearthly scream rang out in the room and for a second everyone stood still staring at Kala. Something had snapped inside her.

'ORDEERR! SILENCE SILENCE! Guards!'

The special judicial magistrate threw out Sunny's bail for the next month and till then she was to remain in police custody. There were no concessions for the girl whose bail plea had been turned down twice, consigning her back to barrack 36 of Bheesha Jail.

PUTRID SUMMER

She had been punished long enough she thought. The birds huddled together and stared disapprovingly. There were little patches of dirty mud where she stood. It was over three hours now. Six-year-old Sunny had been standing there for more than three hours in the suffocating heat of the garden. Her punishment for wetting her bed. The sun which had been soft and harmless and a welcome end to a horridly cold night had become menacing and cruel now. It beat down on her neck and made her head swim. But she would not move she thought. Let her Papa find her like this, she swore stubbornly. The sweat which had gathered at the nape of her neck now dribbled down her back into the crack of her bum and then down her thighs. Sunny always waited till it reached the thighs, she had a habit of rubbing her thighs with the warm liquid in between... It felt better, since she knew that her step-mother would get more pissed, a stolen sin in the long hours of punishment. In front of her, Kala knitted non-stop on her dark wood rocking chair. The needles attached to her stepmother's hands puncturing the air around her at breakneck speed. Her eyes fixed on the little Sunny, she created strange patterns on silk fabrics, her needles going.

—ATTACK SPLICE CUTT ATTACKK SPIN CUTT SPLICE—

When the silk got over she attacked the lowly cottons, her fingers moving with dizzying certainty. Jabbing the thicker contours of the cottons into mouldable shapes with such ferocity as if she wanted to jab out the actual essence of the unyielding raw fabric...

—SPLICE SPLICE CUTTT CUTTT ATTACKK ATTACKK—

Sunny always got frightened, and sucked her thumb when Kala started knitting and stitching. But over time, Sunny fancied she understood the language of the needles. She imagined the dancing needles were trying to tell her something. She imagined they were her friends. They warned her of Kala's state of mind. Fast snippy ones when angry. Soft snips when calm. Uneven ones when Kala was raging. That's when she would want to run away.

The stones now glistened moist and black and slimy from piss. Sunny felt like a voyeur of her own plight, a pretend tourist. Watching from her cot, two-year-old Dannie stared with huge bright eyes. Sunny resisted the impulse to cup her eyes against the rising sun. She wanted the worst to happen. But it never happened. The silence sat angrily, making the birds in the garden even more depressed. This was the longest she had been punished, she thought chewing her lips. And she wondered whether this time Kala would punish her all night. She imagined herself as a tree. She imagined her legs slowly becoming wooden, and her soft skin turning scaly and black and hard. Maybe she was turning into a wood fairy. She imagined her legs getting sucked down into the ground and growing roots. And when her punishments used to be over, she moved around like how she thought a wood fairy should move. But today, standing in her own piss and sweat for so long, Sunny did not feel like a wood fairy, or any fairy, anymore. More like a horrid witch. Maybe that's why she smelled so much now. She let herself go again. The muddy spot had transformed into a bad toilet, a hot fetid swamp. She knew she would have to clean the mess herself, after her quota of punishment was over. But just making Kala angry and pissed off would make up for everything. It gave her a thrill of delight.

'This Sunny had worms, this big, when I first saw her. Ate mud off the floor, little jungli!' *Kala indicated with her arms*

'This big worms inside her guts. She was being eaten alive from inside! Almost out of her mind like her mother,' Kala would say blackly.

'Dirty monkey, you have inherited your mother's madness—both of you were dressed in dirty rags... and this Sunny's intestines were hangings out of her arsehole! Both of you used to shit in the garden. Your mad mother did not even teach you the concept of a toilet.'

'Your mother was some item! A mother of two who still had the time for affairs on the sly! Whore got what she deserved. Chod kar chalee gayee – museebat – *she abandoned you and went off with her* yaar.'

Kala ranted and raved and cursed the girls and their dead mother. And when unchecked, the anger and hostility transformed to verbal assaults and severe beatings. Sunny would take refuge in the darkest and remotest corners of the garden, under the bed, behind the sofa, in the attic, in the store room, and sit and suck her thumb and curl up like a snail or in a tight foetal position, all the time curling her long strands of hair with a finger and more often than not soaked in the hot broth of her own urine. When caught by Kala, the child would be struck dumb with terror. It became worse when Sunny got into the habit of wetting her bed, Kala found macabre ways to punish her. She took special pleasure in punishing the young girl, perhaps maddened by her special beauty which reminded everyone so much of Tabu. Apart from keeping her hungry for hours, depriving her of milk, making her drink bitter tonics all the while hurling the filthiest abuses at the girls' mother, Kala added whipping to scare the already tormented child. When everything failed, the woman came up with more odious ways to cure Sunny. She rubbed chilli in the little girl's vagina till she screamed in distress. Sometimes she sprinkled boiled rice over Sunny's urine soaked mattress and made the child eat the rice. The terror-struck child could not understand why she was being made to eat rice in urine, and she started wetting her bed during the day too. It would have got worse had Suhana not complained to Vishnu. For a long time after their father came back, the frightened girls huddled in a corner with hands over their ears, and holding little Dannie, to stop listening to Kala's piercing screams.

'I will talk to the media, the magazines. They will write about you again now that they have stopped writing about your films. You will be famous again! You and your jungli *monkey girls.' Kala beat her breasts in shameless frenzy, frothing at the mouth falling into a state of feverish delirium scaring the twins and their father into long silences. Her aggressive hatred and violent behaviour frightened Vishnu terribly. The final straw was when he saw Sunny eating mud off the floor and squatting and shiting in the garden. He just could not take it anymore and asked Bina to help. The ageing Bina sent her nephew Kalidas to help Kala, his sister. But what was obvious even then was that the filthy and unkempt Sunny with her matted hair, all tangled with burrs, and disturbing golden eyes and dirty clothes, eating mud off the floor in the day and wetting the floor in the nights, was transforming into an uncommon unsettling beauty. It was clear to all that Sunny was becoming a carbon copy of the stunning creature that her mother was.*

25

'Opinions are like arseholes. Everyone has one,' bragged one of the officers to his groupie subordinates, looking pleased as punch with his smoothness.

'Boys. It's here. Right here where fear is,' he said glibly pointing his stubby ringed finger at his head while the fresh recruits listened on in rapt attention.

'I say the only race in police is khaki,' he continued. ACP Bhonsle rolled his eyes and moved away from the group of policemen into the last empty spot in the far corner of the smoke-filled officer's mess. It was still a Tuesday night but inside here it was always a Saturday at a cricket match. The smell of greasy burgers was over-powering and he could hardly breathe amidst the stench of the burning oil. He wondered why the café even bothered to install bins—nobody seemed inclined to use them. Spotting no empty tables, he made his way back downstairs to order his food. The young boy who took his order looked older than his years, tired, world-weary, uninterested. His order arrived, a huge veggie-burger, large fries and a chocolate milkshake. Kabir absent-mindedly popped a French fry in his mouth. It tasted as bad as it looked. Greasy, unhealthy and fattening. But ACP Kabir Bhonsle felt grateful that the shitty place had taken his mind off the case, even if only for a bit.

The strenuous investigations in the open-and-shut case had only yielded confusing results. The intense media scrutiny had trebled the pressure on his team to demonstrate a movement in the case. Kabir Bhonsle had organized the most concentrated, rigorous and exhaustive step-by-step approach to the case. But the court hearing had left him and his men drained and annoyed. They had been asked to present a reworked summary layout based on the courts' new format. And now even after days of determinedly supervising the crime-scene documentation papers, re-writing notes, overseeing the arrangement of motives and facts to facilitate proper in-court presentation and reconstructing the scene of the crime and the chain of events in chronological order, with no opinions, no analysis, or no conclusions to rule out bias, he was not sure about the case. Kabir believed the only way he could make a headway in the case was to iron out the irritants, especially those who seemingly had no relation to the murder. It was not strictly legal but he had photocopied all the official documents of Kalidas's case and poured over it, scanned every detail, till the facts were ingrained in his brain. His team had lost count of the hours they had spent sifting through the mountain of material in the form of scribbled notes, account numbers, stubs of cheques and dinary entries KD had left behind in a box hidden behind the boiler in his apartment. Putting the whole thing together for court hearings was proving to be nightmarish. The re-processing of all the information into a new layout was arduous, and not surprisingly, his overworked team was full of unhappy and groggy men at the moment. Puffy faced and slack-jawed from the long hours, Shinde had slumped on the chaise lounge and dozed off.

'Why is he sleeping?'

'Double shifts, just a couple of hours of down time before the next shift kicks in,' Holkar said.

'Tell him to get up. Take a shower. Eat and get back to work... Shinde, *chal utth*!'

Shinde instantly wide awake, bounded to the attached kitchen and fixed himself a bowl of roasted dalia and milk and voraciously spooned the cereal into his mouth, before pausing to catch his breath. In response, Holkar rushed to the refrigerator, grabbed a container of orange juice and after a greedy swig childishly kept the carton for himself.

'Excuse me—Bhonsle Sir.'

'Not excused.'

'Man can't be excused to take a *pisshaab*?'

'You should say take a leak *bhnchot.*'

'Leak...Piss ya Pishaab ... *matlab mootne se hai. Gooooing* sir....'

Kabir could not be bothered either way.

'Recently I was asked to give an opinion on the crime scene of a cold case investigation which had occurred more than fifteen years earlier. The Dannie case. I agreed to take a look at everything to give my interpretation of the crime scene. I ordered the reports and pictures from the original files. You know what they sent me? A measly one paragraph narrative!!' Kabir shrugged and got up while gulping down his now cold burger with the tepid fizzy.

'Sir, the content of the Panvel farmhouse lockers.'

'Found anything?'

'Same thing. Naked photos of girls and boys. And lots of photos of Dannie. His niece. Remember Dannie?'

'Yes *bhenchod* I remember Dannie.' Bhonsle regarded the huge stash of photos and tapes and private letters dumped on his table. Pausing for a moment, Kabir pored over Dannie's pictures, as a child of three, five, ten. Even as a child it was evident that she had uncommon beauty, indicative of the star she would become. And one of the most sculpted heads he had ever seen. What surprised the officer was that the actress looked remarkably tiny till her early teens.

A pale-faced office-boy shovelled into the room listlessly trying to figure out where to place even more sealed packets on the already full table.

'*Abbey kya?* There is more stuff? Motherfucker keep it on the table—let me finish this crap first.'

'Anything important?'

'*Bhonsdi ka*...boy photos, girl photos, more chics...pervert *saala*...stubs of cheques, papers with studio addresses, producer details, too much useless information.'

'You know what they are running on TV? Some fantastic theory floating in the media about the motive for KD's murder... the latest one is that he had fallen out with a bootlegger!'

'One thing is for sure. Mr. Unpopular had an unending list of people who had a bone to pick with him. The only living blood relative KD left behind is his psycho sister Kala. His business partner Silky is pissed off and he even managed to upset the Bawlas.' Kabir regarded the exhaustive material in front of him taunting him with its hidden truths and wondered just what had he succeeded in establishing? He impatiently waved to the skinny office boy signalling him to dump some more courier packets on the table and instantly felt bad for snapping at the boy. Poor sod. A late-night shift was no beachwalk in a station full of grumpy policemen. They were all snappy and tired and angry, at having to rework the summary, when all they wanted to do was to hit the field, down stiff ones, crack the case and head home. Not necessarily in that order.

'Hey boy! Come back. Have some tea. Give him some tea and pakoda.' The thin pasty-faced boy, unnerved by the sight of scores of angry men in khaki looking pissed like hell, looked like this was the last place he wanted to be in. 'Boy don't be scared. Have this tea, okay. Take this money and buy yourself something to eat. And that's an order—' His men guffawed as the boy snatched the money from ACP Bhonsle's hands and almost bounded out of the room.

'Back off...! The poor boy was scared shitless.'

'Hey give me a knife. *Maadachot* this is tight—letter *bhi bhejengey chain lagaa kar*—'

Kabir struggled with the last remaining bundle and finally managed to open it. More photos. Shit.

'*Ayuuuikk*? Whathefuckkkk is this!!'

Kabir stared at the photos, but nothing made sense for some time. He sat stunned for a moment, trying to understand what he was seeing. Then with a loud expletive which surprised the assorted men in the room, ACP Kabir Bhonsle's team saw him doing the fastest sprint out of the room yelling at the doorman to stop the office boy. But the thin boy had disappeared into the dark.

'HEYYYYY GET HIM!! GET THAT BOY—GET HIM !! LOOK FOR HIM—MAADACHOD HE WOULD NOT HAVE GONE FAR—'

◆

Sister Sachcha stood across the road melted in the shadows and staring at the ACP across the night traffic and the pelting rain. No one noticed the skinny white-faced girl who with one last look shrank into the back seat of the waiting taxi, guiding him expertly to an unmarked alley through an old tunnel between two building supply lots. They passed dumpsters stuffed to the rim and graffiteed walls on an uncertain road and the taxi driver looked doubtful.

'*Madam aapko idhar hi jaana?* What is here?' The rain was pouring hard enough to distort everything but she could recognize the route clearly.

'Home. I know the way. *Rasta aagey se hai.* There is a way from here.' Another quarter mile of weaving through cracked asphalt and dirt-choked roads, the alley angled and turned into another alley to the left of which was a car waiting for its passenger. The taxi driver stared at his hands full of money as the girl got into the waiting car which sped away. She stared indifferently at the flyovers and film hoardings and night crowds and psychedelic city lights whizzing past her, till there was just skies and trees, and to the far north, the smog-glazed outline of mountaintops. She could not get out of the city fast enough, the city which had sucked out her identity. The memories of another life came rushing back. Another lifetime. When her face was plastered on these very hoardings. They used to call her Dannie. Dannie the Dream Girl.

She had sworn she would never look back, and she had never regretted her decision for a moment. She was finally at peace. The girl who had landed up at Anattā ashram many years back had moved on. She had left behind her career, her family and her identity. She had thought she had forgotten her past, but it had all come rushing back in a single paralyzing instant. The constant feeling of helplessness of always acting. Never being.

Dannie had never wanted to be an actress. But her earliest childhood memories were of talcum powder and paint and lipstick and eye shadows and dresses and perfumes. She had come to hate the cloying smell of perfume her dresses always seemed to reek of. Always powdered and painted to perfection. Her mother Kala would have nothing less for her wonder baby. She made it clear to her that she wanted to see her daughter become a superstar, and would often tell her tales of their gorgeous grand-aunt Bina, the dream girl of the seventies. That was the only time she ever saw her mother not chewed up with hatred for her father and cursing her two step-sisters.

And Dannie fulfilled her mother's deepest aspirations and more. From the age of three to eight, Dannie was the most adorable and irresistibly charming child star, a big money spinner. She had the biggest of films and worked with superstars. Baby Dannie won many film awards and became the little queen of many jubilee productions, the little princess who wore golden dresses and was plied with chocolates and cola so that she gave perfect smiles. At the peak of her career, she earned more than twenty lakhs per movie. That was impressive money for a child actor. Gripped by a maniacal success drive, Kala made sure 'baby' did not reach ten till the longest time, and Dannie roamed around in kiddy clothes, her hair in kiddy braids and ribbons for the longest time. What she hated the most was the strict diet of bland boiled food she had been put on so that her face and body remained uncorrupted and uncorroded. But biology took its course and then a frantic Kala, scared of baby's screen death and offers drying up, took to tying flat strips of ribbons across 'baby' Dannie's chest to keep it from spouting breasts. But fact was that the adorable wonder baby was changing forever. And there were always younger perfectly formed babies around.

Baby Dannie's career as a child star was over by eleven. After a few TV shows and an attempt at a reality show, she was on the verge of becoming a ghost celebrity, when she was suddenly discovered by Dream Star. The cameras unexpectedly started loving the magical way her face was changing. The cameras transformed her off-screen pasty face and skinny form into the most compelling and sensitive faces the screen had seen in a long time. Dannie the wonder baby had magically transformed into Dannie the dream girl. The audience was drawn to her magnetic aura. And when her first film turned out to be a stellar hit, she landed a three-film deal with Dream Star. The world was at her feet. The studios made sure she parted ways with her mother, by instating a handler for her, a secy, apart from a huge expense account, and set her up in the most beautiful part of Mumbai in a sea-facing pad with every luxury money could buy. And instead of her mother, she was now busy making the producers and studios happy. And she was good at it. Always acting. Never being. Till she fell in love.

When Dannie discovered love for the first time, she realized how much she hated men touching her. How much she hated touching them. How long she had gone on like a puppet without emotions which she thought she should be feeling for a man. The fact was she had never felt anything for men. The day she saw Monalisa on the sets of her film, she broke out in a cold sweat, her knees started shaking, her heart pounded madly. Terrified, for an instant she thought she was having a heart attack, till Monalisa looked at her and smiled and she felt warm and complete. She remembered she was so delirious with happiness that she gave a perfect shot with her new hero, the dashing young dream lover Prince Sulaiman Capure, and got a standing ovation. Even Prince had joined in. And she was ecstatic.

Green-eyed Monalisa was the most beautiful girl she had ever seen. Her bisque doll come alive. She could not believe her eyes. Dannie quickly found out the bronze nymphet Monalisa was a fifteen-year-old model who had been roped in from KD's agency by the studios for a bitsy item number. Their first love-making was sheer magic. They kissed each other desperately tearing off each other's clothes. Taking each other decisively. She found surprising strength in Monalisa's fragile body, and she returned the love with unexpected boldness. Soon they were two happy lovers in a crowd. They managed the impossible in Bollywood. They managed to keep their affair a secret. No one suspected them, and Dannie and Monalisa kept their love for each other close to their hearts.

A superhit film later, Dream Star Studios had already started shoots for their next two biggies with Dannie, and the promos were out. She was on top of the world. And then her world came crashing down. Dream Star Studios' patriarch received a secretly shot DVD of her unedited love for her girlfriend. Dannie and Monalisa making love to each other in the vanity van, in her apartment, in her bathroom, in her private pool. The studio was terrified that if the truth about their heroine came out, it'd spell doom for their multi-crore films riding on the hit pairing of Prince Sulaiman Capure and his dream girl. The actor's fury unnerved her, scared as he was at being hooted out of the theatres with his lesbian heroine. Except Dannie was determined to come out after their next film hit the theatres. The studio warned her with dire repercussions but Dannie returned the signing amount. She had made up her mind. However, two days before the wrap of the final schedule, Dannie was summoned to Dream Star Studios and was shown the sex-tape of her little Monalisa with two men. The tape left nothing to the imagination. It was a Monalisa she had never seen before, a nymphet in the throes of passion as two men tried to fill her. Her hungry hands on their bodies seeking love vociferously. Dannie froze, her world closed in on her. She ran out of the office like a pathetic drunkard, her heart thundering as the truth seared through her like acid. Dannie's make-believe world had come crashing down and she saw herself confined to playing Dannie the dream girl again and again. Hardened from the betrayal, Dannie threw Monalisa out of her house and left on a hectic all-India and overseas film promotion tour. Monalisa disappeared from her life. Her film's opening day raked in an impressive 30 crores and the trade analysts projected a monster collection crossing 100 crores. It was during the celebration party at DS Studios while they were announcing their new project with the hit Dannie-Prince pairing, that she received the letter from Monalisa. It was a simple letter written before Monalisa cut her wrists.

'Dannie—you called me shameful! You saw my shame and you blamed me—the two men in the video are not my lovers... They forced me apart and raped me for hours. What you saw was the two men tearing me, plundering my body and ravaging me. But you said I was the whore! I was called into your van by your uncle KD, he said that you were waiting for me. And then he gave me something to drink which took away my strength leaving them free to do anything with my body. I was raped Dannie. One of them was very vicious and I can't forget his drunken breath on my body when he pierced me repeatedly...I was stitched Dannie, in places you cannot imagine and I was in a private nursing home, hoping and praying everyday that you would come for me. They showed me the recording of my shame. Said they will tell everyone that they were my lovers.Said you believed them. And you did. But it does not matter now, it's too late. Always be the dream girl that you are—Monalisa'

It all hit Dannie in a terrible moment of clarity. The conspiracy to get her lover discredited and out of her life in the most horrid way. Monalisa's sordid tale tore Dannie's heart and in one moment of decisiveness, she decided to stop acting. No more acting. The dream girl had to die. She had killed the dream girl and gone on living.

And now the past would also be laid to rest. Sister Sachcha thought of her long terrace garden patch—spectacularly beautiful, sang with cicadas and mynahs. Outside the car, the city's dark smog was clearing up as a faint eastern glow split the sky. The grey air punctured by a soft yellow light revealed the countryside she longed for. Sister Sachcha could not wait to get back to her garden at Anattā.

26

The two appeared very much in love. There were fifty photos of Dannie in various stages of undress with a girl. Kabir stared at the explicit pictures of the two girls. This was no act.

'Vanished. Within seconds.' Shinde rushed in panting, followed by two policemen equally out of breath. 'I think the car was waiting. Took off in a flash. It just went whipping into the alley and then disappeared.'

'What car make?'

'It was one of our Mumbai taxis.'

'Ohh! No wonder. That's smart. I mean there are thousands of those on the streets at any time. You were probably even looking at the wrong one!'

'*Bhenchodd.* I did not think of that.'

'Pictures of Dannie again? And I thought KD was the perv here. Who has sent her pictures...and such pictures!' Holkar said quietly. The rest of the men simply stared at the pictures stunned into silence. ACP Bhonsle and his men knew if the pictures were what they seemed to be, then they were privy to one of the best-kept secrets of B-town. Dannie, the dream girl, was a lesbian. It was incredible that the heroine who was always under media scrutiny had been able to hide such an explosive secret.

'You know, this girl with Dannie looks very young. Hardly fourteen or something.'

'But why would someone send this stuff to us now, bang in the middle of KD's murder investigation? When all the parties concerned have disappeared from the face of earth! Unless there is a link between the murder and this?'

'But it's too difficult to keep such a big secret in Bollywood–' Shinde said, his mouth hanging open.

'Exactly. So maybe someone got to know the secret.'

'So KD's lesbo niece has an affair. And someone sends us all this proof now! For what?? After so many years?–Play that tape which was in this packet will you,' Shinde was struggling with the tape.

'*Maadachodd* shit it's not playing–wait–'

Kabir looked up at the screen which burst into life.

It was the girl from the pictures with Dannie. The girl was performing a slow striptease. The camera focussed on her face and he noticed the pupils of her large green eyes were enormously dilated. Like it happens when someone is high on opiates. Peeling down to black garter belt mesh stockings and high heeled shoes touching herself, bending, spreading, kneading, playing for the camera. The camera swung to the doorknob and two men walked in. The camera was not focussed on them and all he could make out was that one was broad-shouldered and the other was a lithe-looking man (or was it a tall boy?) moving towards the girl who was lying on the bed. The girl got up and seemed to hug a man and then the closeups began. They pinched her nipples, licked her neck...all the while their face remained in soft focus, unrecognizable. The camera remained on her face and her body in spurts. Then it got aggressive and Kabir looked away. The rapid shift in positions and closeups of contorted faces was jarring and had a sense of unease about it. The edgy and restless way in which the film was shot reminded him of something he could not place a finger on. Like he had seen the film. Only that could not be possible because it was clear as day that he was looking at the contents of the video for the first time in his life. By the time it was over he felt suffocated, angry and sad. Mercifully, the room stayed dark for some time. A video which shocked, and confused and troubled him as much as it did those present in the room. Kabir wondered how a girl could let herself be treated like a piece of meat.

'There are explicit films in showbiz...but this is not explicit. This is sort of off-kilter—it's done pretty creatively almost like—hard to imagine someone shooting so voyeuristically so many years back—what are you staring at now, Shinde?'

'Strangely, I feel I have seen this scene in a film—I swear I have seen this before! I mean the girl was different...older than this child...but otherwise exactly same setup. Young girl, drugged and raped—same men, same angles, even the feel is exactly the same—'

'*Baapre tuzya aaila zavla kala kutra Shinde!* What sort of films do you see *bhenchod?*'

'They are not sleazy films. Let me tell you they are cult films with a huge following—HEYYY now I remember! You know I swear it's that Jerome's type of camerawork—you know his film *The Rape*? He got an award for it too! It has a famous rape scene, you can watch it on YouTube...here wait!' Shinde typed the keywords. Jerome Mangwani's *The Rape* cropped up within a nano-second.

'Just wait and see. This scene is quite similar to what's on this tape *hain*?' ACP Kabir Bhonsle watched intently. Shinde was right. The same edgy unsettled format shot in an identical pacy voyeuristic style which he recognized instantly. The scene from the film had two men raping a drugged girl. It even started the same way!

'But don't you see? This film rape video came much after this sex-tape was made...and if no one has seen it barring the actors and the director, then there is a very real chance—what??' Shinde stopped abruptly when he saw the look on Kabir's face.

'He might as well have signed it,' Kabir said without smiling. It was time to meet *The Rape's* award-winning maverick filmmaker Jerome Mangwani.

'Oh and boss—I think we know who our Dannie's mystery friend is,' Holkar said waving a letter which he had retrieved from the packet, 'seems our talented Miss. Monalisa wrote a note to her girlfriend.'

HARD FROST

It was a sad, grimy run-down little room. Smelling of old memories, stale words, a brackish smell of urine mixed with sweat and food going bad. The window ledge was full of yellow white shit which never came out even with the iron sponge kept in the kitchen. The shit encrusted itself into the glass glaze so deeply that despite Sunheri's best efforts to clean it, the glass looked as shitty as ever. The shit entered the grain of the glass which cast its sickly yellow hue on the world outside. A blue sky turned acidic yellow through the window. The world always seemed skewed to the twins when they looked out of that window. And then there were the termites in their cupboard. And the roaches which roamed freely over their clothes reducing Sunheri to a frantic state. Suhana never bothered as much, but as a result of being in a constant state of fright, Sunny developed huge ugly sores on her feet and legs. Suhana got away with a bad case of lice which made her school-going years miserable.

Kala refused to take any responsibility, there was just this much she could do with Dannie's budding film career. While Suhana did not give a damn, Sunheri desperately wanted to be a star too. Like Dannie. She dreamt of a big room just like Danny's, all pink and silk and lace and fragrant with heady smells and beautiful dolls and fantastic gifts from all over the world. The perks of being the wonder baby of the film industry. In the face of the daily torment of deprivation, Suhana's natural defence mechanism kicked in. She became more intense and developed a solitary character and became an expert in concocting little subterfuges to get out of her daily predicaments. But Sunheri moulded into a creature of opposite nature to her sister. She became the resident contortionist in trying to bend to the wishes of Kala—making big panda eyes when she was reprimanded, forever childishly trying to please Kala for little favours like watching Dannie, getting makeup on, or watching her favourite film on TV, for a chance to hold one of those breathtakingly beautifully Bisque dolls Dannie got as gifts. She dreamt of a knight in a shining armour to come and save her from the world of shit.

KD came to the Kashyap household when he was in his late teens. He was vain, common and shallow, was Suhana's first impression when she saw him. But he had a funny rakish appearance which appealed in a strange way to both the girls. Besides, he saved them from Kala's relentless punishments, and that in the beginning was his biggest appeal. KD smoked on the sly, drank forbidden spirits which he hid in cola bottles, told vulgar jokes, and generally took the role of a rampant cocksman. He bought the girls bright bandanas and bracelets made of colourful beads. A silk scarf for Suhana, which she knew was not silk, and rose-colored hippy shades for Sunheri, whom he nicknamed Sunny. A name she loved. KD drew scandalous cartoons of Kala, with horns growing from her head, with a gremlin tail stuck to her arse, smoke bellowing from her ears. He had the girls hooked to his wicked stories about Kala—how she wet her bed, how she ate mitti, how she licked walls, how she shat in her school every day till class five. It went on endlessly. The more the girls laughed the more absurd and bizarre the stories became. Suhana was by then sure that Kalidas was inventing them just to make them laugh but it didn't matter. In fact she was overwhelmed that someone was actually trying to make them laugh. So what if he was lying. It got so wicked that she had to physically stop herself from laughing aloud during dinner time when the three used to exchanged conspiring looks. Vishnu was relieved the girls were laughing again.

She did not understand why KD had started insisting that instead of holding hands they sit on his lap when he told them Kala's secrets. Sunheri would laugh and jump into KD's lap screaming 'me first'. KD would not stop speaking and the twins would listen mesmerised but Suhana was not unaware that KD had started holding and touching Sunheri more and more. And when he first started fondling her near her panties, she sat turned to stone. Nights became frightful times of lying in shame and days were shameful times of sitting in fright. He was all of twenty-one and he used to seek out the girls and spend time with them. Kala was happy to get the girls off her back and even threw a veiled barb at Vishnu about how her brother was also pitching in to look after 'the orphans', how her family had become babysitters. Vishnu never answered. Suhana knew something about her Dad's silence. She shuddered at the thought of what would happen if her father found out, and locked herself on the terrace for a long time staring at the circling crows.

At times like this she would long for her mother. She remembered her mother in little parts. An essence here...a breath there...a touch some other time...a picture in the magazine...a face on TV. She would hold her breath and try to remember as much as she could. The full lips, the aquiline nose, the soft golden eyes, the full-throated laughter, the cool polyester saris and low-cut blouses knotted in front of her breasts. In her mind she would zoom into the image of her mother's face but the features always remained miserably out of focus. In the beginning she believed if she concentrated hard enough she would see her. Sometimes she held her breath till she turned blue in an attempt to make god give her a sign that her mother was watching them from around the corner. Of course, Mother never came.

Not even when the troubling thing started between KD and Sunheri. Suhana was bewildered when her sister seemed to increasingly prefer to stay in his company. The more she tried to talk to her, the more stubborn and angry she got, and Suhana tried putting up with KD so as not to antagonize Sunheri. In her own childish way she was sure whatever was happening between them was definitely not good for Sunheri. Suhana decided to keep a watch onSunheri whenever KD was around. One fateful day she discovered some white powder, which was definitely not talcum, in Sunheri's almirah, along with some graphic pictures of her. A terrible feeling of shame washed down like hot oil down her neck, watching her sister's tacky nude pictures. Suhana lost her temper very badly that day. More than KD, it was Sunheri who bore the brunt of Suhana's unmitigated rage. A screaming match between the sisters ended with Sunheri refusing to speak to her again and KD, backed by Kala, warning her to back off. A frightened Suhana revealed the truth to Vishnu. KD was barred from entering their house ever again and Kala took Dannie with her never to return. Sunheri howled and yelled and threw such a fit that she had to be locked in her room. It was too late for her anyway.

❖

27

Six naked male models draped themselves on red velvet couches, in Jerome Mangwani's dimly lit studio.

'I want wow. I will sock them on their balls. Smack them right between their eyes. And you cunts will help *naah?* Good girls get out now!! They want shocking? I will give them outrageous...won't we cunties?'

It was a busy day at Jerome Mangwani's ultramodern state-of-the-art studio J-ARTS VFX. The shock photo catalogue's clients were very demanding. Jerome could not afford to disappoint this select gang of connoisseurs who truly appreciated his stylized shadow stills and were willing to pay a whallop for the yearly J Calendar, a collection of twelve pictures, one for each season. Except they refused to compromise on the shock value, quite like his films. However, Jerome was both happy and nervous. Happy because the pictures were turning out even better than he had hoped. And nervous because two police officers were waiting for him in the lobby to finish his shoot. Let them wait. Fuckers.

'Bitch your face should say I want to be raped! Okay boys. It should say I want to be the biggest *randi* here. It should say I am naked, come fuck me. Ladies, we are going to kick them in the teeth with this one.' Jerome inspected his male models drily, poking and pinching their skins.

'Here's the scene—boy gets a trick knife from a costume shop. He uses it to grab and rape. Actual sex at knifepoint scene. The trick is that the knife always retracts into the handle. Somehow on that day the knife stays intact. Ohhhh! Someone has substituted the trick knife with a real one. A very sharp steel knife. Shockkkk!! Poor boy had no idea—that's what I want...heyyy where are the black drapes—where is this frigging orange light coming from—'

Outdoors, the air was muggy and the arid noon sun turned the sky into a blazing fireball. But inside the studio it was scarlet cold or a purple winter night or pretty much anything Jerome wished. Kabir Bhonsle looked impassively at the gigantic J ARTS which flickered in full neon glory, the lights reflecting in the glass and steel of Jerome Mangwani's swanky production house, waiting for him to wrap up his shoot. Kabir scrutinized the indoor shooting studio built on three levels, the biggest in the city.

Who could have thought Jerome Mangwani had started as a small-time snapper delivering video cassettes on a bicycle to bored housewives, sleazy men and horny kids from the video cassette library he tenanted. The library gave him access to a large collection of movies and that was where Jerome, who never managed to complete class tenth, spent his waking hours dabbling in rudimentary filmmaking and production, including stints as an assistant to various small-time directors of C-grade films. His desperation to succeed led him to a disastrous TV innings with a flop show and his first couple of films with low-key junior artists was largely ignored at the box office. Jerome forayed deeply into the blooming parallel world of C, D and E-grade hindi films which could do without A-grade actors and big budgets. The films with a heavy dose of erotica and cheap thrills only needed girls desperate enough to do anything. Jerome expressed his wildest fantasies through these films. What separated his films from the other D-grade films was the excellent production and above average actors. Jerome rapidly cast himself in the role of a small-time filmmaker and his zero-budget reelers became known for their violence and gore and soon had a cult fan following for the fact that the films were high on violent edgy sexual content. Jerome became the uncrowned king of erotic violence. But he soon got bored of the D-grade two-reelers which got him money but not the recognition he thirsted for. His controversial morbid films with their sinister obsessive handling of violence and eerie comedy set him apart from the beginning. It was marked as the Jerome style of filmmaking. Through his works ran a strong sense of voyeurism. There were talks about how he did the dead scenes, in which he used real corpses from morgues. Of course it was all hushed up in the name of creative license and simple fear of the studios he represented. Unrelenting graphic violence, wall-to-wall fist fights and shoot outs, and edgy tense sex with an underlying sense of menace, shock filmmaker Jerome had found his true calling in shooting the very dark, sinister, seedy and depressing.

'Hello Officer *jee* I hope they are taking care of you? *Saaheb ko pilaaya thanda?* Just one more thing and I am all yourss, it's a bussssyy day—'

And before Kabir could open his mouth to answer, the director swished out of the room, hissing to his assistants.

'About the women libbies—they are getting a *juloos* against my last calendar today. Remember to get the media. I want full coverage.' Jerome's recent nudie calendar featuring six vagina close-ups of models for a select few connoisseurs from around the world was in the line of fire from media watchdogs.

'My vagina calendar has all these women lib aunties screaming bloody murder...it's such fun—all the panel discussions on TV—*mere liye muft ki* publicity. They had no problem when my penis calendar was launched. But they have an issue with vagina—' Jerome yelled self-righteously, his audience a bunch of stoic police officers.

'How typical!' his boy-faced assistant bleated. 'How did the pictures leak out?'

'You know we kept the launch secret—it was a private showing at this farmhouse but a reporter bitch clicked several graphic pictures and leaked it—the press is a *maadachod.* Soooo Inspec—Officer *jee* what can I do for you??'

'You have got a very striking studio.'

'What, this little place?!' he said delightedly, 'Yes, the best in Mumbai.. ! I got this multi-level baby built three years back...'

'Must have cost a lot.'

'Yes officer *jee*—but what is this about...'

'Don't worry we are not from income tax,' his assistant pitched in.

'We just want your opinion on some photos and a DVD film delivered to us. It's a small video, a bit grainy—maybe you can help us with who or what type of cameras shot it. Who uses such cameras or maybe just in case you recognize the style of shooting—'

'Sure sure! I will do my bit as a citizen—let's see what you have Officer *jee—!*'

'Jerome this will not take long, you have my word. I have with me our official photographer...*chota mota*, not a biggie like you. Cameras and videos are his passion too. He has a theory on this DVD, but I am not sure–'

'Oooo it's nice to see policeman *photowaala*! I will just close the curtains and door to stop the light–give us a better *dekko*? Jerome clapped his hands and a few boys pulled in heavy black drapes on the window. The screen flickered on and a pale white light washed the room in its ghostly glow. It was the sex video of a girl and two men shot in a dark vouyreistic edgy style.

'Hey who is this? What the f-f-fuck. These are not-' Jerome's face lost colour, his eyes bulged as he gawped at the video now playing on his computer.

'Do you recognize this? Shot in sepia some eight years back. Very edgy work.' Jerome sat ramrod straight, the whites in his eyes widened. He made cud-chewing motions with his lips as if trying to bring up the right word. When he finally spoke his voice was weak and trembling.

'You will find no scandal here–it's all proper–'

'We are willing to test that hypothesis–'

'Urk–where did you get this?' Jerome's voice was hoarse with fear.

'It was hand delivered to us. Don't even bother to deny it Jerome. We have seen *The Rape*...quite a coincidence that they are exactly similar? Down to your camera angles. It has your print all over.'

'It's a coincidence, I have nothing to do with this.'

'Let your fans decide that, *haan*? If this clip hits the net along with your *The Rape*–you yourself said people recognize your signature style–let's see what your fans have to say? You will trend majorly. Heard you are very active on Twitter... how many followers do you have? We will get their opinion.'

'It's not a crime to shoot porn—even if we assume I shot it, of which there is no proof.'

'Sure. Many won't believe. But some will and they will talk—and you are not exactly Mr. Popular I am guessing. You know the industy better it's all a matter of perception here. Ohhh...apart from the fact that the underage child in this video committed suicide, the press, the media—I don't think they will be very sympathetic with your "just a coincidence" theory.'

'Uhhherk—' Jerome's face had turned purple and his throat apple was bobbing out dangerously.

'You didn't know she was underage, did you? You know what...we can finish this questioning in the station also. Maybe one night in the cell will refresh your memory? But you may not like the company there—the men there...how they would behave with someone like you...'

'What do you want to know? I have shot so many of these cunts. They come to be heroines and are willing to dance naked, and then cry rape—' Jerome whined.

'Don't use that word. This girl here is a child,' Kabir warned Jerome darkly, 'Did you know her?'

'I know thousands of girls—it's impossible for me to remember these cu—girls I mean, they all come to me to be shot—'

'This one did not come to you. You went to her to shoot her with these two men.'

'So I shot her having sex with two men. I can't be arrested for that. Not a crime. I don't know anything else, it's too long back,' he said with a nasty scowl.

'You did not shoot a girl having sex. This is an explicit film with an underage girl—a felony in every country. Even the countries whose film festivals premier your films. They have very strict laws about this sort of thing abroad you know. '

'Uhhhhh' Jerome let out a painful moan.

'Why did you shoot her?'

'There is no proof–that will connect me.' At this point Jerome stopped moving except his mouth which was frantically opening and closing like a fish.

'The people you are trying to protect will be the first ones to disown you. There is nothing which links the studios to this. But you–do you know she was not even thirteen–I can imagine the headlines. Shock director and ace photographer Jerome Mangwani felicitates rape of a child. No one is going to bother about going into trivia like the proof...a national film award-winner a perverted sex fiend! Everyone knows your signature style you scumbag! You are a sexual predator of the worst kind, the sort who would feed on desperate young groupies, junior artists and dancers to satisfy your demented fantasies–if this gets out, there is always a leak you know, someone puts it on the net–people recognize your art–and they start talking–it goes viral! Sure, maybe nothing happens. But then there is always the chance that people get it–they get the shit you did–you will be over. Finished. Banned. And in jail of course.' Jerome was suddenly looking very tired and very pale.

'I did not know it was rape–how would I know her age? What do you want to know?'

'You know what they do to people like you in jail? Because that's where you are going. I can hold you for questioning for 24 hours without a warrant,' Kabir said.

'O god–ohhh god–god god please god no! KD...KD told me to shoot the film for someone. He said they were willing to pay big,' Jerome sobbed.

Nothing like a little bluff to get you through a day, thought ACP Kabir Bhonsle smiling.

'Don't fucking play games with me. Who else was involved apart from KD?' Kabir's tone was hard.

'I—they—O god! I don't know who they were. There were always people conveying messages to KD. I was a struggler then...I was offered a huge amount...I needed the money to set up my studio—no one was willing to help me, no one would understand my art, not one of the fat fuckers would give me work—who was I...a nobody—I didn't think I was doing anything wrong—I cannot cannot go to jail! Please!' Jerome's face was glacial.

'You shoot a child getting raped and you suspect nothing? You are going to jail Jerome for a very long time. Did you know her name was Monalisa?'

'Ukkkk,' Jerome choked and his eyes bulged out in fear and he burst out. 'Please listen—the man said this fucking lesbo—I am just conveying please—this lesbian chic was messing up his girl. He didn't say who and I didn't ask. You don't start up in this industry by asking too many questions. You need to prove you can be of use. He needed something drastic to convince the girl that this cu—girl I mean—was as queer as a straight line! I was to shoot a sex-tape so his girl could be convinced. He said she should look like she was enjoying the sex. I didn't ask too much.'

'Who were the men Jerome?' Kabir asked again.

'I swear I don't know. And they were just fucking her. I didn't know it was rape. I don't know who the girl is—maybe a model I don't remember—please you got to believe me—I didn't know she was drugged. I didn't even know it would have two men.'

'I will not repeat myself again. And I am tired. We know you are lying and we should do the rest of this at the station. Do you know how many counts you are staring at?' There was no doubting the menace in the policeman's voice.

'Please...this can't get out—please understand I was not ever planning to use the tape. Just that I was in a sticky situation, needed money and he gave me a lot of money. I am just...just a cameraman. Poor man trying to take care of my business—'

28

Nisha Poddar was not born pretty. But then she had never been the one to be handicapped by what nature gave her. She believed what god did not provide, the doctor did. Her mousy limpid hair, uneven jagged teeth, spotted patchy skin had, over the years, been tweaked, pinched, squeezed, pulled, tugged, nipped, pumped, slashed and beefed to unrecognizable dimensions. But the rich black hair, smooth skin, upturned nose and capped teeth she spent fortunes on did not give her the coveted dream girl look she desired. She, however, had learnt to not give too much of a damn. Two disastrous love affairs with actors, who had used her for good reviews and free sex, had revealed the true face of Bollywood. But she did not give a damn. And she had her trusty vibrator. However, Nisha Poddar got her biggest orgasms from being the most feared journo in tinsel-town.

She had just received an invite from Prince Sulaiman Capure. He was throwing a party at his Panvel farmhouse.

You are invited....NISHA PODDAR.
If you got this card you are special to Prince.

No one could tell it was a fake.

Celebrations will continue...in Dubai. Come and be a part of Prince's celebrations in UAE. Let'scelebrate Prince's next superhit 'INDIAWALA HERO'.

Nisha was thrown by the gargantuan ego of the superstar. Proclaiming the film to be a hit even before a single print had hit the theatres! His hyper PR machinery working on an overdrive had already begun sending thank-you-SMSes to the whole of frigging Mumbai for making the film *Indiawala Hero* a runaway success! The party was scheduled to be held at one of his Panvel farmhouses. Which one...she wondered. Out of the stack of five farmhouses which dotted the Panvel road, famously named after his five dogs. She had had the occasion to meet his fat pugs and ugly mongrels at one of his parties. Aurangzeb after the emperor who had a thousand concubines. Ponty after his distributor. George Bush and Razia Sultan just because he could. And Lukhkha. Of the five the only one who truly deserved his name was Lukhkha.

She had seen the ugly monstrous mansions jutting incongruously in the pristine hills near Panvel. She hated them. A farmhouse?? How dare he call it a farmhouse? It was anything but—she had heard colourful, wild and gross stories. For starters she knew the only thing that grew inside was Prince's ego and the party boy's hidden stash of marijuana. And the people who came to the parties were even more bizarre. Full of fame whores and boob-grabbers with puffy wigs and weaves, cunt flashers and chints roaming in fur-lined thongs with fake busts and buttlines, wearing blingy shit and trashy sheers and pointy shoes and stilt sandals with faces treated as MS paint canvases and ten-inch mascaras which would give Lady Gaga a complex for no goddamn reason at goddamned four a.m. Maybe she would go there and wish for a drug bust if only for the pleasure to see the fucks with towels on their faces. What she dreaded was the despo creepos who managed to enter these parties which always like some Darwinian process of evolution, evolved into raves. Nisha stood looking at herself in the mirror. The yoga and pilates were really working. She was happy with her short streaked hair, a new look inspired by some socialite she saw at the fashion week. Lots of Indian jewellery and turquoise too. She selected a white shimmery short dress to show off her shapely legs...and whistled at herself approvingly.

Nisha Poddar stared at the glittering velvet and gold card for a long time, humming Queen's *Tonight I'm gonna have myself a real good time—a reeeall good timmme*—to herself.

She just hoped Nargis Khaled would keep the second part of her promise too.

29

'I have carefully studied the report you have prepared regarding the said notes. I have scrutinized the significant features of the signatures and writings on the photograph. By the enlargements and by lucid reasoning I have no doubt that the probability of the two being from the same hand are exceptionally high. Please keep in mind that while comparing two handwriting specimens, the correct rule is that the paper and colour of ink should be the same for both the specimens as far as possible. But seeing this is not the case here, as is hardly ever, I can only talk in probabilities—' Kabir carefully read the meticulously highlighted letter sent to him by Virat Bhave, a highly skilled forensic expert, a recognized examiner of dubious documents with more than forty-seven years standing devoted to examination of questioned documents relating to courts, banks, government undertakings, private cases and court matters with regard to detection of forgery.

'I am also attaching a note by a graphologist, which I thought was necessary in this case. I am sure you are aware that graphology is the analysis of handwriting in relation to human psychology. In the medical field, it can be used to refer to the study of handwriting as an aid in diagnosis and tracking of diseases of the brain and nervous system or even indicate the presence of opiates in the system. The written strokes reflect changes in the central nervous system such as ones undergone during Parkinson's disease or extreme alcohol usage. What I am trying to say is that emotion, mental state and biomechanical factors such as muscle stiffness and elasticity are reflected in a person's handwriting. The report of the graphologist and mine, both done independently, seem to suggest that the author of the two notes is one and the same and is suffering from extreme emotional swings which could be due to alcoholic abuse or substance abuse or circumstances—'

'You have read this twice already. What's the point?' Shinde interrupted.

'Point is that we have been BLOODY idiots.' Kabir said. He picked up photograph with it's eyes gouged out and read out loudly: '*To the biggest bitch in the world Uncle KD is watching*— Basically what Virat Bhave is saying is that unless Johnny D'Souza and KD somehow possess identical motherfucking fingers and identical motherfucking nervous systems—they are the same motherfucking person.'

'You have said this twice already since yesterday—' Catching the ACP's scowl Shinde stopped abruptly.

'He must have given a fake passport copy of an authorized person, along with a resolution authorizing the opening of the account, a fake proof of residential address some easily forged legal junk! Singapore and Malaysia are essentially what Switzerland was to money laundering in the 1960s. It's all too easy for someone who knows how,' Kabir said.

'I have sent KD—I mean—Johnny D'Souza's bank a query on the other assets he may be holding—they are feeding me customer confidentiality and bad for bizness shit—' Shinde said.

Kabir looked again at the hateful words carved on Suhana's photograph years ago by a man now dead. The deep fury and anger which KD must have felt on being humiliated and thrown out of the house on Suhana's instance. And the extreme fear he must have felt when Silky discovered about Johnny D'Souza. Because the fact was Johnny D'Souza never existed. Kabir could not believe he had fallen for the oldest con in the game authored by a small-time hustler. An address in Singapore, a fake name and a scanned photo of an untraceable man, and a fake signature was effectively all it had taken for KD to open a corporate bank account to route his ill-gotten gains. It was embarrassingly clear to ACP Kabir Bhonsle why Johnny D'Souza could not be traced. Johnny and KD were one and the same person.

'At least one thing is for sure. Jerome Mangwani knew nothing. A man like him would have broken down—so KD uses Jerome at the behest of someone to make this video.'

'Basically it seems it all started with Monalisa's rape made to look like a sex video. Monalisa's letter implicates KD in her rape—So KD gets Monalisa's sex-tape made with Jerome but why? What did he have to gain if Dannie-Monalisa broke off? And if not him...who gains from their breakup? That's #1,' Kabir finally said.

'The two men on the tape who are they? Porn actors or are they involved in this? That's #2,' Shinde added.

'Obviously KD knew about this sex-tape and knew who is behind it and the slimeball smelled easy money, creates a fake id of the phony Johnny D'Souza so no one suspects what he is upto. That explains a lot of unexplained money coming in at regular intervals in the fake account after Dannie's disappearance. Too many coincidences—all point to one big blackmailing racket which exploded in his face. Brings us back to who was KD getting the tape made for? And did the people he was working for find out about his backstabbing? Obviously KD took the risk but was at the same time scared enough to go to huge lengths to hide his identity. That's #3,' Kabir said grimly.

'I think the lure of hot cash proved too much—and he thought he would get away with it. And did too for so long—succeeded once, got into the habit—but finally bit more than he could chew. Blackmailed the wrong people.'

'Going by bank details, KD opened this fake Johnny D'Souza account seven years ago. Must have been pretty good at fooling everyone—so this goes on, Johnny keeps making money. Come to think of it, phony id is exactly up his alley. He had been in for something like this before. I think he just got lucky or unlucky depends how you look at it.'

'Till Silky got inquisitive about Johnny D'Souza. He must have shat in his pants—! After all he did to keep his identity a secret.'

'And all the time Silky thought KD was scared of Johnny!'

'What that man was mortally scared of was loose-mouth Silky blurting out the name somewhere and then—he must have planned to dispose of Silky before he left for Dubai.'

'But someone got to the truth—'

'The truth that there was no Johnny fucking D'Souza. And that KD was a blackmailing prick. But Sir—KD had closed his fictitious Johnny D'Souza account a week—'

'A week before he was killed—'

'Perhaps—KD was scared that his cover had been blown??'

'And—he realized that 'someone' had got to know that he and Johnny were one and the same. And maybe that 'someone' could be angry enough with him to cause him harm. Major harm.'

'That's motive.'

'That explains why he wanted to run to the Middle East ingratiating himself with Salem Hassan. KD paid the price of his unending greed and Sunny got caught in the crossfire? The lipstick on KD's face, the powder, the panties in his mouth, I think all that was just to mislead investigation. Point to the drugged item girl who had a history with KD.'

There were too many ifs for Kabir's liking and he was unhappily aware that their conjecturing would not get him closer to the truth unless he got some real evidence, something which would stand in court. But Kabir could no longer ignore the truth staring at his face. Who benefitted most by breaking Dannie's scandalous liaison with Monalisa? It was someone who had quite a lot to lose. Someone who was powerful with a vast amount of clout. Someone who had a lot at stake. Maybe someone who did not want the truth to affect the fortunes of Dannie's films at any cost and had moved in to control the damage. By the looks of it, the real beneficiary of the breakup appeared to be DS Studios with crores at stake on Dannie, their new-age-gen-next heroine launched with so much fanfare. The truth about their 'gen-next' heroine's sexual orientation would have been much egg on the face, unacceptable for the old fashioned studio.

'Sir, the articles you had asked for—' Kabir studied the yellowed film magazines. Eight-year-old editions of *Star Truth* had been difficult to find. The stories were there for all to see. The stories which had created such a scandal years ago. Kabir went through the tabloid scoops on Dannie and Prince's notorious night together and wondered how far would a studio bend to protect their prized asset? An elaborate hoax, a complicated cover-up machinery set into motion by a mammoth PR machinery was not so unimaginable. So, did the studios deliberately plant false stories to protect their asset, the heroine of their three big budget films? And worse, did they have a hand in something deeper and more sinister? Kabir was dismayed. Proving anything against a powerful studio based only on conjecture and speculation was foolhardy. But the point was DS Studios could have cut their losses and simply not announced their new projects with Dannie. It was too big a chance to take if the truth about Dannie got out. The public could be very unforgiving and that was a risk which no studio would take. Why did the studio announce new films with Dannie when they knew that she was risky asset? Unless the studio did not know.

It was just not adding up. Kabir's head was spinning when he saw the eight missed calls from Suhana. He stared at the caller name and took a long drag of his extra bitter cigarette. Obviously it was something important. Why was he wasting so much time thinking of what to say! With growing dismay, Kabir realized he would have to take a moment to steady his voice. It won't do to sound like an excited schoolboy. What the fuck was happening to him.

'This is ACP Kabir...is that Suhana? Sorry I was busy in this new development—I—'

'Hello whoever!! You have reached my voice-mailbox. Okay so I am out and you know what to do right after this beep—' and then a beep—Kabir had cut the call abruptly. He did not like talking to machines. Why had she called him, there were eight calls from 11 p.m. to 2 a.m. Why the hell was she not picking up the phone—

Kabir's phone buzzed. It was her.

'Ya hi–'

'Hi–'

'You called–' They spoke at the same time.

'I had a call from...from Nargis,'Suhana said.

'Nargis Khaled?'

'She insists she has something to tell me. Us.'

'Last time she talked about her little black book on Bollywood stars' secrets and next morning she feigned ignorance claiming that drinks had made her memory foggy. I don't have time to listen to her lurid tales of how much dick she has sucked in Bollywood–sorry–'

'She said it's something to do with what Prince did–she says she will expose him–'

'I think our Nargis Khaled is feeling the chill of being left out of the limelight. Now she wants to be famous too–'

'She said she needs to tell us something about Sunny and Prince. She is on her way to meet you. She says she has some plan. But it will cost.' Kabir was not sure about Nargis. Last time, Nargis had created a sensation by declaring to all and sundry that she was in the possession of a book which would unleash a tsunami in Bollywood. Nothing came off the threat, not even an apology for making false claims. Nargis then claimed on Twitter that she had a cache of pornographic photographs showing Bollywood's leading stars indulging in sexual acts and also dope on Kalidas. But she retracted her statement within 24 hours saying the police had confused her with their extended grilling and tough tactics.

'Hi I am here.' The intercom rang. It was Nargis.

'Here?? Where?!!'

'Outside your office. Can I come in?'

'Wait for me at the café.'

◆

The fifty-feet by 20-feet rectangular hall with unpretentious metallic chairs, drowsy rubber plants, bare windows and a small colour TV served as the basics at the newly done up café at the station. Looking totally out of place on the red metal chair sat the gorgeous Nargis Khaled, dressed in simple jeans and tee, almost impossible to recognize without her hooker makeup.

'Can I have a cigarette?' she said the moment he entered the room.

'Ya sure.' He liked the way she smoked a cigarette, flicking away her cigarette leaving a trail of sparks and ash on the floor. She had a way of showing off her long legs. Men sized her up and she looked pleased at all the male attention she was getting. 'You look all shaken up. Is this your rainy day?'

Nargis Khaled lit up another cigarette and took a long drag to calm her shaking hands. She stared at the lights blinking on the counter as if trying to make up her mind.

'Where's my cash?'

'Safe. But we need to know what are you selling?'

Nargis gave him a long hard look. She sucked at the cigarette for a long time blowing smoke rings, 'You know we need to expose what happened at Sulaiman's farmhouse party—'

'—aaand how do you propose we do that?' Kabir sighed.

'We go to his party and expose it. He is giving one tonight to celebrate the premier of his film '*Indiawala Hero*,' Nargis said greedily, eyeing the mutton steak and beer placed before the police officer by the café boy.

'Go on. You must try this—it's worth the fat—'

'Ooo I don't—'

'C'mon....or would you like iced lemon tea...?

'Yeah that too. Gosh I am starving,' Nargis did not need to be prompted again and was already tearing into the juicy steak with her fingers.

'You were talking about the party.'

'Yess we go there.'

'Yes, and of course he is sending us a gilt-edged invitation! C'mon what is this Nargis—you came here with this cockamamie idea?'

'Yes. I mean yes he has invited us.'

'He has?'

'I mean he does not know it. Yet.' She chuckled and winked. 'I have managed already.' Nargis dipped her hands in the finger bowl several times to carefully wipe out the last trace of grease from her meticulously manicured nails. Reaching into her handbag, Nargis retrieved two beautiful black and gold invites with a flourish. 'For you and Suhana—'

'How do we know they are not fake? How did you get them?'

'Honestly there is nothing big boobs and bleached hair and unending legs cannot achieve! Let's just say the event manager's son was very appreciative of services rendered.'

'So how does going to a party help?

'I have sent one on behalf of Prince to Nisha Poddaar too!' She said with a crafty smile. 'Yes THE Nisha of *Bollywood Truths*—of course she knows it's a fake—all I can say is that Prince's reputation will be worth less than the shit that goes inside his nostrils every day.' Finally in the glory of limelight, Nargis Khaled stroked the gilted invitation card like a winning ticket. Their conversation was interrupted by a hyper Shinde.

'Sir you need to come and see this. Now!! Please!'

'Don't worry about me Officer. Carry on. I will stay and finish my lunch. Don't exactly have a jealous husband waiting for me!' Nargis said, noisily slurping a lime ice shorbet.

◆

'*Maadachod* this better be good.'

'Wait till you see Sir. Good is not even close. It's a mental blowjob! The bank where Johnny D'Souza had an account seemed he had a locker too. The bank found a DVD. Seems they came around after they saw the contents of the DVD. Said they thought it was their duty to hand over this article. It's being couriered but they sent me a link to the video.'

Shinde placed the laptop on the table jerkily and pounded the play button. There was nothing startling in what he saw. Two men spread out on the bed fucking a girl, their naked arses on display. One bleached and tight and the other hairy.

'You motherfucker. You got me out to watch these two fuckers fuck? I have seen this shit before what the–'

'Sir, sit back and I will show you the difference–now THIS is the video link which Johnny D'Souza's Singapore bank sent.'

Shinde pressed a switch and another movie showed on the screen.

This one had no title, no actors, no credits, just grainy jumpy action. The setting was the same vanity van. There were no shifts of context either. The stationary camera had full-view long shots and occasional close-ups that seemed less concerned with eroticism and more with identification of all the actors involved in the film and the identity of the person making their film. There was no mistaking the profile shot of Jerome Mangwani holding a camera. The men too were acting differently. There was no mugging for the camera like they didn't know there was this camera. A hidden camera. This camera concentrated more on the faces of the two men assaulting the girl. A jolt of electricity shot up his spine. Kabir suddenly sat bolt upright. He rushed to replay the player and stared closely at the men who were fucking Monalisa.

It was there for a single frame, a fraction of a second—the side view of an unmistakable profile. Grainy but without doubt, Kabir stared at the picture in his hand. The proof of the involvement of the biggest name in Bollywood in subverting the truth. There was no mistake. The slim-faced boy with a stunning profile and a probing nose, the boy who raped Dannie's girlfriend eight years back, was Prince Capure, the demigod at the box office and the blue-eyed boy of DS Studios. Then an upcoming actor. And the other man in the picture grinning vacuously alongside him was Munjal. A much younger and better looking Munjal.

'Well well!! So our KD *nee* Johnny D'Souza was being a very very bad boy. He gets Jerome to shoot a video and then records him shooting the tape along with these two characters—!'

The complete silence in the room was broken suddenly. 'Hello boys! Please tell the ACP...Ohh there you are...I am leaving. I have a video to shoot!' All heads turned to gape at the gorgeous item girl looking incongruous in the plain room full of men in uniform. 'And the cards are not fake. See you there!'

Before Kabir could say anything, Nargis Khaled bounded out of the door without noticing Prince Sulaiman Capure and Munjal's naked arses on display on the computer screen.

30

You are invited.

The ornate invite mocked her. Sitting in the car she stared incredulously at the black velvet and gold card.

If you got this card you are special to Prince.

Getting ready for the party was not as easy as she had expected. She changed her outfit five times, finally settling for a blue silk asymmetrical dress that flattered her tiny waist outlining the sexy curve of her hips. Her jet black hair was parted sideways and fell silkily, curling inwards over her slim shoulders, outlining her lily white skin and her cool olive eyes—light green flecks when she was calm and dark olive when angry. Sitting next to ACP Kabir Bhonsle in the car she felt strange. A month back she would have laughed it off if someone would have suggested a date with a cop. But lots had changed since then. Besides, the man sitting next to her did not feel like a cop. He was not judgemental for one. He looked like a grad student today, all buttoned up in a new shirt and new shirt and she was sure he had put some gel in his hair. Not a strand out of place. Kabir caught her staring and flushed. He ruffled his hair with a strong hand and Suhana smiled and looked away.

They entered the kilometre-long lit entrance of Prince Sulaiman Capure's farmhouse, the swankiest of the eight he had. A line of cars snaked their way up to the star-shaped driveway where huge billboards of the superstar's latest films *Indiawala Hero* and *Metal man* towered over all. Flimsily clad female and male valets and escorts waited to lavish personal care on the occupants of the Porches, Ferraris, Volkswagens, Bentleys, Limos, Rolls Royces, Mercedes, Excaliburs and some SUVs.

'This place is fucking freaky,' Suhana felt goosebumps on her arms.

No backing out now.

'Shit I hope Nargis will be there,' Suhana said anxiously.

'Do you really think Nargis Khaled is going to miss the one show she is going to star in!' Kabir smiled.

'You know I don't know what to make of you,' Suhana said, adding, 'Tell me what would you do if you were not doing this job?'

'I would be home watching game shows.' he said, handing over the keys of his car to the valet. Suhana and Kabir managed to enter without creating any excitement even in the small cluster of paid photographers. Girls covered with gold paint, sporting outlandish humongous feathery headgears and little else, carefully scrutinized each invite card, a final check before letting guests into Prince Suleiman Capure's rambling den. Each guest was given their own headgear.

'Good, now I also have horns!' Suhana said wearing hers.

It was called the DEN because of its monstrous design. Like a demon's lair exuding vulgar carnal extravagance from every inch. Mysterious pungent ingredients hovered in the air, mixing with cigarette smoke and brutish vapours of the most potent kind to create an exotic atmosphere. Rich aromatic ethers, familiar and alien, blended with the compelling heady fragrances of beautiful people, creating an intoxicating outlandish atmosphere. It shouted absolute glamour and absolute power as if programmed to persuade impulsive and reckless fantasies and actions.

You put snowballs up your nose
And fingers down your throat
That's why your skin glows
And you weigh less than your coat—

Thirty rooms, five swimming pools, a shooting range, a mini zoo which housed exotic species and several banned ones too. The visitors entered from limestone steps and climbed to the immense landing guarded by statuary snarling lions. The entry hall was big enough to skate in, could accommodate a hockey field, said someone. Three storeys of white marble and a souble-carved white marbled staircase like in old Hindi films. A monster-sized chandelier glared indignantly from the gold leaf coffered ceiling, reflected from the black marble floor polished to glass. Guests chatted and gossiped in the backdrop of gilt framed portraits of Prince Sulaiman Capure in his different films hanging between columns of ruby red velvet drapes restrained with thick gold chords.

'Hellooo bitch. What a degenerate pervert sicko place. I am shitting tripping loveeing it!' Two women she did not recognize accosted her.

'Who are they?' Kabir whispered.

'Everyone's your best friend when you're flying high...' Suhana drawled intimately.

'I met the *hijra bawas* last night. Danced the *kaif kaif* with my camera around my neck, went into a trance at chaar a.m. in the morning dude!'

'Shhhhhhhhhh let her go. Don't look now but OMG her pussy is showing what a cunt-shop!!! What is she wearing...! You know what she did at the Singapore film awards...she turned up in a completely see-through "dress" with just some loose netting on the front and a few pieces of thread round the back....she was so drunk that when called on stage to hand over an award, she got confused and thought she'd been given an award. She then gave a rambling speech thanking everyone for giving her the non-existent award, and much to everyone's embarrassment ended up singing!'

'Yaa so whttts the fk synff miffreshhj, brrphhhtt,' she spoke with the cigarette dangling from her mouth, 'I mean did you expect to meet Virgin Marys here? I mean she has been the mistress of his friend who is also an award-winning director from down south. She was with him for a year. And then they exchanged their mistresses. But her director boyfriend got the other girl pregnant and she made tapes and he had to marry her! And this one is stuck with the other one except now she has become the concubine to her own lover. And they are still making their little "award-winning" movies mind you!' Young girls dressed in little more than nothing bantered casually on Bolly twitter trends of the week.

'...the much-married star who had two-way mirrors installed in his guest rooms to see them fuck.'

'...the hero who could not get it up unless he saw two women together.'

'...the super-stud who had just married his banker fiancée after dumping his gf of eight years. Love sure. He is on the prowl already. His van a frigging harem.'

Just general gossip of the general tinsel-town folk. Suhana and Kabir moved across the party without being challenged or recognized kept their eyes and ears peeled for Nargis.

'After giving crabs to half the men in Bollywood, madame has joined some ashram...she is Mother Prem Asha now! Creepy woman got new breasts after joining the ashram!'

'You did not hear this from me, but she got her lowest set of ribs removed to look like a stick...hey do I know you? You look so familiar!'the model stared at her curiously.

'Yelo!! Sweetiesss! Naughteee naughteee girls! Discussing the changes in Maa Prem Asha's anatomy in this parteecular social setup hmmmm? Yaanowatt it would be the most hardcore thing anyone's done with their body since that dude hung a bowling ball off his dong last time.'

'Shoving cocaine up your ass is extra-strength crazy—that bitch there is so much into new age methods to remain young...pops semen packs on her face and you know last time she passed out at an after-party and had to get her stomach pumped after ingesting a gallon of semen!!'

'Yucckk jeez! A gallon of semen? How desperate. Does it work?'

Suhana noticed Kabir was no longer with her and sighed. It was just too easy to get lost in a place like this. She would have to summon searchlights here, god why did she let go of his arm. She craned her neck over the pulsating crowds and reached her phone. Just then she spotted Nargis going into the LAIR but hesitated calling out to her .A separate entrance into the cordoned off area of the farmhouse. Guarded by Prince's five dogs. Aurangzeb, George Bush, Razia Sultan, Lukhkha and Ponty. The dogs looked too gorged to care and she easily walked into the dusky club smelling of coffee and cognac and stuff she could not recognize. The DJ played out his illegal intentions from his console.

I'm gonna burn down this hotel

I'm gonna fill the pool with drugs
I'm gonna bring a gun through customs
I will snort and I will heroin OD—

As she entered, the intermingled but not unpleasant smells of smoke and sweat and too many people instantly assaulted her nostrils as she inhaled deeply. Ahhh, the smell of hundred percent nicotine, she thought guiltily as she pushed her body through the pulsating crowd. Finally finding her way to an empty barstool in the corner, she caught Kabir's eye, shook her head and smiled downward. She motioned to the bartender.

'Gin...and tonic,' she mouthed, and he nodded and melted away into the cries of a hundred other thirsty patrons. By now her eyes were adjusting to the imminent darkness. Bright spots of neon beer signs on the wall stood out, illuminating the faces and cleavage and six packs.

'Man look at this party go! A'int it summing!' Two awestruck models discussed the party.

'Prince funds this shit? It's huge!'

'Prince's money! Of course not. It's his financiers who do it. People who want a no-holds barred party and no questions asked—the special guests from Dubai, the connoisseurs for whom there were the huts populated by Filipino boys and Ukrainian girls—the LAIR!'

She had heard about the LAIR. The infamous den that came alive with blue and red lights only at night, and this was such a night. It was here that the 'special friends' slouched in the silky confines of water beds waiting for their bid-and-fuck binges to the background of orchestras, the pussy pound, dozens of zoned-out naked girls slushed around in waist-deep water, serving caviar laced with LSD and booze and uppers.

'Wonky to wild to way out demented. I love it.'

'You can make me out to be some drug-raging beat-your-ass-in-the-Waffle-House fucking rockstar. I'm all that. Do I know you honey?'

Suhana turned back. Prince Sulaiman Capure stood right next to her looking deep into her eyes. Suhana froze.

'I am just a fan,' she said. 'Can I get your autograph please!'

'Sure honey—You know this fan once asked me how do I manage to be all what I am and I said because I am a frigging fucking superstar!' Prince Sulaiman Capure flashed his famous dimpled grin.

'Sure. A fucking superstar. That's what you are,' said Suhana.

And he was gone. Just as suddenly as he had come. Even before her gin and tonic slid in front of her the star had disappeared. She saw him dancing off into the throng, smiling and touching a dozen other men and women intimately. She could not believe it! The superstar had simply not recognized her. Suhana didn't know whether to be happy or annoyed but as she crumpled the autographed note she realized she just had had a fantastic piece of good luck. She took her first sip of the simple mixture, cold and icy, slightly sweet and tangy against her lips. She held the drink in her mouth for just a moment and let the ice and gin and lime pulp wallow against her tongue... Abruptly she felt a pair of hands on her waist, and jumped at the sensation. Turning quickly her eyes locked with Kabir's intense gaze telling her to shut up.

'Shhh we are being watched. We are the only ones not snorting or snuggling—' he said as he lifted her off the barstool in his strong arms. His hands fell from her hips, and her skin bristled at the touch. Goosebumps erupted on her arms, despite the heat. Out of the corner of her eye, she saw Nisha Poddar watching her with interest. Suhana blushed but held her stare for a good minute.

'Ffffck! I think it's roll time.'

◆

Sitting in the darkest corner of the LAIR, Prince called out his bulldogs Ponty and George Bush when his visitor were announced. Ponty raced George Bush excitedly and there was a sound of a tussle.

'Get off, Ponty...George Bush, get off me!!' A rough voice commanded the eager dog who had attached itself to his boot. Prince smirked. The sight of Ponty and George Bush mounting Munjal's leather shoes and pumping away always brought a smile to his lips.

'Down boys. DOWN. Can't help it, Munjal. The boys think it's a bitch.' Why Ponty had taken a liking for Munjal's shoes stumped him. Watching Ponty and George Bush in action, Prince's pet bitch Razia Sultan bounded towards Chotta Munjal slobbering him with wet kisses.

'Where is he?' Munjal asked looking around as if expecting someone else.

'Get off Razia. Get her off. I will kick her,' Chotta Munjal yelled hotly his eyes bulging out.

'Dhanna Seth is on his way. And be careful Chotta. She is a classy bitch. Very good pedigree—a lady! Request Razia.' Prince's eyes glittered dangerously. 'Maybe it's time you check who was skinned to make that leather shoe of yours!' A frenetic Razia rode the boot for a few minutes and then with a loud appreciative howl dismounted and waddled off to a corner, looking at the boots longingly.

'At least she finished soon. *Arrey* Munjal, tell your brother to have a sense of humour–' Dhanna Seth walked in laughing hysterically at the sight of Razia shagging Chotta's shoe. Chotta kicked the bitch and stomped off in anger, roughly pushing his way through the crowd. Munjal did not call out to his younger brother. He stared at the miniscule crystals of the pristine white powder in front of him, wrapped in white paper kept thoughtfully on the marble table. He refused. Today his mind had to be clear.

'Seth there is tension. Our artists are complaining about the overheads distribution, equipment hire–even advertising publicity and phone calls were being deducted from the cost of the film before they received their shares.' Munjal had no time to waste.

'It's not cheating in the criminal sense. Show me their contracts as to where it is mentioned they will get their profits before or after these deductions. Munjal we have made iron-clad contracts. Their bleating will not get them anywhere–relax, take a snort–and get me a girl.' Dhanna Seth smiled genially.

Munjal wondered about the studio head's newfound confidence. He remembered the time when his men had started hustling local cinemas with such great success that Dream Star Studios had come flocking to him. The meeting resulted in nothing less than a cannibalistic incestuous deal. The studios had agreed to pay Bawlas a percentage, and in return he had agreed to trample on the wage and other claims and grievances by the members against the studios. At the same time he upped the membership fees. Dhanna Seth with a couple of powerful studios concocted a formidable body to mediate personal, professional and labour disputes with the

Bawlas while quietly, they snuck in two top lawyers with a thick bunch on types of contracts.

'I am tired of being robbed,' Munjal said quietly.

'What happened to them?' Dhanna Seth asked Prince spying the superstar's fat mongrels Aurangzeb and Lukhkha slumped out in a corner.

'*Bigad gaye hain.* They are spoilt. Too drugged to move,' Prince replied.

'Send them to rehab!' Dhanna Seth said.

'This is their state after rehab. Now they want only medicines,' Prince said.

'Bloody dogs! You know Munjal, the problem is not the producers. It's your own men —your brother who is handling KDs shit now—Chotta Bawla is out of control. Too hot headed !' Dhanna Seth said. 'He is already heckling producers, demands token quota for junior artists, beats up directors if some extra he fancies is left outside the frame.'

Munjal knew Chotta was no KD, but after the latter's death, Chotta seemed to have come into his own. His modus operandi was simple. Every morning Chotta would scout locations from his van with his men. When he found a production that did not employ junior artists, he worked the phones with threats to mob the set. Most producers complied or just paid up, to get rid of him.

'I cannot remove him. This will make me look bad with the men,' Munjal shot back.

'Not as bad as your own men made you look Munjal. Look at Chotta!! The word is your boy is mad—*tyachya majhi satakli*! And your motherfucker KD—the police are all over. Bad for business. Bad for our image. It's always the trusted ones who bite us in the arse—and we end up looking like *chootiyas* and *chors.* The police needs an excuse to sniff around us—maybe you should just move out for some time...! I am getting a drink.' Dhanna Seth said walking off. Munjal's burning coal black eyes blazed with fury and he exploded in anger.

Bhenchod rattle snake KD had done more than just bite him in the arse, Munjal thought in his head, recalling the first time he had met KD. He had handpicked KD personally because of his immense ability to cause mischief. He had smelled Kalidas's dubious talents from a mile off. KD fit into the profile of an all-round hustler and Munjal had been on the lookout for people who could keep the revenue flowing from studios. KD had been recruited on the spot. And talented he was, whether it was organizing disruptive flash mobs within minutes to milking studios or stopping shoots. With his high-handed ways KD rubbed many producers and studios the wrong way, but for Munjal it was not entirely a bad thing. He needed men like him to keep the studios buckled up. Initially Munjal Bawla did not take the complaints against KD seriously, after all he was one of his best bawlas. KD, with his Kashyap *khandaan* connection, found it easier to jump into the cracks between the studio and the labour, and bleed both sides, by playing up the unions on one hand, and striking under-the-table deals with the studio executives on the other. But then things started getting out of hand. His scouts gave him lists of hundreds of shoots which had been stalled by KD without informing Munjal, there was no record of revenue collected from these jobs. Or like when KD got a small fortune by not calling a projectionist strike but sent only half the proceeds to the Bawlas, routing the other half to his own company. Munjal was stunned to know that KD had, right under his nose, taken over well-appointed garages of a local goon and had secretly started brokering vehicles to the film studios, by routing them through his private company.

And then when Silky Mehta came to meet him, Munjal Bawla was rendered speechless. The truth exploded in his face with one word.

Johnny D'Souza.

'Maybe Dhanna Seth is right. Go to Dubai or something,' Prince suggested... 'Till this blows over.'

Munjal did not answer. But his strained face said it all. Prince and Munjal stared at each other but Munjal kept his thoughts to himself. He was a troubled man. The case should have been closed by now. They had everything. The witnesses. The murder weapon. The girl. She claimed she had blacked out, had attacked him and not killed him. But Munjal didn't expect anyone to believe her; after all she had a motive and the evidence was stacked against her. Everyone knew she hated KD and wanted to kick him out of her life.

But the police, that Bhonsle, his men had informed him, seemed to be taking a personal interest in the case. That was dangerous. It always got dangerous when it got personal. The ACP did not seem to be in a hurry to wrap the case and get his medals, and was fussing too much over the details. The police had already spoken to Silky and had visited the item girls. So long as that Poddar kept talking about Prince Capure and Mangwani, it was fine. But just in case the police came sniffing around him and the Bawlas he would be ready to make his move.

Maybe going out for some time would not be a bad idea, Munjal thought.

'Why can't you use your pull with Poddar? She is hinting at KD's connection with me. It's bad for my business. Give the bitch an offer she can't refuse—' Munjal told Dhanna Seth when he came back carrying a drink and holding a doped out model on the other arm.

'It's different this time. You really just need to go somewhere for some time,' Dhanna Seth said, kissing the model who looked ready to sleep on his lap.

'After all I did for you?' Munjal said

'And you were paid very well for it. Every time. You got your cut.' Dhanna Seth said

'If it was not for me your hero would have been laughed out of town. *Hijron ki film banatey—saale chakke aatey dekhne—*' Munjal said.

'Watch it Munjal—Dannie is done with. She decided what she wanted to do with her life. And don't act as if you don't know how much that cost us?' Dhanna Seth said.

'It would have cost you much more *agar woh apni dulhan ghar laati sasur jee*—prince of romance and virgin mary. Bollywood *ka* immaculate conception…ha ha!' Prince said and roared with laughter.

It all seemed so long ago. Prince Sulaiman Capure knew shattered reputations would have taken a lifetime to build, but Dannie had not cared. She was not even ashamed when he had threatened her with making the footage public. He was shell-shocked when she calmly stated her intentions to be with her lover. Bitch dyke. He knew he would be laughed out of town. Who would take him seriously ever if it got out—he would as well kiss his Bollywood's romance king dream goodbye—they would call him the Prince of Queens. She would have destroyed him. She had to be stopped. Convincing her that her girlfriend was two-timing was easy. And quite pleasurable. And all was fine till,in a terrifying development, they received a mail from a Johnny D'Souza. It was a simple e-mail.

I have photos.

Prince had ignored it. And then another SMS had come.

I have a DVD.

Thinking him to be a fan, they tried all tricks to engage him, Prince had magnanimously replied:

Okay you have my attention Mr. Johnny...what can I do for you? I will do anything for my fans!

First, I am not a fan. And second, I said I have photos and DVDs. Stuff which you won't want anyone to see. Especially not your fans. And especially not the police.

You fuck! My secretary is tracing this IP code right now—

DVD of you and Monalisa. Sending attachment.

It was not possible. How was it possible?

He had started asking for money to keep his mouth shut. It began with small amounts, but soon the demands shot through the roof. Johnny D'Souza managed to squeeze the pips out of him for the longest time till he was hysterical with fear. Munjal Bawla had come to his aid, with no mean help from Silky Mehta.

'You know, Munjal, I am not going to go to war over you. But at this time if I am pressed to deliver answers, I will,' Dhanna Seth said.

'Just like that?'

'It's business.'

'Don't worry I will take care of everything.' Munjal didn't sound so sure.

'Not this time. I think Dubai is a better idea. Dubai *mein* Palm *jumeira ghoom ke ayengey! Go to Salem's house*', the ribald party was interrupted by a corncake voice belonging to Nargis who had descended on the group. Dressed in a sheer dress and hair dyed burgundy, she came with a pair of lap dogs.

'Yooooo fucker. You raped me for years! Yoooo promised me the part you gave to Daisy! You motherfucking two-faced dickhead! Nargis Khaled screamed.

'Who let you in? Who the fuck let her in?' he said in complete disbelief. 'Hello lover!' Nisha Poddar suddenly walked in. Prince Sulaiman stared incredulously at Nargis and then Nisha and back again.

'—who let these cunts in?' the actor screamed in annoyance.

'You invited me. And I am here,' Nisha said shoving the card in his face.

'I never sent you any frigging card—you bloody lying bitches—' Prince pushed the girls roughly.

'Hey chill, Mr. Jock. I am sure your fans would like to know what actually happens at their superstar's fancy parties...' Nisha said craftily.

'You meddling whore! WHY do you stick your nose where it does not belong? Bitch you don't know what's going on here! You menopausal old bag!' Prince screamed at Nisha.

'Yeah. That's fine with me Prince because I am having real fun finding out. You can read about it in the papers, dearie!' she threatened.

'I will kill you, motherfucking cunt-shop. This is a private affair and you are intruding. If you think you can just walk out of here and type shit about me I am warning you—'

'You don't scare me. I have taken you out before, haven't I? *Gunnd ka* Prince! Forty, fat, and finished,' Nisha smiled goading him to cross the line. The superstar exploded in anger.

'*Teri aukaat kya hai saali, do kaudee ki* journalist writing shitty stories about me! I promised myself I will slap you when I see you next—but I will do better—.' He hissed nastily and promptly planted a kick on Nisha's rump. He missed and tumbled over Prremm Pandeet's bulky bag.

'Hey—sorry Shah—*arrey* you are not Shahrukh—HEYYYY—WHO the fuck are you?' prince looked at Prremm Pandeet with incredulous eyes.

'Sir myself your biggest fan Prremm Pandeet. Myself from Kanpur!'

'Enough!' Nargis grabbed a plate full of chilly prawn sizzlers and dumped it on Prince's head leaving his face beetroot red.

'Just wait bitch! When I get hold of both of you I will tear out every hair off your moustaches!!!!!' The actor pounced at Nargis who jumped aside. The struggle left one of her breasts hanging out with very little to cover her modesty and Prince lunged to grab it. An amused Prremm Pandeet gleefully recorded the entire tamasha on his secret camera stuffed in his bulky bag.

'Throw these bitches OUT!' Prince hollered as he began walking away. Nargis exchanged a look with Nisha. She had other plans. She still did not have the explosive shots she needed.

Nargis purposefully followed Prince into the men's room and pushed and abused him. A furious Prince rushed out and gripped Nargis around the neck with one hand and tightly pulled her hair with the other. Prince, by now mad with rage, pulled Nargis's hair. Her head jerked back sharply and she lost her balance and fell down heavily on her arse. Prince did not let go of her hair and she was by now screaming loudly in pain.

'What's going on?' Someone asked.

'He is hitting a woman. An atrocity. Physically manhandling a poor actress,' announced Nisha.

'It's all on tape,' Prremm Pandeet said indicating his camera.

Prince's bodyguards, two beefy monsters summoned by a panicky Chamanji took over and pushed Nargis away from Prince. The sizzling item girl delivered a vicious right hook on the star's left cheek. Prince let out a roar of pain and stumbled and fell down clumsily on all fours.

'Oh god. My nose is broken. You whore, you brrroke my nose!!' The star screamed in anger and lunged at Nargis, who now stood straddled between two beefy bouncers.The star and the item girl were embroiled in a vicious fist fight even as the bouncers struggled to keep them apart.

'We are just meat for you?? Pieces of meat?? YOU FUCK. I will expose you.' Nargis knew her moment had come. This was even better than she had dreamed. She was getting back at him. *She*, an item girl, was getting her revenge from Prince Capure, the Bollywood star. She was finally becoming famous. Nargis knew that with every second she prolonged the fight she upped her chances of infamy. She was already imagining the reality show offers, maybe a vamp role or why not her own show? Nargis was loving every bit of it and lopped one more punch at the star.

'Bitch, you need help,' Prince had had enough.

'This is a fucking circus,' Nisha Poddar exclaimed melodramatically, her eyes glued to the shocking events taking place in front of her, fingers frantically pounding her cellphone.

'Better. Much better than a circus,' hissed Prremm Pandeet.

'Complete madness....mayhem...what a racket! It's so goddamn craziee I love it! I am just waiting for Nargis...she has promised to hand over the footage she has shot—' Nisha yelled deliriously to someone on the phone.

But she had one more important call to make. Nisha took out her tablet to search for ACP Doble's number, the cop who had a penchant for crashing raves with a hockey stick. 'Who needed a man...this is orgasmic...!!' she thought happily, stepping diligently across the glittering red carpet which was by now littered with sullied and torn posters of superstar Prince Sulaiman Capure in *Indiawala Hero.* She rushed out typing furiously on her tablet her latest story. There was nothing that excited Nisha more than a hot story. And this one promised to be a bomb of a story.

But where was Nargis? Last she had seen her talking to a guest whose side profile was startlingly like Shahrukh? Was everything okay?

Nisha was sure of one thing. No one would take this story from her. With or without the footage, she would see to it this story made headlines. Nargis was taking too long and her phone had been switched off. But Nisha Poddar did not care. She would get her shots even if the bitch bailed out.

It was show time!

By the time the police busted in on Prince's party looking for drugs, no sexual activity could be seen, other than the fact that one actress was naked except for a large blanket. Which by party standards, she might as well have been in a burka. The party-goers claimed that 'The men weren't having sex, just nude in bed, which, you know, is totally normal.'

'I am going to sue every fucker. Every motherfucker who hey—hey stop it stop this! I will call the SSP...you policemen cannot harass my guests like this just because I am famous. I am going to sue every cunt.' His self-esteem had taken a beating and his bruised ego was bursting out all over the place.

Suhana turned to Kabir and said, 'Let's get the fuck out of here.'

31

The newspapers gave the raid at Prince Sulaiman Capure's farmhouse front page treatment. Complete with purple prose, witness quotes, people covering their faces photographs, and articles which lauded the police for their 'lightning operation' exposing the most predatory drugs trafficking ring in the industry. The photographs showed police teams smiling and standing besides bundles of white powder and shapely forms in designer outfits covering their faces with *kafaas*, Dolce gabbana scarfs and Armani tees.

'191 invitees detained, 710 gram cocaine worth crores with tonnes of charas and ecstasy tablets seized in the raid. The cops, led by Inspector Doble, have identified the drug peddler as Romeo who has still not been arrested, but his accomplice, the party DJ has been put behind bars. According to the police, Romeo supplied banned narcotics to the high-profile rave party busted at the farmhouse belonging to superstar. The police have stumbled upon a list of city's hotshots who were regulars in the 'drugfests' they organized. As per the police, the duo smuggled drugs from abroad and sold it to youngsters from wealthy families at a high premium.

They organized parties at posh areas like Ballygunge, Alipur and Salt Lake, and supplied banned drugs and booze. The police were tipped-off by a mysterious caller and they unearthed what they say is a mammoth haul of narcotic substances. It's shocking that the drug peddler Romeo has still managed to evade arrest. Insiders claim the peddler, who is supplying banned narcotics to high-profile persons, is influential and if he would have been arrested a lot of skeletons may have tumbled out—

Prince Sulaiman Capure's PR issued a statement saying he was shell-shocked that such going-ons were happening at his party. The superstar's PR stressed that Prince Capure is extending all possible help to the police as he feels that it's most important to rid the industry of the menace of drugs.

But the word was out on the street. The superstar was to be questioned on far graver charges than a drug bust-up. Words like sex-tape were being dropped.

Shit rolls downhill as Prince Sulaiman Capure was about to find out.

32

Kala could not believe what was happening. Her daughter Dannie was being called lesbian. And the police inspector was calling her non-stop. What did he want from her? They were saying the police had Dannie's pictures doing shameless things with a girl!

'They are mad. They are all mad,' she said ferociously. Diva, her bitch, growled in protest, her nap disturbed.

She glowered suspiciously at the tabloid with her pink-rimmed glaucous eyes. The savage slash for a mouth contorted into a mean grimace. Swelling had disfigured her legs and the soft blubbery face was now crisscrossed with lines smothered in fat, her nose shrunk into a stump and muddy browns remained of what were once clear eyes. Time had been cruel to her. Kala's apartment was strewn with liquor bottles and stale food. But she was used to the cloying smell by now. Lately she had started hearing sinister voices, saw cracks in the road when there were none, experienced distorted views of ordinary objects, saw dead foetuses bobbing around in the garden and lizards in the bathtub. She almost attacked a neighbour's child who was playing with fire crackers bizzarely accusing him of planning to set her house on fire and roast her alive.

How dare that police officer try to tell her that she had been betrayed by her own brother? They were all in it. Sunny smiled at her from the magazine. They had featured her on the front cover.

'Look at her, a slut! A murderess...a whore! Just like her mother. Too free...tooo easy! Painted strumpet who flaunted herself. She is always asking for it...little tart. How many men passed through her bed in one night, god knows! The brazen hussy!' In anger she picked up a bronze statue presented to her by KD and threw it at the table. The glass table shattered into a thousand or more fragments. With a start Diva jumped out of her basket and scooted off in terror, giving her mistress a look of utter contempt.

'Go go go! You also go. Dannie-gone-KD-gone-Vishnu-gone-Tabu-gone-Diva-gone-GO.'

Maybe he was hiding. KD was like that. Crafty. Maybe Dannie was hiding. They were all hiding from her. But she would get the answers. The diary was giving her no answers. The police said they had confiscated it from KD's locker. How dare they open his locker? Her brother would be very mad at them when he finds out. Then he will teach them a lesson. Like he had taught that Sunny.

Or was it Tabu? Why were they calling Tabu Sunny... Didn't they know? She was Tabu. Just look at her face. Tabu had fooled everyone pretending to be Sunny. But she had not fooled her! She, Kala, had caught Tabu's lies.

Stupid police. And that stupid diary. They said it had been written by Dannie. Full of horrible lies. Everyone seemed to be lying to her. Even Dannie lied to her. That horrible letter she had written before she disappeared, why did she make her see that?! It was so cruel of her trying to tell her she loved that girl. That girl on the tape. How could she lie like that?

And now, how dare they say that KD would do those dirty filthy things to Dannie? Her Dannie would never write those lies. Would she not have known that her brother was making her do those filthy things with the producers? Would not have her daughter told her anything? It went on and on till Kala felt her head would burst.

Her poor brother, she felt so bad for him. He had seemed so nervous lately that she had called him to check on him only to be told to mind her own business. She had not prodded fearing boycott from his side, she could not risk that. At her age she had no one to take care of her and KD would at least send her the money in time every month. At her age there was hardly anyone who was kind to her. And only recently he had given her an expensive stole and perfume... He seemed to have a lot of money lately...But...

KD had become so secretive. Insisted she call him on his landline and never on his cellphone. That night when KD had called her from the hotel, he was screaming with so much pain that she was frightened. He was abusing and yelling about Sunny attacking him and her blood had boiled and he was swearing that he would kill her. When she told him to call the police he had become mad at her and asked her to come with first-aid and his Quad drug, the one he took to control his HIV. He wanted to get back on his feet and kill Sunny. But their call had been interrupted by a knock and then she could not hear something for a few minutes.

She thought the phone had been switched off when she heard a man speaking to KD in a voice which made her heart freeze. Kala had gone through what happened next, so many times in her head she remembered each word.

'Ha ha she has decorated your face already! Your whore has slashed you bad KD or should I say Johnny D'Souza! Your Sunny

whore has made our job easier dumbfuck 'Dee–Soo–zah' You thought we will not know??' This was Munjal Bawla. Kala would recognize his menacing voice anywhere.

'Please have mercy!!' KD was blubbering in pain. She strained to hear and caught words like 'fraud', 'secret account', 'cash stashed' and 'blackmailing'. The man was calling KD 'Johnny D'Souza' and Kala was confused.

'The police would note that the previous occupants of this room were probably dissatisfied clients haan? *Or unhappy broads? Equally deadly, mind you,' a new shrill voice interrupted. Kala found this voice scarier.*

'Chotta–ugghiiiikkkk–don't hit me don't hit me–' KD referred to the shrill-voiced man as Chotta.

'Uh! Ohhh god!'

'There is no god here. God has left Mumbai...long time ago.' Munjal said again, '...your whore left her lipstick...let's decorate you Mister Dee–Soo–zah! What's in this? Amitrips! Fucker is taking painkillers–you won't need any of this where you are going bhenchod.'

'I have HIV. I am dying anyway–'

'Whattttafuckk? Don't touch him! Chotta's high-pitched voice rang out.

'Bastard is lying.'

'No please check the drug it's for HIV control,' KD sobbed.

*'Ok! so we won't touch–no hands–tie him up truss him like a turkey –I saw on YouTube–called 'auto-asphyxiation' I think–you will die much more painfully now–*dekho haramzade ki phhatt rahee hai! *I don't appreciate that you kept a lot hidden from us...the money too? Now that hurts you know...after all I did for you??' The voice had dropped to a whisper and for Kala it was difficult to make out who was talking now.*

'You saw that on YouTube Chotta!! Ha ha—what a way to go Johnny boy! Blank cheques in Mumbai...dumping in Dubai... haan? *That was where you were going without me Johnny boy!!'*

'A lie...it's a lie...please there's no proof—aaaaaaaghgrk—'

'Sorry. I should have waited till you told me. You know you should shut up or I may just fillet you and skewer you with this poke—might just peel your skin off your greedy hands? You know you have inspired me—I am now branching out into bigger things—

'Please—have mercy—I am sick—'

'Johnny boy I read on Google that the number of lashes on the right eye are always more than on the left eye. And the size of nails on the right hand is always longer than on the left hand—I always wanted to find out if that was true. Arrey *you will also find out, infact you will get the front row seat*—maadachodd!'

'This is—look at this, you know what this is—the stuff you give your cunts—now you will take it except we will shoot it through the needle and it will go straight to your brain—so either you tell me or I will plumb it out of you—question is what will come first!

'You know you have made me look like a chutiya. A CHUTIYA. Years of hard work, my entire life goes in setting up the shit and then a haramzada *comes and fucks it up,' Munjal said.*

'Respect is most important. What will other men think? That you got away by screwing us? So let's all do it. It takes a loose nut you know. Just one loose nut. So you can't blame me if I wanted to see you fixed. Screwed tight. REALLY TIGHTTTT. Say goodbye to your shitty life.' It was Chotta.

'She should have completed the job you know. But they always have a heart...these cunts. Us....we will not make that mistake, will we? Kill him Chotta,' Munjal said.

'Chod dey *Chotta...Munjal...Bawla...I have worked all my life for you—tell your broth...Chotta—don—please—no—donn—kill me—chodhhh erkkk uhhikkkkkkkkk—'*

His noises reduced to a hiss and a sigh and petered down to painful gurgles.

'Chotta are you sure he is dead?' Munjal said.

'Bhai—you are insulting me,' Chotta replied and laughed.

She had sat frozen for what seemed like eternity, her brother's dying screams echoing in her ears. When she came out of her haze, she had picked up the phone to go to the police but then television news told her that they suspected Sunny of killing him and she had kept the receiver back. But she had to stop them from spreading such lies about her brother. She had to make the call now. NOW. With shaking hands, Kala looked up ACP Kabir's number. They would need a formal statement. When the doorbell rang, she opened the door expecting the police, wondering how had reached so soon.

She opened the door and stared.

But it couldn't be.

It could NOT be.

But it was.

It was Dannie. Her Dannie.

But Dannie was dead wasn't she? Was it Dannie's ghost?

And Kala's head swam as she fell into the ghost's arms. Sister Sachcha gathered Kala and gently placed her on the sofa and closed the door behind her.

33

The exposé marked the beginning of the end of superjock, superstar Prince Sulaiman Capure. The shocking secrets of scandalous filmy parties and the outrageous behaviour of reputed producers became grist for rumour mills. A botched attempt at a cover-up utterly failed. The floodgates were opened and let loose a rising tide of innuendo. It came out that lots of big Bollywood names were involved in several scandalous parties and drug scams which were hushed up with bribes.

There were shocking allegations of Nargis Khaled being in possession of a video which had much more explosive stuff, the claim hotly denied by the item girl as completely fabricated. A video which had three naked girls, who looked worryingly underage and were mostly screaming, and a totally stoned superstar who had sex with one girl, then moved on to another and then to a third one. But after the video was leaked on YouTube and became viral, there was little the studio could do, and Prince was fed to the wolves. No one could stop his manslaughter by the media. The pictures left little to imagination. Was half of Bollywood infested by drug-crazed zoned-out nymphomaniac immorals, was the question the public was asking. The press was already openly talking about a 'well-known Bollywood personality' being accused of committing lewd acts on pre-pubescent girls, supplying drugs to minors, committing perverse acts and sodomy. Names of top-notch DS producers cropped up in connection with the disgraceful acts. Dream Star of course has denied any connection with the event.

Nisha Poddar has announced her intention to write a detailed book on the whole affair.

Chamanji sent out a press release.

'Nisha Poddar should be institutionalized. Coming to our party, planting stuff, accusing our guests...Please don't even drag Prince into this. Casting aspersions on the characters of such reputed people! People who have got national awards and actors and producers?? We are all respectable people here with families. The so-called journalist is a pathological liar...and quite stupid to think she will get away with this sort of defamatory criminal reporting. My lawyers are right now filing a case of defamation against her.'

There is more bad news for Prince Sulaiman Capure. Shit has hit the box office fan. The much awaited *Indiawala Hero* is being likened to the coldest turkey of last year's Thanksgiving. A huge let-down, with critics penning it as an 'inter-galactic disaster', and 'totally lame' and 'pathetic', and complaining that Prince's dancing was out of tune and his dialogues out of sync. *Indiawala Hero* is set to lose about 200 crores.

Nishapoddar@thewholetruth said:

'What a crock of shit! It's not a film. Indiawala Hero is a collosal joke.'

No one could really say how much it's losing. But then that's the issue with film-business. You never really knew what the real budget was anyway. Bollywood isn't very open with numbers. Of one thing there was no doubt. *Indiawala Hero* is definitely near the top of any list of worst films. DS Studios is getting ready to toss Prince Sulaiman Capure to the wolves, and have removed two of his new films from circulation and a half-shot new film has been consigned to cold storage.

Meanwhile, the Mumbai police ACP Kabir Bhonsle has met the superstar, rumour has it on much more charges. Something to do with some sex-tape. Sources close to Prince Sulaiman Capure say the superstar is doing his duty and co-operating with the police on a case not connected to him in any way and the misunderstanding will be cleared soon. Some people swear they heard him drunkenly cursing the media for his troubles.

'I am going to sue every fucker. Every motherfucking reporter who takes my name—they are dragging me down because I am famous. I am going to sue every cunt.' His self esteem had taken a beating and his bruised ego was busting out all over out of control.

Shit really rolls downhill perhaps the superstar is finding out.

EPILOGUE

He always hated the smell of airports. The people standing pretending they were not interested in the other's business yet prying eyes, scooping out details like vultures peeling out flesh from a cadaver. Especially the old ones. He hated the way they stared at him directly trying to dig their beaky eyes into his flesh. Stupid armpit of a people pretending to be better than the ones travelling economy. If only they knew—they would not be staring at him—they would be pissing in their pants—if only he could show them!

If Chotta Bawla had had his way, he would have shot the people standing in line ahead of him and got the pilot to takeoff to Dubai at gun point. But all he could do was snarl at a couple of snotty kids with red lollipops in their sticky hands. The lollipops had started leaking and were staining their tee-shirts crimson. It reminded him of coagulating blood. Like KD's blood, he thought and smirked. Of course he had been very careful and used gloves to tie truss and strangle KD—making sure not a single drop tainted him. After he reached home he had scrubbed his body head to toe in hot water several times and had visited the doctor for a checkup. You never could be sure about these fucking viruses!

But suppose if the *maadachod* had not told him about it—Chotta shuddered to think of his hands covered in KD's infected blood.

The line was moving faster now and Chotta Bawla was finally relieved but his smile froze on his lips when he saw the policemen running towards him.

EPILOGUE

NARGIS KHALED

The announcement came in the evening.

'A huge misunderstanding has been created by Prince Sulaiman's jealous rivals to tarnish his image. The actor wants his fans to believe in him. The fictitious rape charges have been dropped as there was no truth in them. It was a misunderstanding between Prince and Nargis.'

Nargis was being cast in Prince's new film as the solo lead. There were whispers of a tape floating whose participants were not doing legal activities but the rumour was quickly debunked by Nargis Khaled's new PR.

For any interviews with the press, Nargis Momani Khaled would now have to be routed through her new secretary and manager, Prremm Pandeet.

DAISY KATTA

She became the new no-panty girl. Actress and item girl Daisy Katta flashed her fanny to one and all in a major wardrobe malfunction during a music video shoot a few days ago. According to sources, Daisy had to change several outfits in quick succession and had chosen to go panty-less for convenience and to save time. What she forgot was that mobile phone cameras have got so sophisticated these days that even a split-second movement can be captured on a high-end mobile phone camera.

'I want to announce to my dear friends I have just signed *Sabse Badhee Supermodel* by Tunti Shah. I am talented and I am willing to do anything for my talent—if Tunti Sir has taken me he has seen me prop—my talent.'

'Daisy Katta is the self-proclaimed supermodel. She takes her role too seriously and that makes her a director's apt choice,' said a beaming Tunti. 'While working with Daisy Katta I realized that she is the only supermodel of Bollywood...our very own Angel—eena Jolly!!'

PATRALEKHA PARIHAR

Digital Dolly has changed her name back to Patralekha Parihar. She has joined Bawla's film wing and taken it upon herself to get Bollywood rid of 'outsiders' and 'foreigners' who take away jobs from Mumbai's local artists.

Speaking in the presence of various TV news channels she said,

"I would not want to comment but I must say this is so sensitive topic. It's our culture. My job as an upright citizen is to expose people like Nargis Khaled—that woman has underworld links and was involved in a betting racket in Pakistan—Why are we tolerating her in our country where thousands of girls are struggling for work?*Kya India ki ladkiyan marr gayee hain??*

Patralekha Parihar added, 'I have heard Nargis is making a lot of illegal money or black money here and depriving Indian actors and girls of an income. She takes signing amounts from producers and financers. I do not want to specify what she is doing, but the income tax authorities must investigate her source of income. These girls from *baahar se* do films and item dances for a pittance. That hurts us hardworking girls. There should be an investigation against her. She has used various unfair tactics to get her visa extended time and again. And she is making lakhs of rupees every month which are illegally repatriated to her foreign accounts. Any person on a work visa in India cannot accept payments in cash for services rendered. The payment has to be made by account payee cheque only right?! But this *chaaloo* Nargis Khaled has been receiving payments mostly in cash and allegedly, has been using a hawala to repatriate the money to *benami* bank accounts in Dubai and Pakistan—'

Patralekha Parihar has also filed a complaint at the Amboli Police Station against Nargis.

'I am getting calls from people who are threatening me with serious bodily harm, abusing my family for speaking the truth—am I wrong if I point out these producers...do they keep searching for porn stars on the internet? With so many Indian girls ready to do hot scenes and other glamour roles, what was the need for Nargis Khaled? Next they will auction Nargis's panties? If these producers want money so bad they could have appealed to all Indian women, they would have donated their underwear to them so that they could raise money for the publicity for their films. Through you my good friends, I am appealing to all my well-wishers to join me in my Facebook campaign at facebook.com/india.chodo.nargis.khaled. I am now complaining to Information & Broadcasting Ministry, the Home Ministry and other Government of India departments against this woman—we must save India—'

EPILOGUE

The testimony lasted for about two hours in the newly constructed courtroom of the city court. Richly panelled in solid teak, the hall was an extravagance in woodwork. As opposed to the massive exteriors, the actual floor space of the rooms was pretty budgeted, dwarfed further by the huge table placed ceremonially in the middle of the room. Honourable Wanchoo sat on the high backed judge's chair resplendent in a red robe and sash and a horsehair wig, which fell on to his shoulders. The jury box to his left at right angles to the public gallery had the jury seated in anticipation. The barristers wearing eighteenth century cravats pacing the floorspace made the whole atmosphere even more religious.

The last few days had been hectic. After Kala's testimony there was no doubt about the identity of the killer. Thankfully his men were able to nab Chotta Munjal just before he was about to board his flight to Dubai and was now in custody of the Mumbai police. The elder Munjal had been caught in his office. He had not even tried to escape but simply smiled and shook his shoulders when he told him about the sex-tape.

'You don't get it Mr. ACP? This is my city. People come to me with problems. I solve problems. The way I see it that's what I

did. A sex-tape—awlright a rape tape, but so what? You think this city cares about a dead slut from years ago? Or a dead hustler? It's about money. About commerce and I protect commerce. As for the proof what do you have? A fraction of a second picture on a video—good luck proving that. You will put one Bawla in jail another will come—we are everywhere. I will be out before you know it and then I will try my best to get Chotta out—eyewitnesses are so unreliable these days—and you just have an ear-witness! But that boy...such temper...some jail time may be good for him. Who knew the pimp KD's old hag had an ear in the room—' Munjal had laughed.

ACP Kabir Bhonsle could not stand the claustrophobic heat of the courtroom, and walked into the packed corridors looking for an empty spot to sit in, uninterrupted. The media build up was huge but the officer found that he couldn't seem to keep his mind on it. He found himself staring at the hundred-year-old building. It amused him that he had never even had a speeding ticket in his entire life. Security was tight and scores of constables stood in plain sight, keeping their long burly bamboo lathis handy. Uniformed crowd pounders stood on the roads and across the street keeping a wary eye on the people. He had been expecting the news and was prepared when she walked out free.

Sunny looked calm and mockingly unconcerned with the circus around her. They stared at her stupendously. As she walked out, legs in breeches, gum boots, a low-cut leather corset, head totally bald, a hush fell over the crowd. Her golden gypsy eyes still undecipherable, her remote beauty just as disturbing. The onlookers, shocked to silence for a moment, gasped collectively at her shaved head which seemed to make her beauty appear alien. She walked unconcernedly like a monk, her naked head shorn of its glorious tresses even more provoking than before, the twin snakes tattooed on her neck glinting wildly. The crowds stared at her with a voyeuristic frenzy desperate to lay bare the secrets that lay behind those mesmerizing eyes. She stood in front of them—a monk for some, a diabolically beauteous devil for others. No one recognized the impressively built police officer in plain clothes standing like a wall between Sunny and the chaotic crowd as he led her towards a waiting car. The car door opened and Suhana held out a hand to Sunny, and Kabir got into the driver's seat. With a final look, the free girl glanced at the farce around her and left with more dignity than anyone around her. Kabir carefully manouvered the car through the tumultuous crowds and with the skill which comes after years of active service in the force, he knew exactly how to lose the paparazzi hell-bent on trailing them. The backview mirror reflected the two sisters and he caught Suhana's eye. Her burgundy eyes were amber...spilling gold...almost like Sunny's. He thought there was something in the look she gave him. Something almost intimate.

Kabir was not sure but he was willing to test that hypothesis.

But first there was the package to be sent.

EPILOGUE

What does a star do when he has been totally exposed, literally stripped naked with his bare arse bonking in the air? Well, he throws a mega party to prove 'Hey I don't give a damn and so you should not too!' If life shits on you, go ahead and throw a big fat monstrously expensive party and hope everyone joins your champagne-stoked and coke-laced tamasha.

And everyone forgets the shit.

Prince Sulaiman's mega party for the announcement of Dream Star's new film *Item Girl* with his new lead actress Nargis Khaled was a rip-roaring success–

Nisha Poddar read aloud her last column on *Bollywood Truths.* She had been on the other side for too long. Always waiting for the handouts, the press, invites the exclusives and the story—always waiting for the next one. And she knew that getting emotional in Bollywood was a complete waste of time.Everyone had an agenda but she was thankful she had been let off without much scarring. Nisha still loved the *story.* She still loved that people confided in her and that *they* disclosed, revealed, confessed their innermost secrets to her. But she reckoned that over the years she had become one of *them*.

Nisha planned to submit her resignation from the magazine *Bollywood Truths* today. She had been offered the plum post of the *CEO Creative Content* of *Dream Star Studios* by Dhanna Seth himself who has meanwhile left on a long vacation to an undisclosed foreign location. She would also be in-charge of Prince Sulaiman Capure's media interactions on behalf of DS. The panicky superstar calmed down when he heard what she had to say.

'Prince you are a fucking superstar—superstars get away with murder—! Stop panicking and believe me when I say people forget shit. Fans have short memories and they forgive their superstars anything—even murder—and goddammit this is just rape! You know what you could go get drunk and run your car over people and kill them and there could be eye witnesses and still you will NOT go to jail—c'mon you know how it works—you are a super fucking star!'

Nisha Poddar started typing the press release for Prince Sulaiman:

These are fabrications spread by people who are jealous of me—They want to destroy me since they know my fans love me too much. The DVD is morphed. It's not me. I don't know Munjal personally. May have met him at some party. We are preparing a statement. Talk to my attorney, the number is—Her chain of thought was interrupted by an SMS on her mobile:

"Dream Star has managed to bail out Munjal Bawla. Sources say he is setting up a big office at DS Studios."

Sure everyone forgets shit.

EPILOGUE

'Sonuvabitch!!!' He screamed when a brutal blind tackle caught him perfectly and he fell down with a wallop, his flesh grating on the rocky ground. His back bent like a bow, there was a sound of bones snapping with a crunch as he suddenly pitched forward and threw his attacker with a swift move. A satisfying conk told him that his attacker's head had bounced off the bumper before he hit the pavement. Blood dribbling from his nose, his gun ready in his hand, he got up and crouched warily besides the body. Suddenly his attacker's head exploded in a wet-red cloud–

AND CUT.

The set erupted in spontaneous applause. Sumraan Ibrahim breathlessly sat down on a chair, taking in the genuine show of appreciation with a smile. His attacker, Nawazuddin, his head marked by a red splash, sat down on a chair besides him and whistled.

Suhana was happy she had decided to send the cast for fight training sessions and evaluation workshops prior to filming. The cast training lasted for twelve weeks and continued through filming. The Korean stunt coordinator, Jung Wu, had diligently trained the men in fight choreography from martial fights to brutal hand-to-hand combat. After Sumraan she tapped into more actors known for their hard hitting roles. Confirmations happened swiftly and the 'still in talks' were dispensed with. Nawazuddin had been a real find. She finally had her cast frozen. The training slashed the production time to one-third, as with the cast coming prepared on the sets there were hardly any retakes. That had brought the grin back to Biddoo's face. That, and the fact that she had agreed to have an item number in the film after he agreed to get her her Korean fight director.

'Yess baby! Absurdly fetishized women in teeny skirts. Who doesn't want to see girls running down naked! I know just the girl for it—' Biddoo had guffawed.

'I am sure you do, Biddoo,' she smiled grateful to Biddoo for getting her Jung Wu.

'It is a cool story and not just like a video game where you're just loose and going nuts.' It was a relief she and Jung Wu were on the same page, though he had a tendency to go way out in some scenes.

'I want to geeeve the audience what I WANT. Not what I think you want or Biddoo wants or Sumraan wants. Glorious fight sequences at one level, loaded macho fantasies of escape and revenge at another. Then I want to yank it all back and stab you right through the eyeball,' he said with passion.

'Jung Wu, I heard you choreographed the latest ZZZ Spy Game video, my son loves it,' Sumraan shouted out to the diminutive Korean who wanted to show Suhana his storyboard. Jung Wu moving his hands like a bird and standing on one leg with his hands outstretched, his tongue hanging out, suddenly stabbed the air with his taut limbs, tearing into imaginary opponents.

'See this! Like this! Storyboard all my ideas for the fight scenes, I have outlined how the hero will move. My stuntmen and stuntwomen know kung fu fight choreography, very popular in Korean films. See?'

'The film includes an imaginary fight club that the men in the alternate reality are part of, where singing and dancing take place. The fantasy sequences include brutal fights and battles. On the other hand, though it's fetishistic and personal, I like to think that my fetishes aren't that obscure.'

'See in Korea it is normal to create a fight of up to twenty or so techniques that would be shot in one take.'

'It's too circular—' Suhana pointed out.

'We will make it linear—' the ever smiling Jung Wu would not give up.

Suhana addressed Sumraan.

'Something blue. The emotion of the film is blue. Your character is combative covered in a black and blue edgy look—light drain out *kar dengey han*—the fight using your duplicate will be shot wide-angle *ekdum* unedited, I want to hide what is going on, camera approach you know tight angles, shaky camera.'

'It's about what the movie *feels* like when you watch it, more than a specific "Oh, it's a story of this person." It has to be stylized. Young men in the movie are under constant threat of being brutally murdered.'

Things were finally looking up.

Watching from his seat Vishnu Kashyap's face lit up when he saw Sunheri enter the sets of MCMM. Biddoo was already running to her and yelling at his assistants for seats and umbrellas for Sunny.

'I haven't done this in a long time. But I have an idea—'

Catching Sunny's eye Suhana smiled.

HESITANT SPRING

The upper peaks of the lavender grey mountains merged with the pearly mist of the sky. The setting sun softened the contours of the pines clinging to the mountain sides with their fringed viridian silhouettes. Heat percolated from the lowlands and by the time it reached Anattā ashram the air had already got cooler and cleaner and sweeter. In the apple orchard, freshly-tilled plots were surrounded by barbed wire and a profusion of green and gold trees cut in low wide arcs for handpicking. Cherry-sized orbs peeked from under the leafy sap green canopies. Outside, the garden was bathed in a beautiful autumn sun, the grass alight with gold. Sister Sachcha walked through the ground cushioned by pine needles and willow leaves looking at the unnamed package which had been delivered in her name at the ashram office. Three bisque dolls. And below it written neatly: The Dream Girls.

Sister Sachcha looked at the new inmate of the aashram.

She had white hair and eyes which were pink-rimmed and glaucous. But there was a sense of peace on the old woman'sface. Her features lit up when she heard Sachcha's voice. Holding the old woman's hand, Sachcha smiled brightly at the hesitant tangy sweetness of almost ripe yellow and green apples in the orchard. The acrid smoke of leaves burning someplace near mixed with the earthy smell of fresh soil. It was clean, hay-scented, warm, perfumed air. Harvest was a mere month away.

Sachcha threw off her chappals and walked barefoot on the soft grass and told the old woman,

'We must think of a name for you.'

ACKNOWLEDGEMENTS

This is a work of fiction, heavily inspired and researched from non-fiction. I have taken liberties with time periods and atmospherics to protect the identities of some people. I have also changed their names and their identifying characteristics. I have unabashedly lifted from many true-life incidents, borrowed from the peculiarities and foibles of many, the darkness of a few people, the savageness of some, and the brilliance of others. So without naming any of you, I thank you all.

I am grateful to the following individuals and the wonderful team at Rupa: Kausalya Saptharishi, my wonderfully brilliant editor, determined and untiring. Nishi Jain, thank you. Vasundhara Raj Baigra who keeps us going with her cheer and camraderie. Ram Ajhur, Rupsha ghosh—thank you. Mita, my agent who heads the Siyahi Literary Agency. Thank you, Prashant. Iqbal, Juhi Sharma for your help. Thank you, Sonal, for trying. I want to acknowledge Radhika, Yash, Shekhar, Nikhil, Siya and Swati, without whose efforts the novel would have been ready six months earlier. But then what are familes for.

www.ingramcontent.com/pod-product-compliance
Lightning Source LLC
LaVergne TN
LVHW091025080826
845145LV00002B/361

* 9 7 8 8 1 2 9 1 3 4 8 0 6 *